W9-BMY-311

ETHNIC REALITIES
and the CHURCH

Lessons from Kurdistan

ETHNIC REALITIES
and the CHURCH

Lessons from Kurdistan

A history of mission work, 1668 - 1990

Foreword by Ralph D. Winter

Robert Blincoe

Presbyterian Center for Mission Studies
Pasadena, California

Ethnic Realities and the Church: Lessons from Kurdistan
Copyright © 1998 Presbyterian Center for Mission Studies
1605 East Elizabeth Street
Pasadena, CA 91104-2721
e-mail: pcms.parti@ecunet.org

All rights reserved. No part of this publication may be repro-
duced, stored in a retrieval system or transmitted in any way by
any means, electronic, mechanical, photocopy, recording or otherwise, without the prior permission of the author, except as provided by USA copyright law.

Cover photo of bridge in Zakhu, Iraq by Mick Germinaro

Library of Congress Catalog Card Number: 97-69533

ISBN 0-9652533-2-5

Dedication

To H.
The mullah's son
who dared to follow Christ

Contents

Tables, Photos and Maps

Foreword

Don't be confused. This book may seem like just another case study of mission work within a large cluster of hard-to-reach peoples—the Kurds. Rather, it is a handbook of mission strategy, employing the fascinating details relevant to missions everywhere.

This book shows the way forward in a specific case, but does much more. In perusing its pages—sparkling with very candid and refreshing, daringly honest language—it is not difficult to realize the pregnant implications for work yet to be done elsewhere in the world.

Nor is it armchair stuff. This book tells the story of faithful, sacrificing, determined, competent workers laboring at great personal cost with virtually no success throughout many decades. Blincoe respects stalwart, determined missionaries. He's one of them. However, his creative new perspective is not only born of years of right-on-the-ground experience, but gains stunning cogency from the advantage he has of being able to stand back and view the entire story. Taken to heart, this book can single-handedly produce a dynamic new era in the greater part of the world of missions.

Thus, I know of no other book which presents a case study in such fascinating detail and depth and yet, at the same time, generates arresting, highly crucial missiological insights. In case you miss any of them along the way, the author devotes a whole chapter to missiological insights at the end.

If "ineffectiveness" is the remorseless pattern of the decades and centuries of the faith of Jesus Christ in the Islamic sphere, then why read the book in the first place? Ah, this remarkable book fairly bristles with insights about how to get beyond centuries-old misunderstandings and move forward effectively. While it does not set out to oppose today's most widely held mission strategy—that of always working through existing or "national" churches—it does nevertheless quietly lay down imposing, absolutely insurmountable evidence that reveals even so widely accepted a philosophy of mission to be simplistic. This thesis leads to many surprising insights into what can actually be done, and must be done very differently in order for Biblical faith (as contrasted to organized Christianity) to make headway in the world of Islam, and it reveals much that can and should be understood equally well in Hindu and Buddhist spheres.

After all, much of the world's remaining peoples are dynamically parallel to the mountain peoples this book so fascinatingly describes. What major political entity today does not enclose offended and threatened minorities for whom the culture or religion of the dominant group is a dead-end street? To the perceptive reader it shows the way forward on the world level into the hearts of hundreds of other minority peoples scattered far and wide.

This book's appeal can readily range all the way from young people contemplating the formidable challenge of world mission, to pastors and mission executives pondering stone walls of failure in many fields, to field missionaries perhaps too close to their work to see the heart of the problems they are dealing with, and yes, even the national workers who are inevitably part of the jumble of reality and without whom nothing ultimately can succeed. All of these need this book to arrest and challenge them in their involvement as faithful disciples of the Living Christ.

Ralph D. Winter
Pasadena, California
March 1998

Preface

A history book of the mission *to Kurds* would be thin indeed; although hundreds of missionaries have lived, worked and in some cases died in Kurdistan, nearly all of them bypassed the Kurds, "seeking in the most remote corners of the land the little companies of Christians" (Richter 1910:316).

And therein lies a tale.

While walking through a Kurdish town, looking for suitable housing, a priest of the Chaldean church invited me to live in his neighborhood. There, he told me, I could learn the Christian language, rent from a Christian landlord, and hire Christians to wash my clothes and guard the house. Together we would prove to the surrounding Kurds that church people stick together. When I took a house on the other side of town, among the majority Kurds, the priest felt disillusioned. And I felt guilty to disappoint him so thoroughly.

Disillusionment, however painful, is preferable to the alternative. Western mission policies had tied their hopes of Muslim evangelism to a revived Christian witness. But the "little compa nies of Christians" long ago sealed themselves off from the Kurds, like a submarine with its hatches closed. When missionaries from the West brought jobs and education to these Christian tribes, and the fury of the Kurdish tribes was aroused, and valuable lessons resulted.

It is the nature of the gospel that we hear it first from persons outside our own ethnic group. Among the unreached peoples, faith will come from messengers who enter their culture and become, so far as possible, one of them. This is how the gospel came to the persons reading this book; this is the legacy which allows us to stand on the shoulders of great missionaries who came before us.

At Ralph Winter's suggestion, I have leaned the title of my book next to Donald McGavran's excellent work, *Ethnic Realities and the Church: Lessons from India.*

Acknowledgments

I am the least likely student of mission history. However, Ralph D. Winter, in his class at Fuller Seminary's School of World Mission, derailed my lesser ambitions. My interest in Middle Eastern studies is as fresh today as it was the first time I heard Kenneth E. Bailey teach the parables of Luke 'through peasant eyes.' My interest in Kurds began with Mort Taylor, Presbyterian mission statesman who prayed for me. J. Dudley Woodberry guided me in the paths of graduate study, and I owe whatever small success as is present in this book to his patience.

My wife's contribution to my life and faith and work is brighter than all the rest. To her I am hopelessly devoted.

TABLE 1
CHRISTIAN COMMUNITIES IN KURDISTAN
sizes are representative, but
not based on actual statistics

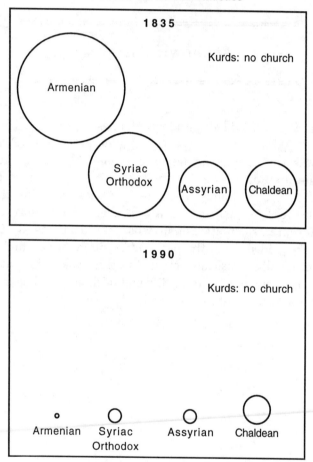

Abbreviations

ABCFM	American Board of Commissioners for Foreign Mission
ABS	American Bible Society
BFBS	British Foreign Bible Society
CIS	Commonwealth of Independent States
CMS	Church Missionary Society
LBI	Living Bibles International
LOMS	Lutheran Orient Mission Society
RCA	Reformed Church of America
SPG	Society for the Propagation of the Gospel
UPCUSA	United Presbyterian Church of the United States of America
PCUSA	Presbyterian Church, United States of America
UMM	United Mission of Mesopotamia
UN	United Nations

Introduction

Kurds are a fragmented people. Occupied by stronger powers on all sides, divided from within, guilty of shedding the blood of Christians, the Kurds are, as Jesus said of the multitude, "harassed and helpless, like sheep without a shepherd." A Kurdish proverb laments, *kurdu heval nînen*, "Kurds have no friends." Few outsiders, it seems to the Kurds, understand them or offer them friendship. In the 19th and 20th centuries, perhaps 200 missionaries lived in Kurdistan; few of these, however, spoke Kurdish or even had Kurdish acquaintances! Missionaries hoped to re-light the mission candles in the historical churches. These churches, in turn, would be a light to the Kurds. The plan failed for three reasons. First, because the minority churches derived fabulous advantages from the missionaries, which history destined them to horde instead of share. Second, missionaries could obtain neither local Christian permission nor government permission to evangelize Kurds; and in those exceptional moments when missionaries did work with Kurds, death brought their work to an end. Finally, Kurds, Turks and Persians resented the missionaries for empowering the church "tribes," a not unreasonable resentment. For these reasons, Kurds in the 19th and 20th centuries continued to live without light.

The rugged Kurdish mountains have bred a rugged people. Since the time of Xenophon (died c. 355 B.C.), foreign armies have complained of the *karduchoi* who harassed them in the mountain passes. Kurds were a bother even back then! Their mountains form a buffer separating Turks, Arabs, and Persians. These stronger powers continue to play Kurdish factions against each

17

other. However, the game goes both ways; Kurdish groups know how to auction their loyalty to the highest bidder.

TABLE 2
WHERE THE KURDS ARE AS OF 1997

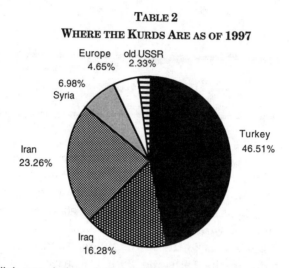

Kurdish population statistics are imprecise. Occupying countries diminish the numbers, while Kurds may exaggerate them. Figures given are median.

Turkey	13 million	Old USSR	0.5 million
Iraq	3.5 million	Israel	125,000
Iran	5 million	Lebanon	75,000
Syria	1.5 million	USA	20,000
Europe	1 million	Australia	10,000

THE WAY OF THE SWORD
HAS BROUGHT MISERY

Kurds have resisted the occupying governments of Turkey, Iraq, and Iran. Ayatollah Khomeini promised Kurds a part in his new government if they would help him topple the Shah. However, after consolidating his power, Khomeini ordered Sunni Kurds to become Shi'a before they could take part as full citizens. Kurds felt betrayed. The Iranian government killed thousands of resisters. In their homes pictures of Kurdish corpses replaced the picture of the Ayatollah; Iranian Kurds swore an oath of vengeance to their dead (Gardiner 1982:4).

Meanwhile, in Turkey, Kurds sustain a hit-and-run guerrilla war against government forces. In retaliation, Turkish troops have destroyed 2,800 villages in the eastern (Kurdish) part of the country. A million Kurds have migrated to Istanbul and other Turkish cities where they hope to start over. Millions more, with no political wishes, are caught between deadly aims of Kurdish separatists and government special forces in southeastern Turkey.

TABLE 3

DEATHS OF SELECTED MINORITIES IN CONFLICTS

(UN 1992)

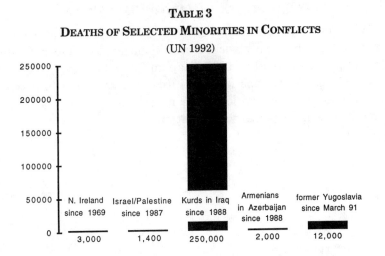

Kurds in the security zone of northern Iraq fear the day that Arabs re-assert control over them. However, if Saddam is patient, the Kurdish factions will fight one another and lose the sympathy of the West.

Syrian ruler Hafez al-Assad meets every dissent with brutal repression. Kurds in Syria await another day to pick up their swords again.

Kurds have one attraction: the West pities them for the abuse they suffer at the hands of the Turks, Arabs, and Persians. That one attraction has dimmed since the Kurds have logged their own record of brutality. Amnesty International has documented the record of torture and murder in northern Iraq since 1991 (Amnesty 1995). Sadly, Kurds are doing to one another as others have done unto them. Islam, which all the players in the region have in common, has not overcome the ethnic divisions of the Middle East.

Rare is the leader who acts for the public good in Kurdistan. Each chief seems to hope that his weapons will give him a victory in his struggle for supreme leadership. The way of the sword has cut the Kurds into ribbons of poverty and ruthless disregard of people beyond their kin.

THE WAY OF CHRIST HAS NOT BEEN TAKEN

What other people has so proved that sinful living reduces them to the "dreadfully wicked conditions" which Judith Grant found upon her arrival in 1835 (Kaplan 1993:25)? Every word of Jesus Christ bears hope for the Kurds. The gospel, which commands men and women love their neighbors and their enemies, must now come in power to Kurdistan.

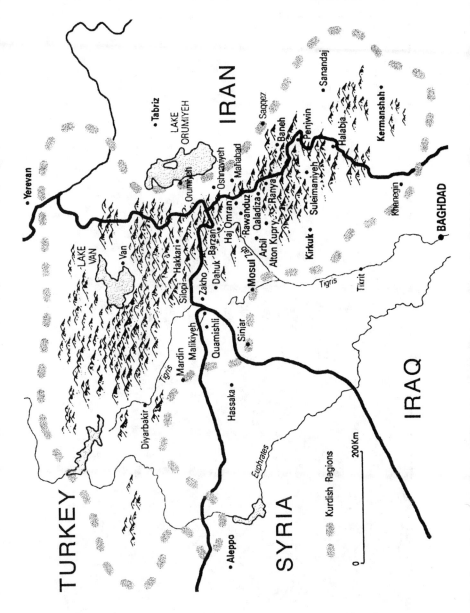

MAP OF KURDISTAN

JUSTIN PERKINS, 19TH CENTURY
(UPCUSA 1936)

Chapter 1

17th Century Mission
in Kurdistan

Missionaries in 17th century Kurdistan needed two months to walk from Mosul to Aleppo. The land is unforgiving; watering stations are still scarce and the weather harsh. Winter winds bite to the bone, and summer heat melts away the senses. For a thousand years caravans moved their goods from west to east and back again along the Silk Road. However, when Vasco da Gama sailed around the Cape of Good Hope in 1497, he proved that Portuguese merchants could bypass the petty kingdoms and customs bandits. From that time, the entire profit loaded in Oriental harbors arrived directly in European ports. The middleman lost out; caravans along the Silk Road vanished. Traders no longer passed through the Kurdish region. Commerce stagnated for 450 years; that is, until Western oil interests laid pipelines in the mid-20th century. Caravans again carry commerce through Kurdistan on its way to western consumers.

A CATHOLIC MISSION ARRIVES IN KURDISTAN

Father Jean-Baptiste of Saint-Aignan walked along this road. Jean-Baptiste was a Capuchin missionary who came to evangelize the Nestorian Christians of western Kurdistan. His experience is a distant mirror for those who followed him in the 19th and 20th centuries.

CATHOLIC MISSION TO THE NESTORIAN
CHURCH OF THE EAST

What were Jean-Baptiste and other French Catholics doing along this road? In the 17th century, French Catholics built mission stations in Aleppo and Mosul and at points between. They were evangelizing the "heretical Christians." Pope Origen IV had issued a decree in 1437, announcing that Nestorians should be encouraged to become Catholics.[1] Accordingly, papal emissaries began a mission to the Church of the East (Nestorians). Its success was so great that more than half the Nestorian population eventually moved into the Catholic Church.

CATHOLIC MISSION TO THE ARMENIAN CHURCH

The Sultan in Constantinople also granted permission for Catholics to work among Armenians. When Armenians converted to Roman Catholicism, they gained an ally in Europe. According to Martin van Bruinessen, Catholics "succeeded in making converts because the French king had acquired from the Ottoman court the right to protect all the Sultan's Catholic subjects" (1992:24). As we will see, the Armenians and Nestorians hoped more than once for a strong Christian partner to free them from Muslim domination and return to them their independent kingdom. Desire for a strong ally has caused the ethnic Christians in the Near East to convert to the religion of the missionary, whether French (17th century) American (19th century) or Russian (20th century). One must understand the vulnerable position of the ethnic Christians; their land was criss-crossed by invading Byzantines, Arabs, Mongols, Turks, Kurds, and Russians. Accordingly, the number one foreign policy goal of Christian tribes has been to seek a strong ally.

MEDICAL WORK OPENS A DOOR

The Catholics built stations in Aleppo and Mosul to serve their growing mission to these historical churches. One day Jean-Baptiste walked on this road; he was stopped by Kurds from Diyarbakir. Their pasha and his brother were both ill, and would the

---

[1]   The rift traces to the Council of Ephesus in A.D. 431.

foreigner please come to examine him. Jean-Baptiste turned north to Diyarbakir and visited the sick men. For several weeks, Jean-Baptiste attended to their needs. The pasha and his brother revived. As a reward, the pasha granted permission for Catholics to open a mission station to the Nestorians in Diyarbakir. As we will see, the healing art often opened the door to Christian mission in Kurdistan.

Father Jean-Baptiste came to Kurdistan from Tours, France (Guest 1993:53). He was a monk of unusual determination. As we will see, only missionaries of indissuadable resolve stayed in Kurdistan.

In 1668 the Pope appointed Jean-Baptiste as custodian of all the Capuchin missionaries in the Near East. In that same year, Jean-Baptiste received news that Yezidi Kurds near Aleppo had contacted his mission, and were inquiring into the Christian faith. He went to look for himself.

CATHOLIC MISSION TO YEZIDI KURDS

Armenians initially supported a Catholic outreach to Yezidi Kurds[2] near Aleppo. The Armenians introduced one Father Justinien to the Yezidi chiefs. Justinien "was fluent in Arabic and knew some Kurdish" (Guest 1993:53). He and Jean-Baptiste spent several days with the Yezidis. The missionaries decided "that the Yezidis were sincere, and persuaded them that the Pope was the true father of all Christians" (1993:53). The Yezidis invited Justinien to visit their community the following week.

When Justinien arrived, large crowds of very excited Yezidis greeted them:

They brought sheep to be slaughtered before him to the music of flutes, tambourines, kettledrums and lutes. The women, dressed in their finest clothes, emerged from black tents with shrill cries of joy. The celebration lasted several days, with ceremonial dances in honour of the Pope, the king of France, the French consul and the Capuchin mission (Guest 1993:54).

---

2   Yezidi Kurds are not Muslims. Their religion existed in pre-Islamic Kurdistan. The subject of Yezidi religion is outside the scope of this book. Refer to Guest, Izady, or Kreyenbroek for more information on this colorful people.

Justinien reported that everyone—sheikhs, the black-robed priests and the tribesmen—wanted to learn about Christianity. John Guest writes,

> Plans were made to hold a mass with kettledrums and tambourines in the ruined basilica of St. Simeon Stylites. . . . The Yezidis satisfied Pére Justinien that they did not worship the devil and that their refusal to curse him was part of a general rule that none of God's creatures should be cursed (1993:54).

"I Thought I Was Seeing a Dream"

Justinien himself was overcome with joy: "When I saw their eagerness to draw to the bosom of the church, their tears and their affection, I thought I was seeing a dream rather than reality" (Guest 1993:54). He celebrated Latin Mass for the Yezidis, evidently translated by three Armenian lay brothers. At the conclusion of worship the missionaries baptized two Yezidi sheikhs and gave them new names, Peter and Paul. One Yezidi tribesman recalled a tradition that his people descended from some old crusaders who fled to the mountains after the fall of Antioch (1993:54). "The only jarring note came from the Armenians, who persisted in fishing despite the Yezidis' plea to spare the hallowed animal lives" (1993:54). Catholic missionaries baptized thirteen Yezidis in the coming months. But serious opposition to the Yezidi mission was about to begin.

Armenian Church Turns against the Mission to the Kurds

More Yezidi chiefs sent invitations to meet the Capuchins; hopes ran high that a movement to Christian faith was imminent. However, at this point disgruntled Armenians put a stop to the movement. Guest explains,

> the Armenians who had originally introduced Father Justinien to the Yezidis now turned against him. They prevailed upon his prospective guide to complain that the missionary had usurped the functions of their chief and that the tribesmen would prefer to deal with one of the other orders. The Carmelites rejected the proposal but the Jesuits, who had targeted the Yezidis as prospects eighteen years before, offered to help. . . . The Armenians hinted that a

subsidy to their Yezidi friends would be very acceptable [if
the Jesuits wanted to win Yezidi loyalty?] (1987:52).

Failure of the Yezidi Mission

The Yezidi mission failed because of jealousy from the Armenians. Having taken cover in the palace of King Louis, the newly
Catholic Armenians closed the door behind them; no Kurds would
be allowed the same protection. As we will see, the Armenian
church often opposed a mission to the Kurds.

Secondly, the mission failed because the Catholic orders competed with one another:

> The ensuing dispute was finally resolved by the French consul,
> who ruled that any missionary endeavor involving actual or
> potential money payments should be approved by all three mis-
> sions [Carmelite, Jesuit, Capuchin]—thereby *suspending all fur-
> ther work among the local Yezidis* (Guest 1993:55, italics mine).

As we will see, competition among missions has greatly injured
the mission work in Kurdistan.

"The Hour Has Not Yet Come"

In 1679 a Parisian named M. Pierre Dupont established a
fund for further mission work among the Yezidis. However, the
missionaries sent out met with no success; the French Catholics
decided "that the hour for the conversion of this unhappy people
was not yet come. . . . They returned, shaking the dust off their
shoes" (Guest 1993:58). As we will see, the missionaries have
felt more than once the need to wait for the timing of God to
begin a mission to the Kurds.

Catholics Continue Their Mission to the Christians

Meanwhile, the Catholic mission to the Church of the East
continued with results. Dominicans actively proselytized Nestorians in Amadia, northern Iraq, from 1759 to 1779. As we will
see, missions competed for Christianized people instead of pio-
neering new work among non-Christians.

Nestorians Who Became Subject
to Rome Were Called Chaldeans

The Nestorians who submitted to the Roman Catholic Church
were called *Chaldeans*. There is no historical connection to the

ancient Chaldeans. Church historian Horner writes that the name Chaldean "was selected to suggest the traditional origin of the Magi who came from the East to celebrate Christ's birth" (1989:41). See Appendix A for an explanation of the various appellations—Syrian, Assyrian, Chaldean, Nestorian, and Jacobite—which all apply to the same Semitic language group. The five names have "caused a great deal of confusion, even among students of the modern Middle East" (Joseph 1961:3).

Non-Catholic Nestorians
Were Called Assyrians

Those Nestorians who remained subject to their patriarch came to be called Assyrians, but not until the 19th century. In 1842, Anglican missionaries encouraged this title, "as an acceptable alternative to the largely pejorative 'Nestorian'" (Horner 1989:22). Contrary to some opinion, the Assyrians and Chaldeans of today are not the descendants of the ancient peoples of the same names. See Appendix A.

Chapter 2

19th Century Mission
in Kurdistan

New mission societies in the early 1800s created, as William Carey foresaw, the means for evangelism beyond Europe. Soon missionaries from Europe and America landed in the Ottoman Empire and Persia. Early missionaries from the Basel Mission and from the American Board of Commissioners for Foreign Mission (ABCFM) walked the ancient caravan routes. Missionaries discovered what the French Catholics had found two centuries previously: ancient churches still survived in cities and villages throughout the region. Protestants quickly decided that these ancient Christians should evangelize the Kurdish, Turkish, and Persian neighbors. Accordingly, the missionaries established their work among the historical churches—Nestorian, Armenian, Jacobite—that resided in Kurdistan. The Protestants directed their efforts—schools, preaching, employment, language acquisition—to the historical churches.

THE GREAT TASK:
EVANGELIZE EVERY PEOPLE

The Protestant mission in Kurdistan began with a journey. In 1830 Eli Smith and Harrison Gray Otis Dwight of the ABCFM left Smyrna (now Izmir) to explore the interior of Turkey and northern Persia. They were the first Americans to undertake the trip. Both men were twenty-nine years old. From Smyrna they traveled to Constantinople, across Anatolia, through Armenia, into Georgia. There, Smith contracted cholera. Too weak to mount a horse, he rode behind Dwight in an oxcart as the pair pressed southeast through the mountains toward Iran. Smith was by now deathly ill and unable to sleep due to constant swarms of mosquitoes. "I lay and wept like a child," he recalled (Kaplan 1993:23).

For three months, Smith recovered at a Swiss mission in Armenia. In November, with snow falling, the two set out again for Tabriz. Smith again fell ill. They were reduced to eating bread filled with "crawling creatures" (Kaplan 1993:23). Finally, on December 18, 1830, with Smith so weak he could "neither walk nor stand," the Iranian city of Tabriz came into view.

They rested all winter to regain their strength. When spring came, Smith and Dwight explored the Lake Urmiah region. Here they met Nestorians, a Christian people with a glorious mission past.[1] Smith and Dwight enthusiastically recommended Urmiah as the center of a mission.

Their two-year exploration concluded, Smith and Dwight returned to Trebizond, a Black Sea port. From Trebizond they sailed back to Constantinople.[2]

What resulted from this exploration? First, the missionaries realized the enormity of the land mass. For hundreds of miles in every direction the "dead hand of the Turk" oppressed the Chris-

---

[1]   The Nestorian Church had been "the most missionary church the world has ever seen," according to Dr. A. Mingana (Stewart 1928: introduction). Samuel Zwemer called the Nestorian Church, "a Church on fire for missions, but later swept away by triumphant Islam":

> Islam's triumph had been prepared by the expansion and then alas! through the failure and decadence of Nestorian Christianity. . . . Weakened by persecution, lured from its true goal by compromise, and exterminated in the end by ruthless savagery, a church once on fire for missions ceased to be an aggressive force, and left behind only the imperishable memory of its past greatness. From the dead ashes we know how once the flames rose to heaven (Stewart 1928: introduction).

[2]   Such extensive travel was only possible because a recent treaty ended the state of war between the Ottoman Empire and Russia: "The Black Sea, re-opened to foreign ships, gave direct access to northeastern Anatolia and the old trade route from Trebizond across the Persian border to Tabriz" (Guest 1987:74).

tian minorities. Second, Dwight and Smith formulated a breath-taking goal: to reach with the Gospel every region of the Ottoman Empire and Persia, and to win some from every *millet* for the Kingdom of God.

This would be a holy endeavor. It seemed to Dwight and Smith that God had preserved the ancient, ethnic churches of the East for such a time as theirs.

THE GREAT EXPERIMENT: REFORM THE ETHNIC CHURCHES

Missionaries drew alongside these ethnic churches to revive them. For Protestants, revival meant teaching the Bible to the laity and emphasizing personal holiness. Instead of priestly prayers, all believers may approach God the Father. The power previously held by priests would distribute to the people, who lay moribund under layers of wrong teaching and superstition. Once revived, these ancient Christians would evangelize the Kurds and other Muslim peoples. This was the strategy of the early missionaries. We might call it a Great Experiment. This Experiment became the guiding star of mission policy in Turkey, Arabia, and Persia. Writes Greg Livingstone:

> The first Protestant missionaries . . . in the Middle East . . . hope[d] that the Christian Armenians, Assyrians, Copts, and Greeks—members of the ancient churches—would (when instructed in the Bible and given new life by the Holy Spirit) become God's instrument for evangelizing all the Muslim peoples of the Middle East and Asia. Accordingly, they devoted themselves to the task of reviving the Christian minorities (1990:31).

Nestorians had spread Christian faith to the gates of China's Forbidden City, as the world discovered in chapter 47 of Gibbon's *Decline and Fall of the Roman Empire*. They could be great missionaries again. To transform the Eastern Church into a mission-minded church, the Western missionaries would act as leaven in the dough.

THE GREAT EXPERIMENT AMONG ARMENIANS

Following Smith and Dwight's proposal, the ABCFM adopted a bold plan. Missionary work would begin among Nestorians, to revive their own sense of mission to the Persians and Kurds. Eli Smith wrote that the missionary should feel

> that *he has found a prop upon which to rest the lever that will overturn the whole system of Mohammadan delusion*, in the center of which he has fixed himself; that he is lighting a fire which will shine upon the corruption of the Persian on the one side, and upon the barbarities of the Kurd on the other, until all shall come to be enlightened by its brightness; and the triumph of faith will crown his labor of love (Joseph 1961:44, italics mine).

"IN THE CENTRE OF THE MOHAMMEDAN DOMAIN"

The exploration by missionaries Smith and Dwight brought results:

> The shah authorized establishment of an American Board mission and school. With this government permission, the ABCFM appointed its first missionary to Kurdistan. The first head of the mission was Justin Perkins, an upright, determined minister from Springfield, Massachusetts (Guest 1993:77).

In 1834 Perkins, with his wife, Charlotte, sailed from Constantinople along the Black Sea route by which Smith and Dwight had returned. The Board secretary told Perkins that his task would be "to enable the Nestorian Church, through the grace of God, to exert a commanding influence in the spiritual regeneration of Asia" (Joseph 1961:44). Urmiah's strategic location delighted Perkins:

> What position could be more important and advantageous, in its bearing on the conversion of the world, for a Christian church to hold, than that occupied by the Nestorians, situated as they are, in the centre of Mohammedan domain, and far towards the centre of benighted Asia! (Joseph 1961:45).

Thus mission work began in the centre of the Mohammedan domain. It was a brave proposal; it required workers of indomitable spirit. But if Nestorians again carried forth the missionary standard the work of western missionaries would multiply a thousand fold.

WHAT MISSION LEADERS SUSPECTED
ABOUT THE GREAT EXPERIMENT

Western Church leaders believed that Islam had rolled over a defective Christianity, and it could be rolled back by a healed church. However, the first Anglican missionary in Kurdistan, W. F. Ainsworth, made an ominous prediction in 1842. He foresaw that Islam would destroy the historical Christians on account of their missionary sponsors:

> This sudden interest, so explicitly and so actively shown on the part of the Christian nations, towards a tribe of people [the Nestorian tribes], who have almost solely prolonged their independent existence on account of their remote seclusion and comparative insignificance, has called them forth into a new importance in the eyes of the Mohammedans, *and will undoubtedly be the first step to their overthrow* (McDowall 1996:46, italics mine).

Rufus Anderson, director of the ABCFM during its years of rapid growth, regarded the secondary mission (strengthening the existing churches) as a substitute for the failure to evangelize Muslims (Coakley 1989). The tinder from the West never lit the wood.[3]

NESTORIAN LEADERS OPPOSED THE MISSIONARIES

Soon into their task, the missionaries were no longer welcomed in Nestorian churches. The patriarch, alarmed by their "low"

---

[3] Rufus Anderson held more than a one belief. In his 1872 book, *History of Missions*, Anderson seemed to indicate that the mission to Christians would not radiate out to the Muslims:

> The main work of winning races to Christianity must be performed by men of the same race. A Moslem will listen more patiently to a Christian Turk (renegade though he may be) than he will to an Armenian; nor has it been found easy to enlist the Protestant Armenians effectively in labors for the Turks (1872b:484).

Thirty years into the mission, Anderson admitted that the Americans may have to do a job that the ethnic churches were unwilling to shoulder:

> Gradually, it may be, some of the missionaries now in the field, who are familiar with the Turkish language, and have their Armenian churches supplied with pastors, will turn their attention mainly to the Moslems (1872b:485).

This is tantamount to admitting failure of the Great Experiment. But Anderson held the course, writing that "the original plan of mission to Turkey has been more promising of good than any other; namely, that of operating upon the Mohammedans through regenerated churches" (1872b:484).

ecclesiology, suspicious of empowering the laity with a knowledge of Scriptures, and disappointed that political benefits had not followed, ordered the missionaries out of his churches. Feelings of disappointment were mutual. Rasooli and Allen wrote,

> It was not the intention of the missionaries to start a Protestant movement, but, if possible, to revive the Nestorian Church, which had sunk into life-less formalities, and to re-awaken its ancient evangelistic zeal. In this they were disappointed. The new wine was too strong for the old wineskins. Opposition arose and after some twenty years of labor they felt they had no choice but to separate and organize a Protestant Church. The project flourished: churches and schools sprang up in the surrounding villages all over the Urumia plain (1957:32).

Missionaries in Urmiah found themselves on a narrow path that allowed little room for maneuver. Unwelcome in the Nestorian churches and unable by law to work with "the Mohammedans" directly, the ABCFM birthed a new sect that it had unintentionally encouraged. Nestorians "came out" from the ancient tradition to form "evangelical" (western) churches:

> It was not their first purpose to divide the ancient Christian communities and create Protestant churches, but this is what happened. Those who accepted the evangelical teaching were often pushed out of the ancient churches, which on the whole resisted Protestant type renewal. The new biblically oriented believers had no choice except to form "evangelical" churches of Christian minorities which exist in Turkey, Lebanon, Syria, Iraq, Egypt, and elsewhere in Muslim cities today (Miller 1971:232).

Succeeding missions arrived like waves to work among the Nestorians of Urmiah, the "centre of the Mohammedan domain"; however, they did not work with Mohammedans! The missionaries could not extract themselves from their commitment to the ethnic churches. Accordingly, no mission to the Kurds began, and no Kurdish church materialized. Like a two-stage rocket of which only the first stage ignited, the mission in Urmiah failed to reach its original goal; it failed so often as to show that the strategy was flawed. Missionaries evangelized an impressive number of

Nestorians; however, these did not in turn evangelize the Muslims.[4]

Missionaries worked with all their might to strengthen the Armenian Evangelical Church, the Jacobite Evangelical Church, and the Assyrian Evangelical Church. Annual reports stopped talking about Muslim evangelism (although individual conversions occurred). Teaching the Christians and preaching in churches became the new target; accordingly, the mission could report successes every year.

This change meant that evangelizing Kurds was no longer in the plan of the American or British or Catholic missions. No longer was there a mission beyond the villages and neighborhoods of the Nestorians, the Jacobites and the Armenians. (However, Alpheus Andrus and Samuel Audley Rhea kept a prayerful lookout for god-fearing Kurds. And a large number of Yezidi Kurds once sought the missionaries in order to become Christians. We have recorded the incident in this chapter.)

THE GREAT EXPERIMENT MADE THE KURDS JEALOUS

At first, missionaries hoped that Armenians and Jacobites would become the mainspring of mission to Muslims. Accordingly, missionaries lived and worked among Christians. In addition, missionaries wrote letters to their embassies on behalf of beleaguered Armenians, Jacobites, and Nestorians. In a hundred ways missionaries empowered their co-religionists. One result was that Kurds felt alarmed.

Missionaries arrived during a power struggle between the sultan in Constantinople and the Kurdish aghas in the east. Before the 1840s, aghas acted as independent fiefdoms: they taxed the peasants and paid their own militias. Aghas even sold Christians along with their land. However, during the 1840s the Sultan increased his power by banishing rebel aghas to western

---

4   Nestorians who did evangelize Muslims were rare enough to be noticed, and we will mention them where we can.

Turkey or to Damascus. He replaced them with Turkish governors. Telegraph lines made possible direct orders from Constantinople as never before. Taxes began to roll directly into the capital. Thus, Kurdish authority was challenged just at the same time as missionaries began to relay Christian complaints to sympathetic politicians in western capitals.

Kurdish aghas were alarmed by direct taxation from Constantinople, by missionary power, and by rising expectations of Christian serfs. The Protestants, though mindful that Christ's kingdom is not of this world, depended on American or British embassies to live in the Ottoman Empire and Persia. Missionaries did not see themselves as representatives of an earthly power, as the Kurds around the missionaries certainly saw them.

Within ten years of the arrival of the missionaries, Kurds slaughtered thousands of Armenians and Nestorians who lived in villages where missionaries labored. This is not to blame the missionaries for the terrorist acts of Kurds. Christians had long suffered the destruction of crops and the loss of their women to raiding Kurds before the missionaries arrived. However, Kurds suspected, and missionaries seemed to confirm, that Christians from the west and Christians in Kurdistan were allying for political purposes.

How we wish that Kurds had welcomed the missionaries! Bringing books and medicine, with their hearts open to help all people, with their moral duty to speak for oppressed minorities, missionaries would gladly have helped the Kurds as much as the Christians. But, like Jerusalem, Kurds rejected the prophets. The blood of martyrs cries out against them. Yet God, in His unsearchable mercy, gave the Kurds other opportunities to believe. In the late 20th century, missionaries returned to the same land, this time to help Kurds, who were now the oppressed minority. When Kurds come to faith, they must renounce the deeds of their fathers, at whose hands so many innocent people perished.

The massacres ended in 1846. Missionaries rebuilt their churches and schools, and started, again, to work alongside ethnic Christians.

OTHER MISSION EXPEDITIONS IN KURDISTAN

The Basel mission and the Anglican mission explored Kurdistan of Persia, though neither was so durable as the ABCFM and later the Presbyterians. The Basel Mission of Switzerland made an early attempt to place missionaries in Kurdistan.

BASEL MISSION EXPEDITION

In 1829 a Scotsman, Robert Pinkerton, visited the Basel Mission in northwest Switzerland. Pinkerton was working for the British and Foreign Bible Society (BFBS) in Russia. He proposed that the Basel Mission undertake a mission to the Kurds, and translate the Scriptures into Kurdish. Accordingly, the Basel Mission planned an expedition.

Christian Gottlieb Hoernle and F. E. Schneider of the Basel Mission arrived in 1834 in Tabriz. Another Basel missionary, Christian Friedrick Hass, joined them there. Hoernle found a Kurdish language assistant in 1835. Hoernle's task was to survey the Kurdish dialects and begin a Bible translation project.

With Schneider and Asahel Grant of the ABCFM, Hoernle twice journeyed through Kurdistan. His findings were "an important contribution to the study of Kurdistan, but Hoernle saw too many difficulties to continue a missionary attempt and recommended to the Mission Board to give up the project" (Waldburger 1983:2). His reasons are cited here:

1. The many dangers a missionary would have to face in the presence of a "primitive, rapacious, bloodthirsty and distrustful people full of hatred against all foreigners and people of a different faith."
2. The nomadic life of the Kurds would make missionary work difficult.
3. The dialectical diversity would make a popular Bible translation impossible.
4. Hoernle imagined the possibility of a medical mission, but did not want to imagine what would happen to a foreign doctor after a medical failure.
5. The complete indifference to education among the Kurds.
6. Considerable financial expense (Waldburger 1983:2).

Thus the Basel Mission decided not to begin a mission to the Kurds.

CATHOLIC MISSIONARY EXPEDITION

Nineteenth century Catholic missionaries arrived in Kurdistan of Persia in the retinue of a French general. The Persian Shah Feteh Ali wrote to Napoleon, asking for protection from Russia. As a result, Persia and France signed the Finkenstein Treaty of 1807. Newshirwan Mustefa writes,

> Napoleon sent a delegation headed by General Gardan to Iran in that year. In the delegation were military experts, engineers, doctors, and also two Jesuit missionaries. These two priests opened an office in Urmiah. Their main task was to oppose the activities of Russia and England in Iran. From the beginning, they made relations with the Nestorians (1992:260).

How could Kurds otherwise comprehend this arrival, than that European powers planned to ally themselves with the local Christians.

BRITISH MISSIONARY EXPEDITION

In 1837 or 1838 the Royal Geographic Society and The Society for Promoting Christian Knowledge jointly approved a two-year "Expedition for the Exploration of Kurdistan"; the primary objects were "to explore central and eastern Anatolia, northern Iraq and the Sinjar and to report on the . . . needs of the Nestorian and Jacobite Christians" (Guest 1987:75). The instructions added that:

> the political and moral state of the tribes of Mohammedan Kurds throughout this district, their languages, superstitions, and other peculiarities, will also, of course, not escape your observations; and it would be desirable to verify the reports concerning the Yezidis, or Fire Worshippers, or . . . Devil Worshippers (Guest 1987:75).

The British led to a mission; Anglican missionaries would arrive in Kurdistan in the 1840s. As American Protestants and the French Catholics before them, Anglicans worked exclusively among the historical churches. Likewise, Anglicans chose Urmiah for their headquarters.

AMERICAN MISSION TO THE NESTORIANS OF PERSIA

Justin Perkins had an "iron will and a robust constitution" (Daniel 1970:47). So did his wife. Charlotte Perkins was six months pregnant when the boat from Constantinople landed in Trebizond. For the next eight weeks she and her husband made their way by horse towards Russian Georgia; the more direct route via Erzerum was thick with bandits. The Russian route had its obstacles as well:

> When at last the young couple reached the Russian frontier, they encountered the first of repeated acts of harassment by Russian officials. For two weeks they were assigned to quarantine, "a hollow, on the bank of a small muddy brook". The scarce food was often unpalatable, the milk generally sour and the eggs "far more than stale." Baggage inspection in the Tsarist custom house, "complete with minute and ribald inspection of Charlotte's underwear," took a full day; after this inspection, a drunken inspector directed that most of the luggage would have to go back to Turkey.

> With no choice but compliance, the Perkinses parted with their baggage and wearily hastened on to the Russian-Persian border, seven days away. At the border they learned their passports must be sent to Erivan, through which they had passed five days earlier, to be endorsed. While a messenger took the documents, the Perkinses camped. "Clouds of sand" sifted through "every joint and seam of our tent, upon our beds, our provisions, and ourselves," Perkins recorded. By paying an exorbitant price, he and his wife managed to obtain "bread and melons, once in two or three days." After seven days of deepening despair, the messenger returned with the passports endorsed. They crossed the Persian frontier. . . . Three days after their arrival [in Tabriz] Charlotte bore a daughter (Daniel 1970:47–48).

By 1836 Perkins had opened a school. Lacking paper and pencils, Perkins taught math by drawing numbers in sand. Each student had a box of sand in which to cipher. After three years the number of schools reached twelve. The number of American-financed schools expanded for sixty years (*see* Table 4).

In 1840 Perkins opened the first printing house in Urmiah. The Lord's Prayer and the Book of Psalms were published in the Soryani, or Christian, script. On December 1, 1851 Perkins began publishing a newspaper, *Sparks of Light*, in Soryani. This was the only the third newspaper published in all of Persia. We mentioned Perkins' written aim of restoring the Christian church for the multiplying of mission effort. His aim reflected his orders:

According to instructions given to him he was to help the Nestorian Church to become able through the grace of God to give new
spiritual life to that region. To the members of the Uniate [Roman
Catholic] churches and to the Muslims he should do good as he
would have opportunity (Vander Werff 1977:115–116).

TABLE 4

AMERICAN MISSION SCHOOLS IN KURDISTAN

(NEWSHIRWAN 1992:261–262)

Years	Number of Schools	Number of Students
1837–1847	24	530
1847–1857	50	498
1857–1867	51	1096
1867–1877	58	2024
1877–1887	81	1833
1887–1895	117	2410

For Perkins, the Assyrians seemed natural allies of the Protestant missionaries:

The early missionaries seem to have regarded this ancient church
as in some sense "crypto-Protestant" because of its antipathy to
Roman Catholicism (caused mainly by the enormous loss of its
membership to the Chaldean Catholic Uniates) and because no
icons were venerated in its worship (Horner 1989:23–24).

Missionary Dwight Marsh likewise felt akin to the Assyrians,[5]
when he wrote that

Nestorius, from whom they derive their name, was born in Syria.
He was a presbyter at Antioch, and in A.D. 428, was made bishop
of Constantinople. . . . His refusal to apply the idolatrous epithet
mother of God to the Virgin Mary was the brunt of his offending;
and if he ventured into dangerous theories on the mysteries of
the Trinity, they received at the hands of the enemies the harsh-
est construction. In fact, Nestorius may with considerable reason
be pronounced the first *Protestant* (1869:107–8, italics not mine).

---

[5] The friendship between Assyrians and western missionaries
explains why the Assyrian Church joined the World Council of
Churches in 1943, when that body was still forming, several years
before the Orthodox Churches joined (Horner 1989:24).

In 1835 the American Board appointed a medical doctor to the Urmiah mission, Asahel Grant. Grant proved unstoppable despite formidable odds. Conditions were so harsh that only a person of indomitable spirit could remain. Such a man was Asahel Grant.

THE ARRIVAL OF ASAHEL GRANT

Asahel Grant was born in 1807 on a farm in Allegheny County, New York. He was 28 years old and already a widower with two sons when he volunteered for Kurdistan. Grant left his sons in the care of relatives, and set forth with a new wife, Judith, in 1835. Contemporaries described Grant as

medium in build, with a dark complexion and bright black eyes; "his aspect was friendly, with a dash of enterprise and enthusiasm." The secretary of the American Board who hired him was especially impressed with "his commanding form and mien, joined with calm decision and courage." These measured judgements fall short by far in conveying the impact upon contemporaries of Asahel Grant's indomitable personality (Guest 1987:74).

Once in Urmiah, Grant opened a medical clinic. He began treating an endless stream of patients, ten thousand in his first year (Daniel 1970:63). He also started a dozen village schools. Very soon, Grant reported the sensational news that the Assyrians were, in fact, the ten lost tribes of Israel! This report seized the attention of the Christian world. Grant based his argument on tradition, physiological affinities, customs and institutions. His conviction was not shared by his contemporaries (Daniel 1970.03), nor by missionaries fifty years later (Speer 1911:20), and is today discarded (Joseph 1961:16). Grant later suggested that the Yezidi Kurds were the lost tribes of Israel (Guest 1993:87).

THE "DREADFULLY WICKED" CONDITIONS

The early missionaries buried their women and children. Judith Grant was first blinded in one eye by ophthalmia, then died in January, 1839. Her twin daughters died a year later (Daniel 1970:64). All four of the Perkins children also died (Kaplan 1993:24). Charlotte Perkins developed epilepsy. It must have been difficult in America to feel the "dreadfully wicked" conditions (Judith Grant's phrase [Kaplan 1993:25]) under which the missionaries lived. The women had married men who could not be stopped. Grant himself contracted cholera, and never fully recovered.

Woes persisted. Two couples, the Hinsdales and the Mitchells, were to join Grant at Mosul, but the Mitchells both died en route, and by the end of 1842 Abel Hinsdale was dead. Somehow undeterred, Grant went ahead with plans to found a base in the Kurdish mountains (Daniel 1970:64).

Grant's early mission success in Urmiah attracted the notice of other boards; in 1837 and 1838 the American Episcopal Church sent Horatio Southgate, to explore the possibility of mission in Persia, in Mesopotamia, and in Anatolia. A French Catholic, Eugene Boré, traveled this ground between 1838 and 1842 and persuaded the Lazarist order "to establish a mission to the Chaldeans in the Urmiah plain; he also started a new Catholic school in Mosul" (Guest 1987:75). We hear nothing more of the Episcopalians. Soon the Basel mission went home as well. The Protestants who stayed were Grant and Perkins. However, Grant was about to build the first house with windows that Hakkari Kurds had ever seen.

GRANT MOVES WEST TO TURKEY

Grant moved westward, in 1842, to the village of Ashitha in the Hakkari region of what is now southeastern Turkey. He built a mission compound among the Nestorians of that region. Grant, ever the trail-blazer, was determined to work in the most difficult locations. A description of the land will help the reader to appreciate the geography of the region. Athelstan Riley pictured it thus:

> The Assyrian country on the Turkish side of the frontier is totally different from that on the Persian. Its chief features are bold and grand mountain ranges, separated by deep and narrow valleys, the fortresses, so to speak, in which the Assyrians have been enabled to preserve the Christian faith amidst the dominant Mohammedan races. There is one valley of considerable size, a small plain indeed, in the mountains, called Gawar; but with this exception, the mountain ranges extend to the Plain of Mosul, where they suddenly cease at a day's march from that town. The

river Zab flows through the heart of the Assyrian country and falls into the Tigris below Mosul. The majority of the population is Kurdish, the Assyrians come next in the point of numbers, the remainder being made up of Yezidis or devil-worshippers, Armenians, and a few Jews. There are also some Turkish officials, but the Porte usually employs Kurds in the government of this province. The Kurds (a Mohammedan people) are the natural enemies of the Assyrians, and live side by side with them. Struggles are almost constantly going on between them, frequently producing actual conflict (Heazell 1913:12–13).

Grant removed from the plain of Urmiah to the "deep and narrow valleys" of Turkey. News of his house traveled to the curious Kurds.

KURDS FELT THREATENED BY GRANT'S "FORT"

"The Kurds were more than irritated; in fact, they felt threatened" (van Bruinessen 1992:180). Windows arrived, the first ever seen in the area, and Grant installed them. Local Kurds thought they were seeing a fort (qal'ah) with holes from which the missionary could fire a rifle. Grant dismissed the "wild reports of my building castles," a rumor which he aptly attributed to "jealousy indulged by surrounding Koords of the influence of foreign Christians" (Joseph 1961:59). The tragic events that followed were not solely sparked by the windows controversy. Yet the rumor of a Christian fortress was one excuse that the Kurds used to plunder the Christian community.[6] A dark chapter in Kurdish history was about to open.

Massacre of Christians

In 1843 tension between Christians and their Kurdish neighbors reached a climax: The Nestorian patriarch, Mar Shimun, and the Tiyari tribe of Nestorians in Hakkari stopped paying their annual tribute to the *mir* of Hakkari. (Since Christians were exempt from military service, they paid a heavier tax than their Kurdish counterparts.) This challenge occurred as the Kurdish chiefs were mobilizing for war against the Turkish army. To Bedr

---

6   Years later, after Grant died, Armenian separatists did use his house as a fort!

Khan Beg of Cizre the Assyrian tax revolt was act of betrayal which involved the missionaries:

> The British diplomats encouraged the Nestorians to stand against Bedr Khan, and they encouraged the Turkish authorities to suppress the movement of Bedr Khan. In this complicated situation, the head of the Nestorians, in 1843, asked for help from the Archbishop of Canterbury (Newshirwan 1992:262).

As the Kurds prepared to resist the Turkish attack, Nur Allah Beg, the Emir of Hakkari, sent a letter to patriarch Mar Shimun to arrange a meeting and negotiate an agreement. "Strangely, Badger, the English missionary, not only did not let Mar Shimun see Nur Allah Beg, but instead made him [Shimun] ask Babi Ali [the sultan] to come and suppress the Kurds" (Newshirwan 1992:265). Badger wrote:

> Nur Allah Beg, the mir of Hakkari, has taken the independence of the Nestorians from them. If the temporary help that they are getting now [from the Christian West] was not there, the Kurds would have made them subservient to their laws, which are the laws of the wild (Newshirwan 1992:265).

So the British consuls in Van and Mosul encouraged the Assyrians not to pay taxes. This lit a fuse. Ottoman authorities, suspecting Grant of stirring a Nestorian separatist movement, gave their blessing to a Kurdish attack on the Nestorians (Daniel 1970:64). Bedr Khan Beg sent troops to enforce the tax collection. Order disappeared; Kurds entered Nestorian villages to steal and kill and destroy. Some 800 Nestorians, including members of the patriarchal family, perished immediately. "Villages loyal to Mar Shimun were massacred or enslaved; mutilated corpses, including the patriarch's mother, floated down the Zab. The Ottoman forces at Amadia made no move to intervene" (Guest 1993:91). The permission to plunder continued for two years. By 1845 some 10,000 Nestorians, a fifth of their number, had perished (Vander Werff 1977:117). Bedr Khan sold other Christians into slavery. This was "the first major conflict between native Christians and Muslims in modern times" (Joseph 1961:64).

Results of the Massacre

Cries from dying Christians reached to the capitals of Europe. "British and French exercised pressure on the Ottoman government to punish this chief and prevent further Christian massacres" (van Bruinessen 1992:180). Accordingly the Sultan sent Bedr Khan into exile, a move the Ottoman ruler was only too happy to make.

Nestorians hoped the missionaries would protect their rights; Kurds suspected it to be so. A correspondent of a London daily newspaper directly charged that "the American, Catholic, and Anglican missionaries were the immediate cause of that outrage" (Joseph 1961:49). British explorer Henry Layard, no friend of the missionaries, visited the area and reported that "there are circumstances connected with the massacres of the Nestorians most painful to contemplate" (van Bruinessen 1992:203). Grant and his Anglican counterpart, William F. Ainsworth, M.D., both wrote books defending themselves against this charge.[7] In their hearts, the missionaries kept to their "instructions that they should not interfere in local politics" (Joseph 1961:48). Kurds must take responsibility for their treatment of the unarmed Christians. Perhaps Layard and the London newspaper had a personal reason in leaving the blame at the missionary door.

Still, perceptions are a kind of reality. Kurds perceived Grant and his friends as government agents protecting the Christians. In his naiveté, Grant assured the powerful Kurdish chiefs and the church leaders "that he had no political objectives." However, as John Joseph commented, "The unfortunate thing is that Grant's mission was nothing but 'political' in the eyes of both Kurds and Turks" (1961:59, 65).

Grant Dies in Mosul

Grant had come up against the limits of human endurance. Eloquently he recorded his feelings:

> All of the romance of that field—if there ever were any—is now sober reality. There is no poetry in winding your weary way over rocks and cliffs, drifted snows or dashing torrents ... I frankly confess that, when in peril, the thought that, should I fall, many will only say, "I told you so," and hand down my dishonored mem-

---

[7] Sadly, these books are unavailable to us; the missionaries who were criticized deserve to be heard.

ory as the only heritage of my children, and an injury to the cause of Christ, has caused me much distress. But be it so (Daniel 1970:64).

Grant moved south to Mosul. There he began to teach the Bible, and especially concerned himself with the Yezidi Kurds. Of them Grant wrote that they "may yet be seen moving forward in a body to the Gospel standard when the restraints imposed of the powers that be are removed" (Joseph 1961:65–66). However, Grant did not live to see that new day. On April 24, 1844, after nine years in the field, Asahel Grant died of typhoid during an epidemic at Mosul.

THE NESTORIAN QUEST FOR PROTECTION

Like it or not, the missionaries stirred up Christian hope for protection.[8] Missionaries wrote to their embassies to pressure the Turkish government; this advocacy brought some relief to the suffering Christians. Eventually, in the 1878 Treaty of Berlin, the Sultan agreed to "improvements and reforms demanded by . . . the Armenians, and to guarantee their security against the Circassians and Kurds" (Olson 1989:5). A British consul arrived in Kurdistan to oversee the reforms. The result was predictable: the consul became "a beacon of hope to the oppressed and repressed Christians of Eastern Turkey, encouraging them to crave for justice" (1989:6). However, as Christians crowded the consul's office to state their complaints, the missionaries found themselves, quite unintentionally, in an adversarial relationship *vis a vis* the Kurds and Turks. One man, Wadie Jwaideh, said that "fear of

---

8   Heazell wrote, On one occasion the Turkish soldiers, who were on the hills, living at the expense of the people while they protected them, watched the sack of a village by the Kurds, and only when the enemy had retired made a silly show of attempting to pursue them; if by any chance the government is obliged to interfere, the surrender to them by the Kurds of half the booty will end the matter. When the nomadic Kurds pass to the Mosul district for the winter, and again when they are returning in the spring for pasturage, there is always robbery and danger of something worse (1913:64–65).

the Armenian ascendancy in Kurdistan appears to have been one of the most powerful reasons behind the shaykhs' attempt to unite the Kurds" (Olson 1989:5).

PROTESTANT WORK BEGINS IN MOSUL

Despite the massacre of 1843–1845, the Protestant mission to the Christians grew. Fidelia Fiske arrived in Urumiah in 1843, and took over the school started by Judith Grant. Under Fiske it became a boarding school. Fiske hoped that the children, away from their parents, would more fully come under the sway of the missionary teachers. In Urmiah, as in Beirut and Constantinople, the missionary regard for educating girls was revolutionary and had a lasting, progressive, effect.

Justin Perkins recommended opening new missions to the Christians in Mosul, Mardin, and Diyarbakir. Dwight Marsh arrived in Mosul in March of 1850.

Mosul is located on the great plain of northern Mesopotamia. Across the Tigris River lie the ruins of Nineveh, which archeologist Henry Layard explored in the 1840s. Marsh and Perkins found some of Grant's converts from 1844. "About sixty men, mostly Jacobites with some ex-Catholics—still met regularly to read the scriptures" (Guest 1993:112). One of them was a Yezidi Kurd who would figure in church history for the next several decades. His name was Jeremiah Shamir.

THE SPIRITUAL JOURNEY OF JEREMIAH SHAMIR

Jeremiah Shamir was born July 13, 1821, in the village of Karaimlais, fifteen miles east of Mosul. He had been orphaned while still an infant. Catholic monks raised him at a church school in Ainkawa, near Arbil. Jeremiah was fluent in Turkish and Kurdish, and he learned Syriac, Arabic, and some Italian (Guest 1993:112–113). He informed his superiors that he would study for the priesthood.

The Catholics sent this promising young man to Catholic school in Mosul. There he met the Protestant students of Grant and his colleagues. The result was a crisis of faith for the Catholic Jeremiah Shamir:

He secretly compared the Biblical texts distributed by the missionaries against those used by the monks. Belief gave way to doubt and he informed the superior that he had decided not to become a priest. Unmoved by three months of strict penance, he fled the monastery [in Arbil] and made his way [back] to Mosul, where he sought assistance from the British vice-consul (Guest 1993:113).

Jeremiah began to study with the Protestants. He impressed Perkins, who took him to Urmiah for further study. In the next year Jeremiah learned some English and Hebrew. In Urmiah

he was spiritually regenerated at one of the mission's revival meetings. In 1850 he returned to Mosul, where it was remarked that "the great change in his whole character made a striking impression on all who had previously known him" (Guest 1993:113).

Jeremiah began to preach under the direction of newly-arrived Dwight Marsh. Marsh supervised Jeremiah's ministry until 1858, when the mission in Mosul closed. Jeremiah remained there until 1864, when he took a job with the English consulate in Diyarbakir. He died in 1906 at the age of eighty-five. [9]

ANGLICAN WORK IN MOSUL

An Anglican named Ainslie worked among the Nestorians of Mosul. Ainslie wrote of his gains among the Assyrians,

The good spiritual condition of the church here has continued without interruption to the present time. Some have presented themselves as candidates for admission to the church, and, after careful examination by the committee, three were accepted and will be admitted at next communion. Last year five were accepted. It is this quiet, steady growth in a church that is, to my mind, the most to be desired.

I have been spending some little time among the villages of this region, and hope to go out next week again. The people are quite ready to listen and some, even of the priests, came to study the gospel. I was interested in noticing *how much I had gained of the Fellahi* [Christian] *language of which I have written*. When the

---

[9] Jeremiah persuaded the missionaries to search for legendary sacred Yezidi books; for more information refer to Guest 1993.

people were talking among themselves in that dialect I was able to understand nearly all they said. This fact gives me great encouragement, and I hope next year to be able to use their language quite freely (ABCFM 1877:243, italics mine).

However, Mosul's climate is a fiery furnace. Summer's heat lasts for nearly six months. Mosul was also a place of disease. Grant had died during the typhoid epidemic of 1844. Henry Lobdell died of fever there in March of 1855. Dwight Marsh returned to the U.S. in 1860. His colleague, Frederic Williams, whose first and second wives died in Iraq, moved the mission headquarters from Mosul to the cooler climate of Mardin, Turkey. No ABCFM missionaries remained in Mosul. Mission work in Mosul was left to a small Church Missionary Society (CMS) band.

MOSUL SHRIVELS AFTER SUEZ CANAL OPENS

After the Suez Canal opened in 1869, trade began to bypass Mosul altogether. The city population dwindled. The canal

provided a fast, convenient means of passage between Europe and India. A few years earlier the Ottoman telegraph line had been extended from Baghdad to the Persian Gulf, connecting there with the Indian cable system, and offering a swifter, more reliable service than the dromedary post. Indeed, in 1885 the vice-consul told a French traveller that for six years no Englishman had passed through Mosul. In 1886 the vice-consulate was abolished (Guest 1993:125).

Thus did mission work fizzle in Mosul. Later, in about 1882 the ABCFM in Mardin began to station a missionary in Mosul during the winter months. The first was Reverend Caleb Gates from Chicago. Gates toured the area, and visited the Yezidis of Baadri in February of 1883. He concluded that "the time has not yet come for work among them" (Guest 1993:125), *the same words* that the Capuchins wrote of the Yezidis in Aleppo two centuries previously.

GEORGE COAN AMONG THE NESTORIANS

Reverend and Mrs. George Coan arrived in 1849. They labored forty years "among the Nestorians or Assyrians, as they are now

called, on the Urmiah plain and in the mountains of Kurdistan"
(F. Coan 1939:11). In 1851 Coan made a long tour through Kurdistan, visiting over sixty villages. After this survey, the Coans
moved to Memikan, Gawar, "to be associated with Mr. Rhea and
open up work among the Mountain Nestorians.... Memikan
was a small, dirty Christian village of some twenty houses situated on the western side of the plain of Gawar" (1939:12).

MISERABLE LIVING CONDITIONS

Frederick Coan, the son of George and Ida Coan, describes the
hardships under which he and his parents lived. Today's missionaries should reflect on the sufferings that his family endured
to follow Christ to Kurdistan:

> It was the middle of November, 1851, when we reached Gawar,
> and just before sunset we arrived in Memikan. We had brought
> from Urmiah a window with four small panes of glass which was
> put in the wall of our room, the only light coming through that
> window. Our own room about twenty feet by sixteen had to serve
> as bedroom, living and reception room, kitchen and school room.
> As the stable and native living room adjoined, with connecting
> doors, it was always filled with smoke or the pungent odors of cat-
> tle. The houses were half underground on account of the intense
> cold. The fleas were so bad that when they retired at night they
> stood in a basin of water and brushed off all the fleas they could
> before jumping into bed (1939:13).

Coan continued his description of the lamentable winter
conditions:

> A narrow passage separated the room from that occupied by Mr.
> Rhea, and through that passage all the cattle had to pass to get
> to their stable. In the winter the thermometer dropped to twenty
> and thirty degrees below zero, and snow fell to a depth of eight-
> een feet, so that sometimes they were in complete darkness. Tun-
> nels had to be made for the cattle to reach the springs to drink
> (1939:13).

"CAN PARADISE BE BETTER THAN THIS?"

Twenty years later, young Frederick Coan returned as a missionary to Gawar in Turkey. Living conditions were no less
miserable:

The people live in the stable for the sake of warmth. At one end of the stable is a raised platform, a foot or so high to get above the moisture. On all the other sides of the stable are the huge black buffaloes, oxen, cows, horses and donkey. The only light that penetrates the place is through a few holes in the roof that are carefully closed at night and throughout the winter. The place is so hot one almost suffocates, and the odors of the cattle and tobacco smoke choke one. Add to all of these the myriads of fleas and other vermin, and, to one unused to it, sleep is impossible. I tried it a few times, and then picked up my cot and went to the street, willing to risk robbers or freezing rather than suffocate. One wonders how so many can live under such conditions. One day we were seated in a small room, so hot that we were all dripping, and so thick with tobacco smoke that one's eyes smarted, when one of the men in all seriousness asked, "Do you think paradise can be better than this?" I told him I hoped so (1939:72).

THE SUFFERING OF MISSIONARY FAMILY LIFE

Family separation brought misery to even the most determined of missionaries. Coan writes of the day his older brother left for schooling in the United States:

All too soon the time came, the most heart-rending in missionary experience, when the children must permanently leave home for their education in America. In 1872 came the sad day when Edward had to go, having already decided to return as a missionary when his studies should be completed. . . . Edward was terribly homesick from the time he left and never got over it. . . . Not many months after he had gone, Father came to the breakfast table with a sad face, saying he had had a very vivid dream that Edward had died. Mother tried to laugh it off, but he could not get rid of the feeling that something had happened. Two months after the dream I heard weeping in the study; going in, I found Father and Mother in tears, and they told me that my brother had died. On comparing date, we found that his death corresponded with the very hour of the dream (1939:28).

Twenty years later, Frederick Coan's own son died of fever in Van. His grave was dug in Urmiah "where it could rest by the side of my brothers and sister on Mount Seir" (Coan 1939:150).

The wife of Samuel Audley Rhea endured another suffering— loneliness. Rhea had married her while on furlough. He allows us to feel his wife's depression, four years into her missionary life in Kurdistan:

> I accidentally found Martha crying today, after our mail came, and I half suspect this matter of associates [that is, friends] was at the bottom of it. These long, lonely winters are rather trying for her; and, though she has a remarkable fund of happy contentedness in her disposition, there are times when the prospect of another winter without an associate is rather too much for her. Still, when the time comes to be shut in again, I have no doubt she will be as happy and content as any one of her missionary sisters (Marsh 1869:226).

However, Martha Rhea did not survive until winter; she died September 16, 1857.

"THE LACK OF PUBLIC SPIRIT"

Another misery was the hard work. Said Frederick Coan, "I have never seen a place where anyone works harder and gets less for it than in Kurdistan" (1939:74). There was another hardship, which Coan calls the lack of public spirit:

> If there is any one thing that universally impresses the traveler in the East, it is the hard way in which everything is done, with physical strength and brute force taking the place of the brain. Then there is also a lack of that public spirit to which we owe so many improvements in the West (1939:178).

This lack of public spirit, which Coan and others observed in Kurdistan, meant a laziness of mind and a disregard of one's neighbor. Each family is set against the others during times of peace. One looks in vain for public projects which benefit the whole society.[10]

At every turn great problems lay heavy on the missionary's mind. Here is a story of a lost musical instrument that would almost ruin one's faith:

---

10 David Pryce-Jones' book, *The Closed Circle*, delves into Arab culture, but his conclusions are meaningful for Kurds as well. "From the proudest power holder down to the humblest family, all are engaged in pillaging whatever they can for themselves, or at best for their tribe and religion, rather than considering the public interest and constructing the commonwealth" (1989:402)

Friends in Hartford, her birthplace, had presented to Mrs. [Dwight] Marsh a superior melodeon. It had crossed the Atlantic and Mediterranean safely to Smyrna, then by steamer safely to Scanderoon, thence through Aleppo, across the Euphrates, past Abraham's birthplace [sic], and by the Tigris at Diarbekir. It had come out of the gates of Diarbekir, and was approaching Mardin. Its eight thousand miles of sea and land were safely completed to its very last stage. It had only once more to be lifted on to a mule's back to reach its expectant mistress in Mardin. When the melodeon should have appeared there, the muleteer entered and placed a bag down with about a bushel of screws, hinges, rods, and the lock and key. His brother, left in charge while he tended the mules, had probably lain down smoking; and, at any rate, when he returned from his mules he found his brother asleep and the box burning up! (Marsh 1869:250).

Traveling missionaries had to hire guards (Turkish soldiers or Kurdish servants), purchase tents, pay for lodgings for days at a time, and, often, pay customs fees. In addition, they sat out winter storms, sweltered in summer's furnace, and paid bribes to border guards or to release captives after raids.

ENTRY STRATEGY—PERMISSION TO PRACTICE MEDICINE

Missionaries entered Persian Kurdistan through Christ's healing ministry, beginning with Asahel Grant. Through medical work, they gained permission from the authorities. Frederick Coan wrote,

We first reported to the government (in Diza) [near Sulaimania] and secured permission to proceed. The doctor's coming was soon known, and many sick began to pour in from every direction for treatment, continuing to come for days after we had left. Diza is the most dusty, uninviting place one can find, for all the sweepings, refuse, and ashes are dumped into the streets and the continual winds blow the dust everywhere. The small town is quite an important center, with roads that radiate into Persia, Kurdistan, Bashkall, the Albak region, Salmas, and Van (1939:86).

By Christ's healing ministry, Protestant and Catholic missionaries served all manner of people. Rich and poor, of all religions and sects, were alike to the missionary doctor. In addition, doctors opened the door to the preaching ministry. Coan wrote of his travels in 1888 with Wishard, a doctor:

> I think we proved how difficult it is to do satisfactory medical work when touring. As a help and adjunct to the evangelistic work, however, the presence of a physician is very valuable. The sick came from every direction when they heard there was a doctor. . . . The doctor brought large crowds that would have been hard to draw otherwise and gave many opportunities to preach and to talk with them. What the doctor was able to do also broke down prejudice and opened the way for us everywhere (1939:112–114).

In the 1880s Presbyterians built Westminster Hospital in Urmiah, placing Joseph Cochran (field dates 1878–1905), a distinguished physician, at its head. Cochran's work so increased the respect for Christianity among the Kurds and Persians that local Christians were less subjected to oppression and violence. A famous story told below relates how Cochran stood alone at the city gate and rescued the city of Urmiah from marauding Kurds.

Joseph Cochran Averts a Massacre

In the spring of 1880 Sheikh Obeidullah, a Kurdish leader, had invited Cochran to come up to visit him and diagnose him. Cochran says, "We had opportunity given us to speak very freely on religious subjects" (Speer 1911:74).

However, in October, Obeidullah's Kurdish warriors surrounded Urmiah and threatened to bombard it. A general panic followed while Cochran, then twenty-five years old, faced Obeidullah at the city gate. Cochran persuaded the sheikh to march away from Urmiah, pointing out to him the many benefits that the Kurds had derived from the medical mission (Richter 1910:307). In this way Cochran averted a massacre. The story spread throughout the land the foreigner had faced down Obeidullah's horsemen. However, Obeidullah's raiders attacked outlying Christian villages:

> Those Koords pierced the babies and killed the helpless women and shot men without mercy. They spoiled the property. All they could carry away they carried in successive caravans. The articles that could not be shipped, they burned in the homes of the owners. (Yonan 1895:9–10).

The following month, internal dissensions sundered Obeidullah's band and it melted back into the mountains. The Sultan in Constantinople moved against Obeidullah, and exiled him to Mecca in 1882 where he died the following year.

COCHRAN'S SON BECOMES A MISSIONARY DOCTOR

Joseph Cochran, Jr. followed his mother and father onto the mission field in Kurdistan. Joseph's mother wrote that "Joe has retained his knowledge of Syriac and Turkish, so he needs only to study the Persian, the Court language" (Speer 1911:54). Mrs. Cochran writes of blessings that accrued from her son's medical work:

> Yesterday some Kurdish chiefs and their escorts were at our house to consult Joe. One had been here last week with his sick son, and yesterday he returned filled with joy, and expressing heartfelt thanks for his son's recovery. He remarked, "Now I shall not throw my hand from off you," and wanted Joe to visit him in his castle. He said, "The doctor can walk in safety in Kurdistan." No one can do this unless under the protection of this powerful chief (Speer 1911:54).

THE POSITIVE INFLUENCE OF MISSIONARIES

We have referred to the senior Cochran's influence with Sheikh Obeidullah. Missionaries often won favor with Kurdish leaders.

THE INFLUENCE OF MISSIONARIES
ON KURDISH CHIEFS

The historian Julius Richter writes of one sheikh who granted permission for missionaries to work in his area:

> From time to time an opening presented itself among the unstable robber tribes of the Kurds. Gul Babaa, an influential sheikh, head of a religious sect which claimed 40,000 adherents, showed a remarkable tolerance; he welcomed the missionaries and other Christians to his remote mountain retreat, was glad to engage in religious discussions, and read the Bible with interest. But as the Kurds are most dangerous robbers and thieves, no missionary could live safely in their mountain fastnesses, and at no time has regular mission work been undertaken among them (1910:325).

Coan remembers another influential Kurd who welcomed the missionaries:

> The governor in Soujbulakh at one time was a very intelligent, powerful Kurd who hated the missionaries and had given word that if they were killed nothing would be said. Later, through the influence of our helper, Saifi-din Khan purchased a Bible and was much impressed by it. When I called on him he was most cordial and in his study, where I saw many French books that he had read, he told me that Christianity was the only true religion. He told me that it was the meeting with such men as Reverend W. L. Whipple and Dr. Holmes and Dr. Wilson that had disarmed his prejudice, saying, "When I talked with Mr. Whipple, I realized I was talking with a holy man" (1939:63).

Later the governor pleaded with Coan "to open a school for the Kurdish boys in Soujbulakh, offering to give liberally towards its support" (1939:63). *Coan had permission from the Muslim government, but not from the Assyrian church, to teach the Kurdish children.*

PROTESTANT MISSIONARIES INTRODUCED NEW CROPS

Missionaries arrived with seeds to improve the crops in Kurdistan. They introduced strawberries, raspberries, gooseberries, currants, tomatoes and sweet corn, and an improved variety of apples (F. Coan 1939:231). Coan also introduced potatoes:

> In my early tours to Mosul through the mountains that lie between the Persian border and the upper Mesopotamian plain, I noticed that the people had never heard of the potato and were having a hard time raising enough millet and corn to keep themselves alive. So I showed them the potato, spoke of its value, and asked whether they cared to have me plant a small patch for them. They eagerly agreed, and so all through, from Khazni on the Ilajan plain to the city of Rowanduz, potatoes were planted. I asked the people not to eat the first crop but to save them for seed.
>
> A few years later, having forgotten all about my potatoes, I was taking the same trip. In the evening at the first village my cook brought in a plate of deliciously fried potatoes. I expostulated with him for making our loads any heavier by bringing potatoes from home. Then he told me he had found the potatoes in the village. As we travelled on from day to day, I found potatoes

everywhere and was told that they were so popular that villages off the road had come and begged for them, so that potatoes had been quite generally introduced. I considered that my potato sermon, and possibly one of the best I ever preached (1939:181).

REVIVALS AMONG THE NESTORIANS

Missionaries reported about a dozen revivals among the Persian Nestorians between 1846 and 1863. Revival started among students and spread throughout the Urmiah region. An awareness of sin opened their eyes to the saving power of Christ; the joy over forgiveness led to a deep interest in God's word and prepared many to serve Him. Vander Werff says that, as a result, "some Nestorian evangelists worked among Kurds living in surrounding villages" (1977:125).

History records a few Kurds from the 19th century who followed Christ. In following Christ, they became like Him. We turn to their stories.

TWO KURDS IN PERSIA
WHO FOLLOWED CHRIST

Coan describes the conversion to Christ of two important Kurdish men; one was Dr. Sa'eed, of whom we will hear more. The other was Sheikh Baba.

THE TESTIMONY OF SHEIKH BABA

The conversion of Sheikh Baba proved Christ's power to reconcile enemies to one another. When Kurds receive the kingdom of God, they must receive it as meaningfully as did Sheikh Baba:

[Sheikh Baba] was led to Christ by one of our helpers and later baptized by Dr. S. G. Wilson of Tabriz. Sheikh Baba was regarded as a holy man whom many Kurds from the region of Soujbulakh[11] would visit to do homage. As a result of his conversion, the villages over which he held control had been all thrown open to our workers and a welcome extended to our preachers and missionaries.

I [Coan] told him we would hold a communion service on Sunday and asked if he did not want at that time to make a public

---

[11] Soujbulakh is called Mahabad today.

confession of his faith and unite with us. He said it was a serious step, but he would think it over and let me know next day, and then sent word that if we felt he was worthy he would gladly be with us. Sheikh Baba arrived with a large escort of armed men, who were stationed at the gate, and entered with his brother and nephew who had both been won to Christ. In that room there were some thirty souls, Kurds, Jews, Assyrians, Jacobites, Chaldeans, Armenians and one American.

Never did Christ seem nearer. At the close of the service I gave him the right hand of fellowship and explained what it meant, and then, to the surprise of all, this dignified leader of thousands, ignoring all others, stepped up to the Jew who had communed and kissed him. At that the whole company broke down in sobs.

To grasp the significance of that service, one must remember it was held in a bigoted, fanatical Kurdish city, where, had the people known what was going on in that upper chamber, a mob would soon have killed every one. Later during the war when the Turks came in, the conversion of Sheikh Baba was reported to them, and when he refused to deny Christ he was hung to a tree and left there until the birds had picked the body clean. Samuel the Jew also suffered a martyr's death (1939:61–62).

THE TESTIMONY OF DR. SA'EED KURDISTANI

Dr. Sa'eed's dramatic conversion to faith in Christ, and his many years of Christian medical work, have been the subject of two books: *The Beloved Physician of Teheran* by Isaac Malek Yonan (1934) and *Dr. Sa'eed of Iran* by Jay Rasooli and Cady Allen (1957). All who knew Dr. Sa'eed Kurdistani were drawn by his love and devotion to Christ:

> Here was a medical St. Paul. Kurd of the Kurds, Moslem Pharisee of the Pharisees, this brilliant powerful young mountaineer of Kurdistan becomes a follower of Jesus at the price of scouring and branding and at the peril of his life (Yonan 1934:intro).

Dr. Sa'eed's Early Years

As early as his ninth year, Sa'eed was giving the call to prayer and reading with mullahs at the mosque. He spent many hours each day reading Kurdish poetical works about Muhammad's life.

While still a young boy, Sa'eed developed a haughty disposition toward the Jewish and Christian minorities around him. When on an errand to such a home, young Sa'eed was known for passing close to a shelf, and with his elbow sending a dish or two crashing down, and then offering profuse apology for the accident! He hoped that the damage would be to Allah's glory, and would thus merit a later reward for himself (Rasooli and Allen 1957:24).

At 13 his father, the mullah, died; at 14 Sa'eed succeeded his father as mullah. Moreover, Sa'eed was initiated in the Naqshibandi order, the youngest member the order had ever taken. His mother and brothers and sisters felt proud of his ambition and accomplishments.

Exposure to the Bible and to the church did not influence Sa'eed except to make him more content in his Islamic faith. Sa'eed describes his first reading of the Persian New Testament:

As I had never seen a Christian Bible before, from mere curiosity I read and read, but could make nothing out of it. It was such a strange book. Through one of my Christian pupils I made an engagement to meet the Catholic priests, to whom I sent and asked for an explanation of certain passages in this strange book. But he could not solve my difficulties, nor explain the passages that puzzled me. So I cast away the book with disgust. Through my pupils I also visited some other Christian homes and even went into their church and saw their worship. The image worship and adoration of pictures, both at home and in the church, the mode of their worship, the vestments, of their priests, the curtain and the holiest place, candles, incense burning and bowing to the eucharist—in fact, the whole service gave me the impression that these poor men and women were nothing but idolatrous. I did not wonder why, *in all the Kurdish poems I had read, Christianity and idolatry were synonymous.* Disgusted and hateful more than ever, I left these Christian Gowers (heathen). I came to the conclusion that Islam was the only true religion of Allah; and how grateful I was to my ancestors who suffered and at the point of the sword were compelled to become Mohammedans, centuries ago, and I owed my orthodox faith to them (Yonan 1934:24–25, italics mine).

Sa'eed Confesses Christ as His Savior

In 1879 an Assyrian pastor, Kasha Yohanna, and two colporteurs trained in Urmiah came to Sa'eed's city, Sanandaj. The pastor wanted to improve his Farsi, and Sa'eed was recommended as a teacher. Through Yohanna's friendship, Sa'eed understood the Christian faith for the first time. Sa'eed gave up the practice of "cutting the Koran," that is, opening it at random for divine guidance. Sa'eed had to wrestle with the growing conviction that his father's Islam was wrong. Due to Kasha Yohanna's virtuous life and compelling faith, Sa'eed at last placed his own faith in Jesus Christ, and turned from Islam.

"A Sudden Explosion"

Accordingly, the young mullah was no longer able to mount the minaret for the call to prayer. Isaac Yonan records the drama:

> You can imagine the scene before you. It is sunset time; the muezzins from a dozen minarets of Senneh have begun singing solemnly the familiar Arabic phrase, *Allahu Akbar*, God is great. But Sa'eed's voice was silent; he did not even show up at the mosque. There was a stir of anxiety among his kinsfolk who daily had listened with pride to the melodious voice of their pious Sa'eed when he uttered the phrase *Allahu Akbar*. While they were thus pondering his fate, Sa'eed came home; but before explaining the cause to the excited groups of relatives, he handed to his brother a letter which he had prepared.

The contents of the letter were as follows:

> In the one only God's name.
>
> My brother. You know that the dangers to my life grow greater every day. To remain in my paternal home is impossible. I am a Christian, and confess it openly to you. If you will murder your brother, my life is in your hand. I cannot escape you; yet death is also a gain to me. If you spare my life I shall be very thankful, and will all my life respect you, and serve you as much as I can. My wish is to flee from here so that you may get more peace.
>
> Your brother, Sa'eed

A sudden explosion of a bomb could not have terrified the family as these words did. "Blasphemy!" they all shouted frantically. All agreed that Sa'eed had been duped by the stranger, the

Christian Gewor to whom he had been giving lessons in Persian in the past years (1934).

Dr. Sa'eed was baptized April 10, 1887, in public, with Muslims present.

Sa'eed's Brother Tries to Kill Him

Sa'eed's brother, Muhammad Rasooli (known as Kaka), at first took seriously his responsibility to kill Sa'eed for renouncing Islam. Sa'eed left Sanandaj, and Kaka vowed to hunt him down. However, in time Kaka himself came to Christ as his Lord. In the town of Hamadan Kaka, along with a missionary, J. W. Hawkes, opened a medical clinic and a school for boys and girls.[12]

Dr. Sa'eed, as a Christian, Discusses Islam

Sa'eed became a doctor, married a Nestorian woman, and settled in Teheran. His medical skills, his bold witness, his piety, and his generosity made him widely known and respected. In later years, Dr. Sa'eed reflected on Islam in these words:

Islam is a system of stolen truths. There is not a thing of primary importance in it which would be claimed as original. I have come to the conclusion that it is a system of apostasy and heresy. I assure you it is worse than heathenism. Mohammed said: If Jesus had not gone too far in the religion of God, I could have accepted his religion. Now, that shows conclusively that he understood Christ well, and knows that Christianity would not give him a license for the things of the flesh that he himself indulged in. So he gave it up and became a renegade, yet availed himself of Christian religious phraseology and gladly put it in the Arabic garb.

In his plagiarism, Mohammed was helped by Jews and Christians whom he had compelled to become Mohammedans and who, to gain his respect and to please him, put Biblical phrases in Arabic form and attributed them to Mohammed, just as the sugar stolen by the brigands resold in the market will still be sugar. The pity of it is that all such stolen truths from the Bible are misquoted and garbled.

---

12 Kaka's son, Jay Rasooli, became a medical doctor and moved to San Pedro, California, where he and I became acquainted.

Any honest seeker after divine truth who can empty his mind of partisan prejudice and religious bigotry, by comparing the Koran with the Bible, will positively reach the same conclusion (Yonan 1934:108).

We have briefly examined the Protestant mission to the Nestorians in Persia. We next study the mission to the Armenians in Turkey.

THE GREAT EXPERIMENT AMONG THE ARMENIANS

Missionaries among Armenians were determined men and women of the American Board of Commissioners for Foreign Mission (ABCFM). However, in just two years, this Great Experiment divided the Armenian Church between the Protestant-disposed reformers and the priestly traditionalists.

THE PROTESTANT MISSION DIVIDED THE ARMENIANS

In March 1839 the Armenian patriarch forbade the reading of books sold or distributed by the missionaries; the Greek Orthodox patriarch did the same. They forbade contact with the missionaries. Beginning January 25, 1846, and continuing through the year, Armenians who continued with the missionaries were excommunicated. Protestants had not leavened the loaf; they had extracted a piece. The missionaries felt responsible for this piece for the century to come.

Unwelcome in the Armenian churches and forbidden from teaching Muslims, only one narrow course opened to the American missionaries. They petitioned the Sultan in Constantinople to legalize an Armenian Evangelical Church. The Sultan granted this petition on July 1, 1846. From that date, references to Protestant work refer not to the Armenian Orthodox church but to the Protestant version, the Armenian Evangelical Church. Reverend Stepan Eutudjian was its first pastor (Fidelis Society 1993: introduction). Having birthed this church, the ABCFM naturally provided parental support. From that time, the ABCFM sponsored the Armenian Evangelical Church. Descendants of those early converts populate churches today in Syria, France, South America, and the United States.

MISSION SUCCESS IN THE
ARMENIAN EVANGELICAL CHURCH

After the missionaries opened the Armenian Evangelical Church, it grew rapidly. Thousands of Armenians in Kurdistan transferred to it. For example, in 1855 an evangelical Armenian church was established in Marash. "Within six years there were sometimes more than 1000 at the Sunday morning service, with 1500 more coming for the afternoon communion service" (Farnham 1985:20). By the turn of the 20th century, a third of Marash's 30,000 Armenians were adherents of the Evangelical Church or the Catholic Church (Kerr 1973: introduction). Similarly in Aintab (now Gaziantep) the gospel had broken into the large Armenian communities "with astonishing results" (Farnham 1985:18).

ABCFM WORK IN AINTAB, TURKEY

Henry J. Van Lennep was the first American Board missionary to visit Aintab. Van Lennep arrived on April 1, 1847 (A. Edmonds 1979:1). He met a well-educated Armenian teacher known as the "blind sage" Kevork. The next visitor was Reverend Thomas P. Johnston; he was not well received, being "stoned out of the city by an Armenian rabble" (A. Edmonds 1979:2). Fortunately, the next visitor, Azariah Smith met with promising success when he healed a woman. This was in December 1847. Smith and his bride settled in Aintab the following year. The doctor devoted most of his time to evangelizing the Armenians. A report in the *Missionary Herald* of September 1851 suggests that the Armenians who yielded to Protestant teaching were abstaining from alcohol:

> It is a matter perfectly understood in Aintab that as soon as a man becomes a Protestant, he abandons his cups. One of the first steps, indeed, towards Protestantism is entire abstinence from all that intoxicates. Temperance has become a kind of test of Protestantism; so that when an Armenian is suspected of leaning towards it, the inebriating bowl is presented to his lips; and according as he receives or rejects this, he is pronounced an Armenian or a Protestant (A. Edmonds 1979:2).

In June 1851 Smith died of typhoid and pneumonia that he contracted through his medical work. His wife returned to the

United States. The hospital, built in 1880, still operates today. Until recently it was known as the Azariah Smith Hospital. Compassionate professionals carry on the hospital's heritage of caring for the sick.

Fred Shepard of Aintab, "Just like Jesus"

Fred Douglas Shepard worked his whole adult life in Kurdistan. A doctor with the ABCFM, Shepard resided in Aintab from 1882 to 1907. He also traveled to Urfa (now Sanlifurfa) and Diyarbakir and Aleppo, ministering to Kurds, Turks, and Arabs. A fellow worker remembers an incident:

> The news soon spread that he [Shepard] was there, and again the sick were brought to him. A room in a house was given him, and all day he ministered to the sick, even until nine o'clock in the evening, when we started on our journey again. The words of an Aintab Seminary schoolgirl, who lived in that village and who called on us, expressed the feeling we all had concerning him. As we sat watching from the window old and young, sick and infirm, deaf and blind, some brought in ox-carts, some on the backs of mothers or husbands, some walking, but all in distress, waiting to see the doctor, this girl said, "He is just like Jesus, isn't he?" And we all answered, "Yes" (Riggs 1920:103).

The hospital and medical department of Aintab College ministered to all the citizens of Aintab. This did much "to allay the existing antipathies against foreigners and the religion they bring" (A. Edmonds 1979:5).

The Cholera Epidemic of 1891: Shepard Takes Command

Familiar to workers in Kurdistan is a careless disregard of hygiene. Shepard's daughter, Alice Riggs, recalls the conditions of Aintab in her father's day:

> All the rubbish and garbage from the houses in Aintab were thrown out into the street, and the dogs were the only ones expected to take care of it. The waste water of the city was carried off by a foul-smelling, open gutter down the center of the street. Aintab, the Spring of Healing, was named after the magnificent, gushing spring, some miles distant, from which the water

supply was brought to the city through an old Roman aqueduct. The water could not have been purer at its source, but as the watercourse ran under every street of the town, each house had its wellshaft through which the bucket was dropped to dip up water from the common supply. Cholera, typhoid, and dysentery germs might, and often did, go down with the bucket; and the spring of healing became the spring of death.

In the summer of 1891, a terrible epidemic of cholera broke out in the city. Dr. Shepard took command. He marshaled all the doctors and druggists in the city, and organized them into "day" and "night" corps, to fight the dread disease. In all the churches and mosques they gave public lectures, telling the people that they must cook all solid food and boil everything they drank.

The Christians obeyed, and fewer and fewer were taken sick. But the Moslems said, "Of what use? If it is written on our foreheads that we shall die, we die; if it is written that we shall live, we live. Of what use is it to cook our food and boil the water we drink?" And in this way many died (1920:58–60).

ABCFM SCHOOLS AMONG THE ARMENIANS

In every city, missionaries in eastern Turkey established schools for the Armenians. The *Missionary Herald* magazine, stirring stories inspired the mission societies back home. Typical was this from the Euphrates College in Harput:

President Wheeler reports that, of the 277 male pupils, who come from fifty-one cities and towns, seven were in the classical department, and 45 in the theological department, and 225 in the three preparatory grades. In the female department there were 238 pupils, coming from thirty-one different places. In a recent visit of the Governor-General and his suite to the college, he spoke enthusiastically to the young ladies, and among other things said, "I am about to open school for girls, and by-and-by shall call for some of you to teach my teachers how to teach" (ABCFM 1877:243).

In 1859 missionaries opened a theological seminary in Harput. One missionary wrote a half century later, "To these graduates is due much of the credit for social and religious changes in ancient Armenia" (Eddy 1913:117). Other schools began in Mardin, Marash and Bitlis.

Armenian Outreach to Armenians:
The Kurdish Missionary Society

American Board missionaries not only established churches and schools and hospitals, they successfully introduced missionary societies. From *Missions in Eden*, we read that Armenians collected funds for Armenians living among the Kurds, and called it the Kurdish Missionary Society:

The monthly concert became one of our best attended meetings. We made it interesting by translating the most interesting papers from the [*Missionary*] *Herald* and other magazines into simple Armenian so that they might be easily understood. We often illustrated these topics by drawings on the movable blackboard. The students in our high school were able to give us a great deal of help in getting ready the monthly concert papers and drawing the illustrations. For example, we would take the Sandwich Islands and give them the history of their evangelization by American Christians. A picture of these islands with the missionary vessel, the Morning Star, which was built by the children, with all her sails set, approaching the land, was very pleasing and had a stimulating influence.

The children in our day schools being anxious to be formed in to Missionary societies like the American children and have a name all their own, we organized, "The Gleaners" in one ward of the city, "The Morning Star" in another, "The Day Spring" in one of the villages, and so on. In order to raise funds for the work we invited the children to bring *paras* (one-tenth of a cent), we held fairs, inviting the mothers to come and buy the articles their children had made. At such times the girls would be ready to sing and to recite, which greatly pleased their mothers and friends and served to interest them in our work. We wished to have the children working in this way all over the field.

Some thought all the money should be used for Home work; but others of us felt this would make the children narrow and selfish, so the Kurdish Missionary Society was formed, which was *intended to care for Armenians who lived in the midst of the Kurds,* many of whom could speak only Kurdish. One of our pastors who could speak Kurdish, travelled extensively in this region and came back to tell us tales of their wretchedness and ignorance which so touched all of our hearts that soon Branch societies were formed in all the churches (Wheeler 1899:100–101, italics mine).

Armenian Outreach to All Peoples

Around 1866, the Armenian Evangelical church formed the "Armenian Harpoot Evangelical Union." According to Vander Werff, it was a mission to all ethnic groups in the region: Jacobites, Muslim Kurds and Yezidi Kurds in the area (1977:112–113). Unfortunately for us, no reports of work exist.

BARNUM'S FORTY YEARS IN HARPUT

Set on a hill above modern day Elazig, the Armenian city of Harput lies northwest of Diyarbakir. Reverend Herman N. Barnum worked in Harput for forty years. He summarized his years of work there in the *Missionary Herald* magazine of the ABCFM. Barnum mentioned several improvements that occurred during his lifetime:

> Upon my arrival, forty years ago, I found one church of 28 members without a pastor. We now report 25 churches which have had a membership of more than 3000, and nearly thirty pastors have been ordained.
>
> The Turks have been affected less than the Armenians; still they have felt the stimulus of our schools. Home life improved, as did agriculture, the arts, and enterprise (ABCFM 1899a:401).

Economic Lift in Harput

Tangible blessings of redemption and economic lift came to the Armenians. But this roused the jealousy of the Turks and Kurds. Barnum makes this telling comment: "The thrift of the Armenians, their growing manhood and independence, are the real secret of the terrible events of 1895" (ABCFM 1899a:401). What does Barnum mean? Barnum's city on the hill, Harput, brings to mind Christ's metaphor of the light that cannot be hidden. The missionaries' agenda was to bless the Muslims by the light of the Armenian community. How hopefully the missionaries must have listened when the Turkish governor spoke at Euphrates College, saying that the graduates would "teach my teachers how to teach." Yet, in the end, Muslims destroyed the city set on the hill. If they would not have the light for themselves, they would deny it to the Armenians.

Harput Twice Devastated

Kurds massacred the Armenians in Harput in 1895–96. This destruction was wrought by the *Hamidiye,* special Kurdish forces which Sultan Abdul Hamid created in 1891.[13] Kurdish civilians also took part in the plunder. It looked, at the time, like the worst possible catastrophe. However, Armenians and missionaries returned to rebuild. Mission work continued another 20 years. However, when the massacres of 1915–1916 fell, all the Armenians fled or perished. The mission in Harput disintegrated with the Armenian nation.[14]

THE GREAT EXPERIMENT
AMONG THE JACOBITES

Mardin became a center of missionary work among Jacobite Christians (also called the Syrian Orthodox or Soryani) in 1858. Hundreds of Jacobite villages existed in southeastern Turkey at that time. One Dr. Williams established a second mission base in Midyat, a three-day's walk from Mardin:

---

[13] The Hamidiye, literally "men of Sultan Hamid," numbered more than fifteen thousand. "They spread fear through the open avowal that their official task was to suppress the Armenians, and that they were assured of legal immunity for any acts of oppression against the Christian population" (Kinross 1977:557). Ironically, the Hamidiye were the forerunners of the Turkish government special forces that today evict Kurds from these same Armenian villages.

[14] In August 1992 I visited the village of Harput. I was amazed at how well-preserved the old buildings of Harput appear. The main building of Euphrates College and the church still stand. New occupants, Kurds, simply moved in, and their descendants remain there today. In the old part of town there is no evidence of improvement. Grass grows through the roof of the round-topped, abandoned church. I ate at a garden restaurant overlooking the plain below. The other persons enjoying the view were Turks and Kurds. I did not have the courage to bring out the pictures and ask the Kurds and Turks at dinner what happened to the previous occupants.

Midyat was the administrative centre of about one hundred Christian Jacobite villages in the area. . . . There were also many Kurdish-speaking Muslim villages intermingled with those of the Jacobites in the foothills below. *Midyat was therefore seen as a stepping stone to a work amongst the Kurds* (Farnham 1985:14, italics mine).

For Protestants, the first stepping stone was reforming the Jacobite church. Evangelism of the Kurds would be a second step, taken by Jacobites themselves. This was the sum of the Great Experiment.

MISSIONARIES LEARNED
THE CHRISTIAN LANGUAGE

Protestant missionaries arrived in Mardin in 1858. They faced "a baffling array of languages. Arabic was the general language of the area, but Turkish was the language of administration. There were also two dialects of Kurdish, two of ancient Syriac, three of modern Syriac, and Armenian" (Farnham 1985:16).

Having decided to learn the Christian language, the missionaries quickly distanced themselves from Muslim Kurds, Turks, and Arabs. One American wrote, "I am able to devote more time to the acquisition of the [Christian] language, which I find is no holiday task" (ABCFM 1859).

CATHOLIC MISSIONARIES DIVIDED THE JACOBITES

Roman Catholic missionaries arrived before the Protestants, and succeeded in converting many Jacobites. In Mardin, a great controversy followed:

> The efforts of Rome a century earlier to reunite the Syrian orthodox with the Roman Catholic Churches . . . resulted in much division and bitterness. Add to this the Christian communities of Nestorians, Chaldean Catholics, Armenian Catholics and Gregorian Armenians living in the area, and it is small wonder that any Muslim on-looker should be confused as to where or even whether true Christianity could be found in this profusion of labels! (Farnham 1985:16–17).

Even the church buildings were divided down the middle. It was not a pretty picture:

Jacobites who had seceded to Rome still worshipped in the same churches, but at different times. Sometimes fights would break out if the first group did not finish on time. Once these became so bad that the local pasha (governor) heard of it and threw all the priests of the town indiscriminately into prison. The problem was finally solved by an extraordinary solution. A decree was obtained from Constantinople that every church should be divided in the middle by a wall, and that each party should take half. So for a time it was possible to attend services on one side of the wall, and hear the opposing group worshiping the same God on the other side (Farnham 1985:16).

Into this brew of tension and intrigue came Protestant missionaries. They attracted godly men who were weary of church conflicts. These men "were quickly attracted to a message in which Christ was preached as one who came to break down dividing walls" (Farnham 1985:17). But the tug of war between Christians went on. Reported one Protestant, "A merchant, a man of influence and head of a large circle of kindred, has renounced popery and has become a decided follower of Christ" (ABCFM 1859:73).

JACOBITE OUTREACH TO THE KURDS

A breakthrough came in 1867, when Protestant Jacobites began meeting for prayer every morning and every evening. Farnham writes that "Old wounds were healed, wrong relationships were put right, and the people began to pray as if they had done nothing else all their lives" (1985:21). He adds that the Spirit of God moved them to consider a mission to the Kurds:

Through prayer they caught a vision for the thousands of Kurds in the area who were almost totally unevangelised ... so they chose one of their own to be a missionary student who would later be sent out to work amongst these neglected people. He delighted in the name of Oosee Sit and was "a great six feet, brawny fellow, with unwashed clothes (he was a tanner), long dishevelled hair, large open features, eyes black as coal, that shine like stars, but so simple in his trust, so tender in his love of Jesus, so earnest in his efforts to do good." Sadly, no record remains of what happened to Oosee; the last mention of him was as he waited for "the melting of the Taurus snows and the winding up of his business to go and study that he may preach the Jesus he loves" (Farnham 1985:21–22).

ALPHEUS ANDRUS AND THE
KURDISH BIBLE TRANSLATION

Williams, the missionary who opened Mardin to Protestant work, died in 1871. A young missionary, Alpheus Andrus, took his place. Andrus worked in Mardin until the outbreak of the First World War. He wanted to evangelize the Kurds:

> With the church in the hands of a local pastor, Andrus was freer to organize outreach into surrounding areas. With a special concern for the Kurds, he was soon engaged in a translation of the New Testament into Kurdish. It was this same love for the Kurds that pushed him out again and again to the village of Midyat, the key to the Kurds and the Jebel Noor beyond (Farnham 1985:22).

Andrus supervised a translation of the Bible into the Kurdish tongue. It remained a manuscript. Much later, during World War I, the Turkish government arrested Andrus as a conspirator (although the United States was neutral in the war). Unfortunately, he was forced to leave without his manuscripts.

THE JACOBITE MISSION IN OTHER CITIES

Nineteenth century Protestants succeeded in other towns where Jacobites resided. Bitlis and Diyarbakir are two examples.

Town of Bitlis

Missionaries worked among Jacobites in Bitlis, Turkey. A typical report follows:

> This is a promising field for missionary operations. The town itself has a population of about 4,000 families, of which only about fifty are Jacobite Syrians. One hundred and fifty are Armenians, and the remainder Mussulmans. There is a large Armenian population in the surrounding country; and though it is a stronghold of ignorance and bigotry, there is an urgent call for the extension of our labors in that direction (ABCFM 1859).

City of Diyarbakir

Missionaries also converted Jacobites in Diyarbakir. Referring to these Protestant Jacobites, the ABCFM Report of 1899 said that "the city congregation has ordinarily ranged from 70 on weekdays to 200 on sabbaths; though on special occasions it has numbered from 300 to 600" (1899b). This congregation continued into the 1980s, when the last Protestant families moved away.

THE MISSION WORK
OF SAMUEL AUDLEY RHEA

Perhaps the outstanding missionary in 19th century Kurdistan was Samuel Audley Rhea. Rhea's contemporaries regarded him as extraordinarily gifted. One of them, Dwight Marsh, wrote Rhea's biography, *The Tennessean in Persia and Koordistan.* Comments Marsh,

> No missionary to Persia, not even Dr. Grant, ever searched out the whole Nestorian field both in Persia and Turkey, so thoroughly visiting again and again every nook and corner, as did Mr. Rhea. His trials as well as his joys directed him to this great work (1869:242).

We now turn to give an account of Rhea's work and faith.

THE SPIRITUAL VOW OF SAMUEL AUDLEY RHEA

Rhea worked in Kurdistan from 1851 until his death in 1866. His private diary reveals his sanctified life. We quote in full the vow that he made his first year in Kurdistan:

> Our Father who art in heaven, in the name of thy dear Son, and in the strength of thy Holy Spirit, I come to thee. Deeply convinced that thou alone art my rightful Owner, that I have been bought with the precious blood of Jesus, I do solemnly surrender my entire being to thee;
> my body, with every organ and member;
> my soul, with every power to think, to feel, to will and act;
> every moment of my time;
> my property, my influence, my plans, prospects,
> interests for all coming time and under all circumstances,
> whether of joy or sorrow, adversity or prosperity;
> to be disposed of just as may please thee;
> to live or die,
> to be sick or well,
> to be despised or honored,
> to be joyful or sorrowful;

my own will forever to be sweetly and humbly lost in thine.

Upon thine altar I lay my all, because I know it is sacrilege any longer to withhold from thee that which is sacredly thine. I do solemnly renounce the dominion of Satan, and of sin in all its forms, and take thee for my Father, Protector Preserver; the Lord Jesus for my Saviour, my sin-atoning Lamb, my Elder Brother, Shepherd and Friend; and the Holy Spirit for my Enlightener, Comforter, and Sanctifier.

With feelings of deep penitence and self-loathing I mourn over years of the grossest and most aggravated sin, in view of which I cannot but feel that I am the chief of the chiefest sinners; and were it not for that precious word, "Jesus Christ came into the world to save the chief of sinners," I should die in despair. In view of these aggravated sins I do look away from myself and all human aid, and without one plea, direct my eyes to that dear bleeding, suffering, dying Lamb of God, whose blood was freely shed for the remission of the sins of the world, and, if so, then for mine. Here I rest my only hope of acceptance with God, when, defenceless, I shall stand before his judgment-seat.

I am deeply convinced of my utter inability to begin or carry forward the life of God in my soul, and this work, which, O Lord, is thine, I do this day commit into the hands of thy Holy Spirit, and do resign my mind and heart to all his holy influences, to be enlightened, baptized, anointed, sealed, and completely sanctified by him.

I rejoice this day that I have the hope that to me, the least of all saints, is this grace given, that I should preach among the Gentiles the unsearchable riches of Christ! To the work of the holy ministry I do now solemnly give myself, praying that I may be anointed by the Holy Spirit: be a vessel sanctified and meet for the Master's use; that I may make full proof of my ministry, endure hardness as a good soldier of Jesus Christ, be instant in season and out of season, and, so long as I have a voice to speak, plead with dying men to become reconciled to thee, only to the praise of the glory of thy grace.

I feel this to be the most solemn act of my life. I never can do a more solemn act. It is a personal transaction between my soul and God, and, though I tremble, I cannot shrink from it; and though looking at my own sufficiency all is hopeless, I believe that Thou, O Father, Son, and Holy Spirit, wilt keep that which I have committed into thine hands.

And now, O Lord, seal to all eternity that which is and ever shall be only thine.

In the presence of God, the Father, Son and Holy Spirit, I make this dedication of myself to all eternity.

(signed) Samuel Audley Rhea
September 16, 1851.
Renewed upon the mountain near Memikan, June 4, 1857 (Marsh 1869:53–55)

"THE DESOLATIONS WHICH REIGN HERE"

In a letter to his family, Rhea challenged American Christians to sacrifice more on behalf of mission in Kurdistan:

> If you had seen what I have seen of the desolations which reign here, and felt what I have felt, never would you regret my leaving you. From the time that I first trod upon missionary soil, at every step I have taken I have rejoiced that I have been sent to these benighted lands; and if Christians in America felt as I believe they should feel, hundreds and thousands would make an offering of time and property and talents to give them the bread of life (Marsh 1869:37–38).

RHEA BELIEVED IN THE GREAT EXPERIMENT

Rhea gave his immense energy to the Great Experiment: grafting Protestant faith and practice into the existing churches. He wrote of one Nestorian who preached to the Kurds:

> Odeeshoo and Khoshaba came from Kerpel, a Koordish village. They say they spoke much with the Koords of Christ, and they listened attentively. There is a very friendly relation existing between many Koordish and Nestorian villagers; many are warm personal friends of each other, and the Nestorians are not afraid to preach Christ among them. *It would not be strange if the Koords should be the first Mohammedans moved upon. Oh what momentous interests are involved in the reawakening and reviving of this remnant of a once powerful Christian Church!* (Marsh 1869:90, italics mine).

Rhea's arrival in 1851 brought renewed hope to the missionary band; "all previous attempts to locate a mission station among the mountain Nestorians had failed. Had God's time now come?" (1869:97). Rhea wrote, "We will labor on until songs of joy go up from every village and hamlet on the plain and among the mountain Nestorians," (Marsh 1869:54–55). He worked hard to learn the Christian language. "No other missionary ever in our field," wrote Justin Perkins, "has possessed a better knowledge of modern Syriac or spoken it so well" (Marsh 1869: 289).

THE ASSYRIAN PATRIARCH OPPOSED RHEA'S WORK

By encouraging Assyrians to read the Bible, Rhea's aroused the familiar opposition of the Assyrian hierarchy. He wrote on January 21, 1852,

> Just at this time there seems to be in several villages a bitter hatred against us and our work. Mar Shimon (the patriarch) has succeeded in infusing his own hostile spirit for a time into many hearts, and the universal cry is, that we are aiming to make away with their time-honored church and the loved customs of their fathers (Marsh 1869:93).

WHAT RHEA THOUGHT OF THE KURDS

Rhea sympathized with the Nestorians who suffered under the hands of Kurds. Kurds would raid Nestorian villages and take what pleased them. Rhea writes his own feelings:

> The Koords are almost all Moslems, of the Soonee [sic] sect, and are very superstitious and bigoted. They are divided into numerous petty tribes and sects. Like most mountain people, they are brave, passionate and rebellious, and often semi-independent. The Yezidee devil-worshippers speak Koordish, and belong to the same race. The Koords are profoundly ignorant, being almost without readers and writers. In ferocity and cruelty, when aroused by passion or in pursuit of plunder, they scarce fall below the savages of our American frontier (Marsh 1869:110–111).

Kurdish Terrorism, as Recorded by Rhea and Others

Rhea wrote, "Koords are treacherous, and wait a fitting time to do a dark deed" (Marsh 1869:136). Other missionaries agreed. Rhea's biographer, Dwight Marsh, wrote, "We all knew something of the treachous [sic] character of the Koords. A number of our missionaries had been robbed by them. I had undergone that process twice and Mr. Cochran once in the neighborhood of Gawar" (1869:197).

A generation later, in 1890, Isabella Bird traveled to the same Christian villages and found them still terrorized by Kurds:

> Many women and girls, especially at Charviva and Vasivawa, have been maltreated by the Kurds. A fortnight ago a girl, ten years old, going out from _____, to carry bread to the reapers, was abducted. It became known that two girls in _____ were to be carried off, and they were hidden at first in a hole near _____. . . . Daily and nightly during the week of my visit Gawar was harried by the Kurds, who in two instances burned what they could not carry away, the glare of the blazing sheaves lighting up the plain (1891:280).

Marsh tells of a powerful young Kurdish chief from Jezirah (now Cizre), Yez Deen Shir, whose infamy was deserved:

> Yez Deen Shir used to visit us at Mosul to while away his time, and had savagely informed us that he would "like to kill every Jew, Yezidee, and Christian," politely adding, "except yourselves, my friends, and drink their blood!" . . . The atrocities committed by him upon the Christians of Jebal Tour sent shudders through the mountains (1869:197).

"Give Me Back My Peace!"

On one of his travels, Rhea mentions the hostility bred into one Kurdish traveler for a stranger who turned out to be a Christian:

> One evening at dusk, near the Khabour, an armed Koord intercepted us. Our Mosul attendant gave him the Moslem salutation. Soon the Koord, discovering that Ablahad was a Christian, demanded, *"Give me back my peace. Give me back my peace"* [italics not mine], meaning to get back whatever was pledged in the prayer, "Peace to you!" He then, as we rode on, deliberately leveled his gun at us and snapped the lock. It missed fire. I have seen many brave deeds, but never one more cool and gravely amusing than Mr. Williams then performed. He had not mounted, but with bridle in one hand, he raised the butt of his riding-whip, and walked rapidly up, shaking it closely before the Koord's face, with eyes fixed upon the Koord's eyes, not striking, but following him up as he stepped back farther and farther, till he had backed him out of the way, and thrown him completely off his guard, when suddenly Mr. Williams whirled, mounted and joined our rapidly-moving party. A half hour brought us, with darkness, to friendly shelter (Marsh 1869:151–152).

After a furlough during which Rhea married, he returned to Kurdistan. Danger from Kurds continued. His wife writes,

Much of the time we dreaded Koords. When we entered a narrow mountain pass, or turned a sudden corner, or saw dark objects or met horsemen, we would think they were upon us. Mr. Rhea's calm trust in the protecting hand that led us through those wild and dangerous regions did much to comfort and reassure us, and through that guiding Power we were safely kept (Marsh 1869:275–276).

RHEA BEGINS TO LEARN THE KURDISH LANGUAGE

Rhea is one of two 19th century missionaries who began to learn the Kurdish language (the other was Andrus Alpheus). He wrote to his parents on May 29, 1855,

I am studying Koordish. I am every day brought in contact with Koords; and for our protection and security here it is important that I know their language. But my chief design in making myself familiar with their languages is that I may preach to them Christ crucified. If my poor life is spared, this I confidently hope to do. They too are immortal, and many among them numbered doubtless among God's elect ones to be gathered from the four winds of heaven. Oh, what a privilege to be the instrument of bringing a wild and savage Koord to the feet of the Lord Jesus! What sacrifices may we not gladly welcome to be thus honored. I do not think it will be a difficult language to acquire. Being a corruption of the Persian, it belongs to the great Germanic family, and is a distant relation of English; it does not sound so strange as the Syriac did to me at first (Marsh 1869:203).

Rhea's diary does not include any conversations that he had with Kurds. He continued his work with Nestorians and did not apply himself to evangelize Kurds.

SAMUEL RHEA'S DEATH

Samuel Audley Rhea died of cholera September 2, 1865, age 38, and is buried in Seir, south of Urmiah. Marsh writes that a massive block of snow-white gypsum neatly polished, was soon placed over Mr. Rhea's grave by his widow, bearing the following inscription:

Rev. SAMUEL AUDLEY RHEA
MISSIONARY TO THE NESTORIANS
Born January 23, 1827; died September 2, 1865
Present with the Lord

On the reverse side the name, office and dates are the same, in modern Syriac, with the Scripture: "He was not, for God took him" (Marsh 1869:351).[15] A memorial to Rhea is also located in Blountville, Tennessee.

TABLE 5

ABCFM MISSIONARIES IN KURDISTAN, 1859

Listed under the 'Nestorian Mission'

Urmiah—
Austin H. Wright, M.D. missionary
George W. Coan, missionary
Edward Breath, Printer
Mrs. Catherine M. Wright
Mrs. Sarah P. Coan
Mrs. Sarah A. Breath
Miss Mary S. Rice, teacher
6 native preachers

Seir—
Joseph D. Cochran, missionary
Mrs. Deborah W. Cochran
four native preachers

Gawar—
Thomas Ambrose, missionary
two native preachers

On furlough in the United States—
Justin Perkins, D.D. missionary
Samuel A. Rhea, missionary
Mrs. Charlotte B. Perkins
Mrs. Sophia D. Stoddard
Mrs. Eliza A. Crane
Miss Fidelia Fisk

Listed under 'Assyrian Mission'

Mosul—
Dwight W. Marsh, Missionary
Henri B. Haskell, M.D. Missionary Physician
Mrs. Lucy Lobdell
Mrs. Sarah J. Haskell
Three native preachers, one helper

(ABCFM 1859)

---

[15] Rhea's own words, could have served as a fitting memorial to his character:

> In a single battle of the great Russian and Turkish [Crimean] war more souls entered eternity than all the missionaries who have died for five hundred years. Honor to the brave! Let them win earthly applause.... But did not the angels look down as approvingly upon those who, throughout the Crimean and Persian wars, held the missionary front in Koordistan? (Marsh 1869:196).

OTHER MISSIONARY GRAVES IN KURDISTAN

Many 19th century missionaries were laid to rest in Kurdistan. With Rhea in the missionary cemetery in Seir are Stoddard, Thompson, Breath, Austin H. Wright, many children, including Rhea's one year old son (Marsh 1869:308) and eight Cochrans. Coan mentions the Assyrian village of Diza, near Memikan (in Turkey north of Kani Masi, Iraq), "where the first Mrs. Rhea, Mrs. Crane, and a child of Dr. Labaree were buried" (1939:71). Buried in a mission cemetery outside of Mosul are Lobdell and Grant. Other graves are that of "Mrs. Stock in Hassan and the little McDowell children in the olive groves of Dihi, Supna, located near Sersink in northern Iraq"[16] (1939:71). Roger Cumberland, whom we will meet in the 20th century, is buried in Mosul.

A CHURCH OPPRESSED

Latourette writes, "Again and again, notably in the 1830s and 1840s, the Assyrian (Nestorian) Christians were massacred by their fierce neighbors, the Kurds" (1975:1209). Richter adds,

> Until the year 1843 the Nestorians maintained their independence against the hordes of Kurds, which surrounded and threatened them. In that year the powerful Kurdish chiefs, Nurallah Bey and Bedr Khan, entered into an alliance with Turkey. While the Nestorians were quarrelling with each other, the Kurds fell with fearful ferocity upon their defenseless opponents, taking possession of valley after valley, and slaughtering 11,000 Nestorians in the space of a few weeks (1910: 243).

There were grievances innumerable. Samuel Audley Rhea made the following complaint:

> The testimony of Christians is not received in courts of justice. . . . In cases of the murder of Christians there is seldom any

---

[16] I visited Dihi in November 1995. A villager showed me the gravesite of a child named McDowell. He said that one day the McDowells had walked to Dihi from a distant village, when a blizzard enveloped them. The child died on the journey, and was buried in Dihi. It is still a Christian village; Saddam Hussein's government destroyed it, but it was rebuilt in 1995 by Southern Baptists as part of the humanitarian relief effort.

redress obtained. There are murderers of Nestorians every day walking the streets who have never been punished in any form (Marsh 1869:292).

CHRISTIANS WERE PROPERTY OF KURDISH CHIEFS

Kurdish aghas regarded Christian peasants and craftspeople as their private property. Van Bruinessen writes, "Even now, some older aghas still speak of *filehen min*, 'my Christians.' And, just as killing someone's sheep is an act that calls for revenge by the owner, so was killing someone's Christians" (1992:66). Van Bruinessen then relates the following atrocity:

> Taylor, the British consul at Diyarbakir in the 1860s, related that, in his time, the Christian [Chaldean] peasants in the district of Botan (called zerkiri, "bought with gold") were bought and sold together with the land on which they worked. Each of them thus "belonged" to a (tribal Kurdish) lord. With horror, Taylor told how, after a zerkiri had been killed by (or at the instigation of) another chieftain, his lord, as a revenge, killed two of the culprit's zerkiri, "although they had no part in the assassination of their co-religionists" (1992:66).[17]

Samuel Audley Rhea observed that the Nestorian Christians were owned, bought, and sold by Kurds. Rhea writes:

> Nestorian Christians in their present condition differ but little from serfs. They are attached to the soil to all intents and purposes. When a village is bought or sold, the rayats go with it, and they can't remove from one village to another to escape the oppressions of their masters. If they do they are almost invariably brought back.
>
>   The Nestorians are kept down in a state of serfdom, because there are so many restrictions and barriers to entering any other employment. They are regarded as ceremonially unclean. Fre-

---

[17] How did Kurds view the missionaries? Newshirwan writes that Kurds and Assyrians got along better *before* the missionaries came:

> Before the arrival of the missionaries, the Kurdish-Assyrian relationship was to a large extent normal. The history of the area does not speak of any long or bloody fighting between these two nations.... The missionaries had an effective role in encouraging the Assyrians against their neighbor Muslim nations, especially the Kurdish nation (1992:265).

quently, respectable Nestorians—in some cases ecclesiatics (sic)—
have been cruelly beaten in the streets because they happened to
touch a Mohammedan. With one or two exceptions they have
never attempted to have shops in the bazaars. Their touch is pol-
lution to a Mohammedan, and everything in the shape of milk,
curds, butter, cheese, fruit coming through their hands is defiled.

They are helpless in the hands of their Mohammedan masters.
The lands which they have been accustomed for ages to plough for
bread may be taken at any time and turned into vineyards by
their masters, and the water belonging to the village, and necessary to the irrigation of the lands, may be, and often is, sold to
other villages (Marsh 1869:291–292).

FEMALE CHRISTIANS WERE
PREYED UPON BY KURDS

From the missionary record we see how Christian families
could lose a daughter to predatory Kurds:

> Of late years the sanctity of the home and family relation of the
> poor Nestorian has become more and more defenceless. [Kurdish]
> Masters, their sons and servants, can enter the houses of the
> peasants, to any extent decoy, allure, or force the female members
> of the family; and, being miserably poor, the offer of new clothing
> and a comfortable living is often a greater temptation than they
> can bear. Within two years more than twenty-five females have
> been thus abducted, some willingly, and others forcibly. There
> were cases in which little girls fourteen years of age were thus
> carried away; and when, afterward, they were brought to our
> premises, and with their broken-hearted parents declared their
> unwillingness to become Musselmans, they were still forced to do
> so. Some of these cases were presented to the sardar of Tabreez,
> but there was no redress. When a girl has been carried off,
> whether enticed or forced, she is kept closely confined for several
> days—in some cases violated—and then brought to the gover-
> nor's—occasionally to our premises—surrounded by a crowd of
> Musselmans, to declare whether she is a Christian or not (Marsh
> 1869:291–292).

Rhea personally witnessed the misery of Christians under the
hands of Kurdish brigands:

> On Thursday, at the dead hour of the night, fifteen artillery-men,
> heavily armed, came into the village of Digga, just under the

shadow of our city walls [Tabriz], rushed upon the roof and dragged from her bed the daughter of Baba, the chief man of the village, a girl fifteen years of age. Her cries for help aroused the villagers. They ran to her rescue, fought desperately with the ruffians, but were overpowered. Two of her uncles were severely wounded; one is now at the point of death. But all was in vain; though the poor girl herself made a desperate resistance, she soon had to yield under the blows of the soldiers. She was dragged by the tresses of her hair from the village, her cries imploring help being heard to the last.

Before light the intelligence of her seizure was brought to our premises. Knowing her well, having often stopped at her house, and from her modest demeanor being satisfied that she was entirely innocent, that it was a most flagrant case of violence, and that without the promptest measures in a short time she would be made a victim of Moslem lust and fanaticism, I resolved to use all the strength and influence of our mission to save her (Marsh 1869:296).

There follows a tense story of government laziness and trickery that delayed justice interminably. The girl herself finally escaped.

THE BRITISH GOVERNMENT LENDS A HAND

The British ambassador in Constantinople, Sir Stratford Canning, championed the human rights of the Christian minorities:

In 1852 the British Embassy in Constantinople heard reports of massacres of Nestorians by Kurds and the selling of women and children as slaves into the Arab parts of the Ottoman Empire. The ambassador of the time, Sir Stratford Canning, actually rescued some of the slaves, buying them back with money raised by public subscription (Darke 1987:270).

SIR STRATFORD CANNING
SPONSORS THE CHRISTIANS

Canning redressed many grievances of Nestorians and Jacobites and Yezidis through his influence in the Sultan's court:

High-principled and staunch in his Protestant beliefs, [Canning] emerged as the zealous champion and protector of Christians, often indeed overriding in scope his own government's specified policies. He protested insistently when in succession a young

Armenian and a young Greek, who had embraced Islam, reverted to Christianity and were executed under Koranic law for their apostasy. He finally induced the Sultan in person to "give his royal word that henceforward neither should Christianity be insulted in his dominions, nor should Christians be in any way persecuted for their religion." This assurance was confirmed and spread through the provinces of the Empire in a public declaration. For the Sultan it earned a letter of congratulation from his fellow sovereign Queen Victoria. . . . To the Christians he [Canning] was the Padishah of Padishahs (king of kings) (Kinross 1977:477).

"FIND OUT WHAT ARE THEIR WISHES"

The Earl of Clarendon, British foreign minister, wrote to Canning, "The government of her majesty with great pleasure wants to find out the level of the success of the efforts that you can make for the sake of this oppressed people. And as a result, find out what are their wishes" (Newshirwan 1992:262). Consequently, the Nestorian patriarch, Mar Shimun wrote directly to Queen Victoria. His letter was read in the House of Commons and the House of Lords. Lord Russell wrote to the British ambassador in Istanbul, "Inform Ali Pasha that the happiness and welfare of the Assyrians is important for the government of her majesty. You should inform him that immediately the Ottoman government should arrange to end their suppression" (Newshirwan 1992:262).

The Archbishop of Canterbury sent a delegation to investigate the situation. It met with the patriarch in Hakkari. In 1886 the Archbishop stationed a personal representative, E. L. Cutts, to advise the Assyrians. In 1888 Cutts asked a Nestorian tribe in Hakkari to "write out a schedule of their losses. . . . I wrote to the British Consul in Tabriz, asking him to try to get these poor fellows some redress" (Joseph 1961:105). Cutts' successor, William Brown, advised Mar Shimun for 25 years, until Brown died in 1910 (Newshirwan 1992:263). Thus did the Anglicans ally themselves with the historical church. Missionaries intended to redress grievances, but the Turks protested that they interfered with internal affairs. The Governor of Van complained to the British consul that the "missionaries were exciting the hopes of the mountain Nestorians respecting political aid from England" (Joseph 1961:106).

HOW THE HUMAN RIGHTS ISSUE
AFFECTED THE NESTORIANS

Kurdish chiefs opposed the interference of foreign consuls in their affairs. Kurdish chiefs "vowed that they would redouble their persecution in order to "wreak their vengeance for the measures taken against them by Turkey at the instigation of the English and Russian Consuls" (Joseph 1961:107). Meanwhile Nestorians believed they were "in some special manner entitled to the protection of England; in fact, they are virtually British subjects" (1961:107). Joseph goes on to say that "such a belief led both to *presumption on the part of the Christians and to an aggravation of the jealousy between the various religious and ethnic groups—especially the Kurds*" (1961:107, italics mine). The missionaries had chosen one side in a political struggle between ethnic groups; Kurds closed ranks to protect their interests.

THE U.S. GOVERNMENT MOVES
TO PROTECT ITS MISSIONARIES

In 1880 the Kurdish chief Obeidullah invaded Persia. As we reported, Obeidullah spared Urmiah because of Joseph Cochran's intercession. However, the incident was reported in Washington, D.C.

> The month following the siege of Urmiyah, R. R. Dawes, Representative from Ohio and brother-in-law of missionary Shedd of Urmiyah, asked the State Department to appeal to the Persian government to protect the missionaries in Azerbayjan. . . . Representative Andrew G. Curtin of Pennsylvania and a former United States Minister to Russia, advocated the establishment of diplomatic relations with Persia. "We have more missionaries in Persia than has any other country," he said on the floor of Congress. "Surely those of our citizens who in self-sacrifice have penetrated the darkness which has covered that historic land, given them the Bible and its precepts, and established schools, deserve the active protection of this government" (Joseph 1961:114).

In 1883 S. G. W. Benjamin, son of a former missionary to Turkey, became the first United States Minister to Persia. The

Nestorians were elated. Missionaries, for good or ill, linked their message to protection for Christians. Was history repeating itself? Missionary work had stalled in fourth century Persia, precisely when Christianity became the official religion of the rival Roman Empire.

MCDOWELL AMONG THE YEZIDIS

In November 1888 Edmund W. McDowell of Illinois set out from Urmiah to meet the Christian tribes in the Hakkari region of Turkey. Along the way he met Kurdish Yezidis and, like Grant before him, prayed that he might convert them. McDowell decided to take up a new work with Yezidis in their villages north of Mosul.

In 1889 McDowell sent two lay assistants to live with the Yezidis in Sheikhan, near Dohouk, as "artisans." These two reported that "the lower classes were open to religious conversation," but that "'the rulers, who are very suspicious would fight [against mission work] to the death'" (Guest 1993:133).

Accordingly, McDowell reported to the Presbyterian Board of Foreign Missions that prospects for work among the Yezidis was poor. All the greater was his surprise, then, when in 1891 one of the Mosul Protestants, Jurjis, reported "that the Yezidis leaders would be interested in learning how their community might be received into the Protestant church" (Guest 1993:133).

YEZIDIS CONSIDER CHRISTIANITY

McDowell discussed the Yezidi situation with Alpheus Andrus, the American Board missionary in Mardin, who was then transferring the Mosul parish to the Presbyterians. How could the missionaries determine the sincerity of the Yezidi community? Andrus suggested a ten-question litmus test for the Yezidis in written form. This McDowell agreed to. Apparently the Yezidis asked for time to review the questionnaire before submitting a formal reply (Guest 1993:134).

What provoked the Yezidis' interest in Christianity? We know that the Sultan in Constantinople had ordered Yezidis to provide officers and troops for the empire, an obligation from which Yezidis had previously been exempt. The Yezidis, in turn, looked for a way to avoid the obligation. Only Christians were exempt from military service. This exemption caused Yezidis to contact the missionaries. However, the Ottoman government acted swiftly, sending a troop of soldiers under the ruthless leadership of Lieutenant-General Omar Wehbi Pasha. He ordered the Yezidis, who are not Muslims, to choose between Islam and severe punishment. "About a quarter of the chiefs refused and were beaten; one of them later died from his injuries. The remainder, headed by the Mir, pronounced the irrevocable words of the Mohammedan profession of faith" (Guest 1993:135). In his report, the General telegraphed to the capital that thousands of Yezidi families had become Moslems—a premature announcement. The Yezidis rebelled, and Omar Wehbi Pasha spilled much Yezidi blood before forcing the Yezidis to conform to Islamic worship. However, their conversion was a pretense:

> When commanded to curse Satan, many of them mumbled the like-sounding word "Sultan." Another reported that the villagers assembled as ordered for the Friday prayer, but that after the preacher had completed his 15 minutes of devotion, his congregation had drifted away (Guest 1993:137).

HOW THE MISSION TO THE
YEZIDIS CAME TO AN END

Ottoman persecution of Yezidis continued through most of 1892. The Yezidi appeal to the missionaries had been the hand of a drowning man reaching for a branch. The Sultan, whose military draft brought Yezidis to the door of the church, now prevented these Kurds from entering in. However, one Yezidi eventually made his way to a monastery in Baghdad, where he sincerely confessed Christ as his Lord. His name was Habib.

THE CONVERSION OF HABIB

In May 1898 Habib traveled south to Baghdad, where he could talk in secret about his new-found faith. A Catholic missionary, Father Anastase, described Habib as "a handsome young man with big black eyes, a thick well-trimmed moustache, an aquiline nose, a healthy pink complexion, a pleasant oval face, regular features, a colossal build and a robust state of health" (Guest 1993:153). Habib was thirty years old when he met the Catholics. He was born in Bozan, near Alkosh in the Yezidi region of northern Iraq. He had worked for seven years as servant and librarian for a Yezidi religious leader. However,

finding his life boring and trivial he had gone to work for the monks. After observing their way of life, he had decided to become a Christian and had come to Baghdad to escape being killed by the Yezidis as a renegade (Guest 1993:153).

After seven months of instruction, Habib was baptized and given a new name, Abd el-Mesih.

Habib/Abd el-Mesih was familiar with the mysteries of the Yezidi faith, including, as he said, the sacred books that were forbidden to outsiders. These he agreed to explain. In a series of articles published in Beirut in 1899, Father Anastase set forth the mysteries of the Yezidi faith.[18] Abd el-Mesih died of natural causes in October, 1899.

PERSIAN KURDS WHO FOLLOWED CHRIST

We have mentioned Sheikh Baba and Dr. Sa'eed Kurdistani, two Kurds from Persia who converted to Christian faith. Another follower of Christ was the son of Imam Juma, one of the highest Muslim ecclesiastics. Frederick Coan writes,

He was converted while studying with our helper, Deacon Samuel. When his father found it out, he demanded that his son be executed by the governor and his body thrown to the dogs. The governor, anxious to save the lad, said it was a "foolish request, for it will advertise to all Kurdistan that the son of the great Imam Juma has become a Christian." Thus was his life saved. Driven from home, the young man and his brother fled to India where they could have freedom to live as Christians (1939:63).

---

18 The existence of sacred Yezidi books is a subject of controversy. Translations came to Father Anastase's hand, which he proclaimed as a great literary find. But their authenticity is doubted today.

Vander Werff describes 19th century Presbyterian churches that contained Muslim converts. Kurds are among those peoples mentioned:

> The congregations at Teheran (1878), Hamadan (1876), Tabriz and Resht included Muslim converts and those at Kermanshah and Meshed were composed almost entirely of such. Jews, Armenians, Nestorians, Muslims, Kurds, Parsis and European knit together as a worshipping family made a fine demonstration of God's reconciling work in Christ (1977:140).

MISSION SUCCESS AMONG ALEVI

Richter and others have mentioned the Alevi Kurds as a point of entry for Christian missions work. Here the Alevi are called Ali Ilahi:

> In no part of Persia do the itinerant missionaries find such an open door and such an interested audience as among this simple village folk. [Shunned by] most of the Kurds, despised by the orthodox Shi'ites, regarded as hopelessly unclean by the mullahs, yet a hopeful field for the Christian preacher. Every year a few baptisms are reported in these villages; not seldom whole families are converted. *The Ali Ilahi villages seem to constitute the strategic point of the mission field in Persia* (Richter 1910:326, italics mine).

Not only in Persia, but in Turkey as well, missionaries had some success in converting the Alevi sect to Christianity, as we will now see.

SUCCESS AMONG THE ALEVI IN TURKEY

Ali Agha, a member of the Kizilbash (Alevi) sect, converted to Christianity. The British Consul to Kurdistan, J. G. Taylor, traveled to meet him and kept a journal of the event:

> Ali Agha—who is more generally known as Prot Ali Agha, from his now professing Protestantism—received us most cordially, and at once gave orders to kill the fatted lamb, which soon was served up to us cut up into small pieces, mixed with garlic floating in a small sea of melted butter. Our host prevailed upon us to pass the rest of the day there; we passed our time in conversing with him on the habits, customs, and creed of the Kizzilbash. Ali Gako is a well informed, highly intelligent, and, in his way, a conscientious man. After studying the Bible he forsook his creed, on the teach-

ing of the worthy and indefatigable American missionaries of Kharput. His life and conduct agree with his professions, although the Moslem, indignant at this preferring Protestantism to Islamism—in which indignation Armenians and Catholics join, from similar feelings that he should not have adopted their form of religion—make him out the biggest villain of the entire Kizzilbash. He was eager to discuss any question bearing upon his new opinions, but rather avoided giving information respecting those he had forsaken (1866:317–318).

The Baliki tribe of Alevi Kurds regarded Muhammad's nephew, Ali, as the Deity in human form, and ignored the founder of Islam. In 1890 this tribe was reported open to missionaries who had been "very successful among them" (Garnett 1891:151–152).

REMNANT CHRISTIAN RITUALS
AMONG THE ALEVI SECT?

Taylor says that the Kizilbash (Alevi) observed "the Christian rites of baptism and the Lord's Supper" (1866:320), a claim that other westerners made as well. A missionary named Nutting reports that Kizilbash confess Christ as the Lion of God, and "it has been handed down to them, that in the last times a Christian teacher shall come to instruct them in the true religion" (ABCFM 1860a:345). It seemed to Nutting that the Kizilbash in the region north of Kharput were dissatisfied with their own religion; there were "unmistakable indications, that the set time has come for us to preach the Gospel in all their villages" (ABCFM 1860b:346). In his next letter Nutting reports the results of a preaching mission undertaken by two brothers (Armenians?), who entered several Kizilbash villages and read from the Bible. But here the information trail ends.

A KURD IN TURKEY WHO FOLLOWED CHRIST

A Turkish believer mentions a Kurd who followed Christ in the 19th century:

A Kurd named Mamo became a Christian and gained a reputation as a holy man. Mamo memorized the Sermon on the Mount. One day, his neighbor robbed Mamo of a bushel of wheat. Mamo saw him struggling to pick up the wheat, and went outside and helped his neighbor to pick up the wheat! The neighbor then ran off, but was afraid to come harvest his own field, adjacent to Mamo's field. When Mamo saw that the neighbor had neglected his field, Mamo harvested it for him, and sent a message to his neighbor that the bushels were prepared. When the neighbor came, it was said that he attracted Mamo's wife to run away from him. Soon afterwards, both the neighbor and Mamo's wife died. This was seen by all as divine justice (S. 1984).

THE FIRST PROTESTANT CONGREGATION IN THE MIDDLE EAST?

Mel Wittler of the American Board in Istanbul put to me a tantalizing question in 1992: Which early missionary began the Protestant church in the village of Hassana[19] in southeastern Turkey? The villagers of Hassana followed the lead of their pastor and suddenly joined themselves to the Protestant faith. The year on the church seal that I saw in Hassana is 1833. Early missionaries walked through the region as early as that date. However, missionaries did not settle in the region until Grant arrived ten years later. Below are the facts as we know them.

HOW HASSANA BECAME PROTESTANT

According to Mel Wittler, the village of Hassana converted to Protestant faith after its Jacobite bishop argued into the night with an itinerant missionary. The missionary prayed that God would give true faith to the bishop and to the entire village. In Wittler's re-telling, the bishop at last yielded, saying, "The religion you have just described is what we believe; we all want to join your church." Accordingly, the bishop delivered the entire village into the hands of the astonished missionary (1992).

Frederick Coan locates Hassana exactly at the village of Hassana today (the Turkish government has renamed it Kösreli).

---

[19] This congregation may be, Wittler thinks, "the first Protestant church in the Middle East" (1992). Why the first? Because it sprang into existence before the historical churches in the Middle East—in Egypt, Lebanon, and Istanbul—broke off their relations with the western missionaries.

Coan seems to indicate that the missionary who founded church there was Samuel Audley Rhea. Coan writes,

> When we reached Hassan, a Christian village seven hours from the Tigris and beautifully situated in a valley surrounded by olive, fig and pomegranate trees, our tents were pitched in a beautiful garden in the picturesque gorge above the village; and, as usual, the sick flocked to us.
>
> Here we had a live, strong church, started by the Rev. Samuel Audley Rhea. On one of his tours, he had made a visit to this place and was much drawn to its young bishop, Yosip. He asked God for his soul and determined to win him to Christ. The bishop was converted and decided to go back with Mr. Rhea to Urumia to take a course of study and return as a preacher to his village. At his death, his brother, Kasha Elea, took his place and was pastor when we were in Hassan. He, too, was a good man, one of many preachers massacred by the Turks in 1895–6.
>
> Hassan was fortunate in that its Kurdish sheikh, the Agha of Shernakh, had always been very friendly to the Christians. He was keen enough to know that they were a valuable asset, for they provided him with masons and blacksmiths to build his castles and houses, and farmers to till his fields.
>
> One good deed of his deserved great credit. He was one of the few Kurds who, when ordered to massacre his Christian subjects, [1895] refused. When he found he could no longer protect them, he opened a way for them to escape to Persia (1939:125).

RHEA'S RECORD OF A SIMILAR INCIDENT

Samuel Audley Rhea was the kind of contestor for souls who would have made an opportunity for debate, such as took place in the church of Kösreli. We read of such a debate from Rhea's own journal of January 20, 1853,

> [It has now been] two weeks since we made a little tour of five or six days among the nearest Nestorian villages. We tried to become one with the people; traveled on foot, sat with them in their stables, ate of their coarse fare, and lay down at night on a pallet of clean hay. I never felt better; had a good appetite, slept soundly and sweetly, and was able to preach without fatigue day and night. In each village little groups of from forty to fifty persons gathered around us, and sat oftentimes from sunset until a late hour at night, listening to the truth. One night, after the

younger part of the crowd had talked rather long and hard, contending for their long fasts and other vain superstitions, two venerable men, whose heads and flowing beards were white with the frosts of many winters, rose and said: "We are all wrong, we are all wrong; these, our friends, are right—they preach the truth; hearken unto them" (Marsh 1869:129).

A SECOND VILLAGE BECOMES PROTESTANT

Four years later, April 28, 1858, another village was completely converted through Rhea. He identifies the village as Shakh,

> Just after Bishop Yoseph, not then of age, had been made a bishop, I found him one day in that churchyard at Shakh, alone, with a little manuscript book, to which he was adding proof-texts against Protestants. Deacon Eremia and myself talked and prayed with him, rejoicing that for any purpose he was studying the word of God. Still later, after Mr. Rhea's visit, the bishop and Ishak were so desirous of communing with our little church in Mosul that they came the long journey to Mosul, were examined and joined us in celebrating the dying love of Christ. Both have since witnessed a good profession.
>
> I am seated tonight where we were seated together more than four years ago—in the churchyard. I have had a very attentive congregation of thirty persons. I have been much pleased with the young bishop, Mar Yoseph. He seems to be quite studious, desirous of acquiring a knowledge of the Scriptures and of teaching his people (Marsh 1869:244).

A THIRD VILLAGE BECOMES PROTESTANT

Frederick Coan had an amazing experience when he converted an entire Assyrian village, Dihi, to Protestant faith. (The McDowell child, or children, are buried there.) This occurred in perhaps the year 1889 (F. Coan 1939:101–102). Dihi is situated near Sersink in northern Iraq. Pastor Joel Werda,[20] of the

---

[20] Joel Werda later attended the Paris Peace Conference after the First World War. For that conference he wrote, *The Flickering Light of Asia* (1924), in hopes that the League of Nations would confer nation status to the Assyrians. His efforts failed, and the Assyrians were made citizens of Iraq.

Assyrian Evangelical Church took up the work among the new believers there.

MISSIONS COMPETED
FOR LOCAL CHRISTIANS

Every missionary sect—Protestant and Catholic, and Anglican—competed for the loyalty of the Nestorian Church. As early as 1842 Grant had urged haste in beginning a mission, to move faster than "the 'true' enemy of the Nestorians, the Catholic missionaries" (Joseph 1961:55). Grant warned that the Catholics were "enemies of truth" who "stand ready to penetrate the Nestorian country the moment the existing obstacles are removed" (1961:55).

PROTESTANTS COMPETED
WITH CATHOLICS AND ANGLICANS

Protestant leaders such as Samuel Rhea and Grant maintained an adversarial relationship with the Roman Catholics. The two faiths competed for the slender harvest among Nestorians, not the Muslim field. In 1852, early in his work, Rhea wrote,

> The leaven of the Papacy is at work. Its silent, poisonous influences are spreading slowly but steadily toward the heart of the mountain Nestorian country. The tide of annual emigration which pours down from all the mountain districts and comes in contact with the ever-wakeful emissaries of Rome, returns more or less infected with the poison. I found poor, deluded Papists in Bass and in Jeloo, and they are not inactive (Marsh 1869:154).

Catholic missionaries were angered when Presbyterians arrived in Mosul, Iraq to convert the Uniate Chaldeans. From their effort, Presbyterians began a congregation of ex-Catholics (F. Coan 1939:98–99). This congregation survived for many years after the Presbyterians abandoned Mosul (owing to the city's heat and disease).

George Coan Consults the Patriarch

In 1892, Roman Catholic missionaries began a vigorous new work among Assyrians of eastern Kurdistan. The Catholics made rapid advances. George Coan, Frederick's son paid a visit to Mar

Shimun, the Patriarch of the Assyrian Church, to discern why Assyrians were deserting "a known friend for an unknown friend." The conversation concluded with Mar Shimun announcing the complete reversal of his intentions; he would now "deny the false reports of any plan to subscribe to the Holy Father as God's viceregent." Mar Shimun, while sitting with Coan, suddenly wished to "subscribe to the American religion"—that is, Presbyterian. Coan demurred:

> I thanked him for the honor, but said that would make people think I had come there to do what the Catholics had attempted. I want here to emphasize this point [writes Coan] for we have always worked in harmony with the Nestorian Church and have held it in great esteem, our only wish being to bring it back to the spiritual condition it enjoyed early in its history. Our aim has never been to make it Presbyterian (1939:155).

Perhaps the Nestorians would have become Protestant if there were temporal benefits. Coan did not offer any; his benefits were spiritual. In consequence the Nestorians turned to the Russian Orthodox Church.

Anglicans versus Americans

Anglicans competed with Protestants and Catholics for the attention of the historical churches. In 1842 the Anglican Church Missionary Society (CMS) sent George Percy Badger to Mosul. Badger had previously served the CMS in Malta and in Beirut, where he managed the printing press. Badger was well-schooled in Arabic. He befriended the Nestorian patriarch, and carried instructions "to warn him against the pernicious doctrines of American dissenters" (Guest 1993:90). "I did not fail to acquaint the patriarch how far we are removed from them in doctrine and discipline," Badger writes (Joseph 1961:61). Badger also pressed upon the patriarch the benefits that the British government could confer upon his people. By contrast, Grant and Coan tried not to entangle their spiritual message with an offering of worldly alliances.

In 1843 the Kurdish uprising forced the Anglicans to leave their work. Badger (after sheltering Mar Shimun in his home in Mosul) returned to England, along with Ainsworth. The Anglican mission in Kurdistan closed its doors for forty-three years. When it returned, it was to Urmiah, where it again competed with several missions for the prized Nestorians.

ANGLICANS SETTLE IN URMIAH

In 1886, after four decades of inactivity, the Archbishop of Canterbury initiated a new mission to the Nestorians. (It will be recalled that the Anglicans renamed the non-Catholic Nestorians, referring to them as Assyrians). Athelstan Riley explored Kurdistan and met with Mar Shimun. Shimun sent a letter with Riley to the Archbishop, in which the Assyrian patriarch wrote:

> It seems to us that there is no help nor support from any other place whereby we might be strengthened; because all are our enemies except the pure and cleansed Church of the Archbishop. And if your compassion neglects her as hitherto it has neglected her, she will be dispersed and perish among her enemies, and in a short time her name and memory will vanish for ever (Heazell 1913:1).

Mar Shimun then listed specific requests: a school in Qudshanis and another in Urmiah, smaller schools for the villages, a printing press, and "it is clear that for these we require money and funds" (Heazell 1913:2). Then followed a request for protection:

> ... the wealth of the labourers has perished by robbery and theft and plunder, and our race is greatly impoverished until what we need even is not collected from the community. On this account our third request is that you would take care for the defence of our nation from those wrongs which in various ways are done to it by our enemies, and especially to our soil and lands, which are bought and sold by royal decrees to the Kurdish chiefs and others (Heazell 1913:3).

Two clergy volunteered for the mission, William H. Brown and Canon Maclean. Anglicans established their mission headquarters in Urmiah, as had the Presbyterians previously. The Presbyterians resented the arrival of the Anglicans in their vicinity, and the matter worsened when the Anglicans announced that they had come to defend the Nestorians against the Americans (Richter 1910:310).[21]

---

21 Of the various denominations working in this field only the Archbishop of Canterbury's Anglican mission has sought not to make

Anglicans Offered More Protection than Americans

From the Nestorian point of view, American missionaries were slow to rescue their fellow Christians from the hands of the Ottomans. Mar Shimun, the spiritual head of the Assyrians, was especially vexed by the Americans, with whom he spent 18 months in Urmiah, exiled by the Ottomans. Upon gaining his freedom in 1850, Mar Shimun turned to an Anglican, W. F. Ainsworth, whom he praised. Mar Shimun preferred the direct political involvement of the Church Missionary Society over the "we-have-no-politics" pretense of the Presbyterians. Moreover, the democratic organization of the Presbyterians undermined the patriarch's control over his subjects. The patriarch understood government by bishops.

Anglicans Competed with the Catholics

Anglican records reveal a rivalry between themselves and Catholics. Nestorians tribes and even whole monasteries sold their loyalty to whichever missionaries seemed to offer more protection. Riley visited Mosul:

> I found a separate Assyrian communion of considerable size that had abjured the Roman obedience in 1873. . . . In the other villages round Mosul the churches are in the hands of the Romans, and the inhabitants, owing to pressure, have outwardly conformed. Two monasteries, Mar Elia and Mar Michael, have renounced the Roman obedience (Heazell 1913:11).

The only Anglican contact with Kurds, judging from the record, was passing them on the paths and charging them with grievances (*see* Heazell 1913:19, 54). One day the British vice-consul visited the Anglican missionaries:

> In June Captain G. S. Elliot, R. E., H. B. M. Vice-Consul at Van, cheered us by a four days' visit to Qudshanis. He very kindly took the Matran to Diza in Gawar, and the civil and military authorities escorted him safely to Persia. The Sheikh Mahmed Sadiq had constantly had men on the way from Qudshanis to Gawar, and on

---

proselytes but rather to educate the people and purify their spiritual life within the ancient branch of the Church owing allegiance to the Patriarch of the East (C. Edmonds 1957:22).

the Mar Bhishu road to Persia, to catch the Matran should he
venture forth. . . . *It was good for me, and so for the Mission, that
the authorities should see me as the companion of one whom they
have to honour*; and the simple people are cheered by seeing an
Englishman, and especially a Consul, passing through their country; they are not altogether forgotten, and they are encouraged
to hope in waiting for better days (Heazell 1913:137–138, italics
mine).

Anglican Mission Schools

The Anglican ideals were high. They came to educate the local
Christians in the Christian faith, "not changing customs which
are not contrary to true religion, but enabling them to worship
with understanding and with intelligent devotion" (Heazell
1913:22).

Four missionaries from the Sisters of Bethany traveled by ship
from London and overland from Russia to arrive at their new
home in Urmiah. They proceeded to learn Syriac, though it came
with great difficulty. They opened a school for Christian girls in
1890. One disappointment they faced was the young age at
which girls were married:

> Fifteen years old is considered "old" for a girl to marry here, and if
> a girl is not married by the time she is seventeen she is consid-
> ered quite ineligible. . . . After their marriage they are mere
> drudges, and there is but little hope of getting hold of them unless
> the husband happens to be a nice fellow (Heazell 1913:42–43).

The Sisters of Bethany worked for eight years, withdrawing in
1898.

MASSACRES OF 1895

Sultan Abdul Hamid believed his government threatened by
revolutionary activities of the Armenians. An incident at Anatolia
College in Marsovan in 1893 lent credence to his fears:

> On January 6, the Gregorian Christmas Day, posters proclaiming
> a revolution and calling for the deposition of the sultan appeared
> on mosques, churches, and school houses. After preliminary inves-
> tigation by Turkish authorities established that these revolution-
> ary placards had been printed at the College, a student and two

native faculty members, Thoumayan and Kayayan, were arrested and charged with revolutionary activity. At the end of January a newly completed college building burned, whereupon the acting president, George F. Herrick, accused Husref Bey, the ranking Ottoman official in Marsovan and "a known robber and murderer," with setting the blaze (Daniel 1970:115).

In 1895 the smoldering hostility between Turk and Armenian burst into an open rebellion by the Armenians. The Sultan unleashed his Hamidiye on the Christians in the east. Plunder of property and the loss of life convulsed all of the Christian communities.[22] The Armenians were unarmed; Hamidiye cavalry, along with armed Kurdish mobs and Muslim clerics massacred thousands of Armenians in a frenzy which no decent people can excuse.

JIHAD IN AINTAB

The plunder of Christian property and the loss of life reached Aintab, where Fred Shepard had his mission hospital. His daughter remembers:

> It was Saturday morning, November 16, 1895. Dr. Shepard was seated at breakfast with his family in the little home on the college campus, half a mile from the city. Suddenly the maid burst into the room, "Oh, doctor Effendi," she cried, her voice hoarse from terror, "it is gone, the city is gone!" Springing from their seats, all rushed to the front door. The air was filled with horrid clamor—shrieks of women, the crack of guns, the shouts of men, the crash of breaking doors and windows, the shrill battle-cry of the Moslem women cheering their men on in the awful work of killing and plunder (Riggs 1920:108–109).

The cheering and the killing spread to cities all across eastern Turkey. Kurds rushed to the Armenian quarter. Murder and plundering began at once. Armenians ran for protection, and found it behind the missionaries. Then came crowding and, in the following days, typhoid. Shepard administered the Committee of

---

[22] Robert Daniel states that, "Although early reports described the Armenians as victims, later evidence established that the Armenians were more often the aggressors" (1970:116). But Daniel should have, but does not, supply his evidence.

Relief and Rebuilding in Aintab. This agency gave out $100,000 worth of relief funds and supervised the building of 900 houses in the next ten months.

There is blood on the hands of the Kurds. They tore open the homes of peaceful Christians. Having no light of their own, they extinguished the light in those around them. Not wanting to learn "the thrift of the Armenians," Kurds in Aintab destroyed their neighbors' houses. It was cruel and indecent. When Kurds turn from the devil to follow Christ, they will cry for shame over the sins of their fathers.

MASSACRE IN URFA

During two months in late 1895, mobs surrounded the Armenian quarter in Urfa. Then, in December, at the sound of a bugle, Turkish troops with maddened Kurds rushed in. They killed all the adult males on the first day. The next day the women and children were burned to death in the cathedral. No one escaped. Then,

> At three-thirty in the afternoon the bugle blew once more, and the Moslem officials proceeded around the Armenian quarter to say that the massacres were over. They had wiped out 126 complete families, without a woman or a baby surviving, and the total casualties amounted to eight thousand dead (Kinross 1977:560).

A similar bugle sounded the beginning and end of massacres in most of the thirteen cities of eastern Turkey. These included Trabzon, Erzinjan, Bitlis, Erzerum, Diyarbakir, Malatya, Harput, Sivas, Kayseri (McDowall 1996:61):

The Armenian massacre of 1895 had showed the Nestorians what fate awaited them, unless they found a protector. Among the Armenians,

> Men and boys [were] murdered and mutilated, little children killed with utmost torture, priests dragged to an infamous death, girls dishonored, pregnant women treated in a fashion which cannot be spoken or thought of. They spared neither sex nor age. The massacre of the Pit of Galo-guzan is one of the most barbarous tragedies which ever occurred in the history of the world. Armenians by hundreds, men, women, and children, surrounded on either side, came in to surrender, with the priest at their

head. The Turkish chief charged the priest with having blinded the people, and ordered that he should be blinded in turn. His eyes were pierced through and his torments were brought to an end with the bayonet. The other unfortunates were butchered by soldiers and buried in one common grave (Yonan 1895:14).

Where was God in the destruction of the Armenians? Why did He forsake them? The Protestants hoped that the Armenians would be, like Isaiah's vision, a light to the Gentiles. The Muslims loved the darkness rather than the light. However a hard message to hear is that the Armenians did not want to love their neighbors as they loved themselves. Armenians, despite exceptions, gambled that they could keep to themselves the blessings of faith in Jesus Christ, while withholding eternal life from their enemies. Did this gamble contribute to their doom?

THE EUROPEAN POWERS CALL FOR AN ENQUIRY

News of these massacres aroused strong protests from Britain, France and Russia.[23] American sympathies were with the Armenians. The Methodist *Western Christian Advocate* suggested that Turkish rule must be overthrown by force. When disorder spread to Constantinople in 1895, Congress nearly did intervene, but the conservative press dissented from American involvement. The Senate and the House agreed to only a mild censure (Daniel 1970:119).

Sultan Abdul Hamid responded with an enquiry. The Sultan's enquiry turned the issue on its head, to investigate

"the criminal conduct of Armenian brigands"—thus hoping to preempt further investigation and prove the Porte's version of events. Following this mockery of justice the powers, reinforced by mass meetings in London and Paris, put forward a scheme for Armenian reform, which the Sultan made a show of accepting in a watered-down version, with a profusion of unfulfilled paper promises[24] (Kinross 1977:558).

---

[23] Germany, however, did not protest the massacres. Trade between Germany and Turkey was booming.

[24] Students of modern Turkey will recognize a familiar pretense in the Sultan's response.

HOW THE NESTORIANS
BECAME RUSSIAN ORTHODOX

A great number of Assyrians converted to Russian Orthodoxy, beginning in 1897. Following are the reasons.

A BISHOP IS MURDERED

The Assyrian bishop of Urmiah perished at the hands of Kurds in June 1896. The bishop, Mar Gauriel, had visited a Kurdish sheikh who was "all-powerful in that district" (Heazell 1913:113). The next morning the visitors went on their way, fourteen persons in all, with an escort of the Sheikh's servants:

> Nothing more is known of them, but that their bodies were found fearfully mutilated, in a ravine some few miles on the Persian side of the frontier. The Bishop was found to have had his head cut open by a sword gash, his stomach ripped up, his head nearly severed from his body, and to have been stripped of all his clothes. His nephew was found in very much the same state. Qasha Dinkha, the Matran's Archdeacon, was found stripped and stabbed in many places, and his beard cut off, the greatest indignity one can do to a priest in this country. His body showed, too, to what great sufferings he had been subjected before his death; it was found to be black with bruises, the result of the Kurds having beaten him with the stocks of their guns. The deacon's body was so fearfully cut about, that before it could be removed by his friends for burial, it had to be wrapped up in a blanket; another, a priest, had his head entirely cut off from his body; another, formerly a chief servant in Mar Shimun's house, was stabbed in seventeen places (Heazell 1913:114).

The sheikh gave as his reason for the attack his fear that the Christians of Tergawar would attack him; but according to the Anglican mission, "most probably his real intentions is to come down and destroy the Christian villages in that district" (Heazell 1913:115). Thus did unarmed men fall before murderers. Is there sorrow in Kurdish breasts today for the blood which their grandfathers poured on the ground?

A SMALL PEOPLE THAT NEEDED A BIG BODYGUARD

Russia, at the end of the 19th century, began to develop its industry in the Caucasus region, north of Turkey and Persia.

Thousands of Christians found employment as laborers and contractors there. "Year after year," wrote Shedd, "the ties which bind us to Europe and especially Russia, are strengthening. . . . The hand of Russia is all-powerful in Persia" (Joseph 1961:120). Christians hoped that their co-religionists to the north would deliver them from the Muslims.

Mar Shimun, now an aged and bitter patriarch, sent an emissary to the Russian Orthodox Church.[25] The Americans and then the Anglicans failed to sponsor his political ambitions. When Russia seemed to promise political delivery from the Turks, Nestorians risked everything on a Russian victory. However, the student of history should remember that the Nestorians did not actually change their loyalty; *they remained loyal to the principle of self-preservation.* Nestorians had joined the Catholics, the Anglicans, and the Protestants in turn, for protection and national survival. Their submission to the Russians was a natural step for a small people that wanted a big bodyguard.

A BISHOP PLEDGES HIMSELF TO THE RUSSIAN ORTHODOX CHURCH

Anticipating a Russian invasion and gambling on victory, Mar Yonan, the new Assyrian bishop, traveled from Urmiah to St. Petersburg and offered to join the Russian Orthodox Church. Rumor in Persia spread that the Russians were ready to give

---

25 In the 1840s Shelmon Arajan, a Nestorian priest from Persia, had visited the Russian governor in the Caucasus, Fortinsoff. The priest asked permission for all the Nestorians in Iran to emigrate to his region. Fortinsoff did not allow this, because he calculated that the Nestorians could better serve the Russians in their own region. Fortinsoff wrote to Nisilrud, the Russian foreign minister, "We cannot let the Nestorians transfer to the Caucasus, but we must make good relations with them. We must protect them . . . so that we earn their trust and loyalty, because in the future we can benefit from them" (Newshirwan 1992:263).

During the Crimean War, 1853–56, the Nestorians expressed readiness to cooperate with Russia, and entered negotiations to join the Russian Orthodox Church. This background puts into focus the events which occurred later in the 19th century.

untold millions of rubles to a converted church. Accordingly, two Russian monks and a married priest arrived in Urmiah in May of 1897. They made fabulous promises, such as:

> The Moslems [are] to be turned over [to the Assyrians]; their land to be taken away from them, and given to those who joined the Russians. . . . All who did not join to have their property confiscated and be banished to Siberia. . . . The American missionaries to be banished (Joseph 1961:121).

Thousands of Christians signed a petition to unite with the Russian Orthodox Church. The monks from St. Petersburg made a grand tour of the Christian villages:

> They were enthusiastically welcomed by the Nestorian population, being accorded a triumphal entry. Men and women sang and danced around them; they were greeted as deliverers from the yoke of the Moslems. The Christians shouted to the astonished Moslems that it was now their turn, and that Christians would soon have their feet on the necks of their old oppressors, and would occupy their houses and fields. Ten or fifteen thousand Nestorians signed their names in the lists of the Russian monks. . . . During the next year, by promises, persuasions and threats, village after village was induced to abjure "the errors of Nestorius" and to sign a paper in which they accepted the Orthodox faith. Twenty thousand of the 25,000 Nestorians in Persia thus joined the Russian Orthodox Church (Richter 1910:311–312).

So it came to pass that the Nestorians switched *en masse* to the Russian Orthodox Church. Nestorians yielded to the Orthodoxy they had spurned at the Council of Ephesus in A.D. 431. The dual nature of Christ was suddenly their orthodoxy as well.

However, the reason for this landslide was "purely political; the people believed that the [Russian] mission was the forerunner of political changes. As one Nestorian priest put it, he 'would accept whatever Church wielded the biggest club'" (Joseph 1961:121). The British hoped to wield that club, but her policy suffered when Nestorians declared their loyalty to Russia:

> As early as 1863 the British Foreign Office had feared that if the Nestorians obtained relief from their suffering by uniting with the Russian Church, then the Russian government would interfere authoritatively on their behalf (Joseph 1961:92).

ANGLICANS WITHDRAW FROM URMIAH

The Anglicans closed their mission after thirteen years in Urmiah. Anglicans more than the Americans or Germans submitted to the Assyrian bishops, and never divided that church. Accordingly, when the Russians came in and the Assyrian leaders requested the Anglicans to leave, the request was honored. Fifty schools were handed over to the Russians, who hired the same local teachers at the same pay scale.

Anglicans moved to Van, to make "a new centre from which to reach the Syrians of the mountains" (Richter 1910:313). Will no obstacle cause missionaries to work among the Kurds?

HUNDREDS OF PRESBYTERIANS JOINED
THE RUSSIAN ORTHODOX CHURCH

Presbyterian Nestorians also caught the Russian fever; hundreds of Protestants embraced the Orthodox faith. Any who refused were treated with scorn, and even beaten (Richter 1910:311). But the Presbyterian mission recovered from the defection, as

> only a few hundreds of members left it, and these soon came back repentant, so that a year later the Presbyterians were able to report an increase of membership. The position of the Protestants towards the other (historical) Nestorians had, to be sure, undergone a complete change, and this change was at first unfavourable. Whereas, before the storm, there had been no sharp split between their congregations and the ancient Church, so that the missionaries had been able to work as preachers and teachers in the Syrian church at large, there was now a deep cleft between the "Russian" Christians and those of the Reformed Church (Richter 1910:312–313).

ORTHODOX RUSSIA:
REVERSAL IN WAR, REVERSAL IN MISSION

Winning counts in the Middle East. After Japan defeated Russia in 1905, Nestorians withdrew their trust. Rumors of Russian rubles were, as it turned out, just rumors. Western missions gained back their ground from the Russians. Political power had attracted Nestorians to the Russian Orthodoxy; the waning of that power evoked a general return to the church of their fathers.

HIGH HOPES AS THE 20TH CENTURY OPENED

Missionaries had high hopes that the best days were just ahead. It was a hope for Armenians and Nestorians, not Kurds:

We are able to declare that, thanks to the abundant help of the Christian people and the astonishing vitality of the Armenians themselves, the Turks have failed. It is true that the Turks and Kurds still tyrannize over and attempt to crush the Armenians. But on the whole the Armenians have recovered from what then [1895] appeared to be a fatal blow (Richter 1910:152).

THE RUIN YET TO COME

When the new century opened, no one could foresee that only fourteen years of work remained for missionaries in eastern Turkey. No one could know that just five years after the 1910 Edinburgh Conference, the Christian population of the Ottoman Empire would be obliterated. Richter has said of the destruction in 1895, "It was as if a destructive hail-storm had passed over a field of ripe grain" (1910:155). The ruin yet to come would nearly annihilate an entire civilization.

SAMUEL AUDLEY RHEA, 19TH CENTURY
(MARSH 1869)

Chapter 3

A Misunderstanding
Agreed Upon

The New England missionaries must have astonished the peoples of the Ottoman Empire and Persia. Who were these friendly Christians from the New World? Why had they come? And such confidence these Americans exuded! They had subdued their own wild country; they assured themselves that they could prevail in the Old World as they had in the New. The missionaries set out to subdue the historical church, and second the Muslim masses. The tools of these missionaries were the Bible, education and medicine. These tools, in the hands of determined men and women, began and sustained the missionary enterprise in Kurdistan.

WHAT THE MISSIONARIES MISUNDERSTOOD

But did missionaries understand that the historical churches wanted a political ally? They wanted a Nestorian El Cid or an Armenian Judas Macabbees to throw off the chains of Islam and restore their kingdoms. They wanted to take pride in their church again. Pride meant earthly power. The Nestorian priest said he would "accept whatever Church wielded the biggest club" (Joseph 1961:121). The historic church seemed to say, "Bring an army along with your medicine, and then we shall re-Christianize this region."

Anglicans knew how to tether their power to the British Empire, and used this connection to attract the ancient Christians. Similarly, Russian priests offered the Czar's protection.

Americans professed to have no earthly power; they were ambassadors for a heavenly kingdom. For Americans, Christ's power was spiritual, and the change in men and women would occur on the inside. This change would create a "new manhood" (Herman Barnum's phrase) in which followers of Christ would work.

However, American schools tunneled beneath the autocratic leadership of the Armenian and Assyrian priests; in reaction, church leaders forced out the Americans and slammed the door against them. So the unstoppable Americans took their converts with them and set up alternative churches. In these new churches a holy discipleship occurred. Economic lift also occurred. Armenians, Jacobites, and Assyrians who joined the missionaries gained the benefits that come from thrift and hard work. Graduates learned to read and think and cherish democratic ideals. But education also spurred converts to emigrate to the New World. The converts wanted to leave the Old World behind. They believed their future would be in the west. One in four Assyrian men left for the west between 1880 and 1910.[1] Forty promising young people emigrated from Harput one day in 1907 (Eddy 1913:119). Today the Assyrian diaspora in the U.S. and Europe and Australia

---

[1] Brain Drain in Persia: Presbyterians maintained an extensive network of mission schools among the Nestorians in Persia. However, bright students left for the West and never returned:

> Since Christians are excluded from the service of the state, and from the most lucrative professions, such students as did not enter the service of the mission were practically forced to emigrate. And such emigration was the easier because of the valuable knowledge of the English language which they had acquired while in the college where English was, almost of necessity, the medium of instruction. The emigration to Europe and the United States, *so disastrous to Protestant missions and Churches throughout the Near East,* increased in proportion to the mismanagement of the Persian government, and the impoverishment of the Syrians through overtaxation and the constant raids of the Kurds (Richter 1910:307, italics mine).

Loss by emigration is a lesson that workers in Kurdistan should ever keep in mind.

accounts for more than half of the total membership of 150,000. *Emigration from Iraq and from Lebanon is unremitting.* Slow erosion continues in both Iraq and Iran from conversions to Islam for prudential reasons (Horner 1989:23, italics mine). The dioceses of the Assyrian Church are located in Iraq (two), and one each in eastern Syria, Lebanon, Chicago, and Modesto, California.

SIGNS OF FAVOR IN THE 19TH CENTURY

Missionaries hoped that the signs of the times portended the favorable year of the Lord for work among the Muslims. Greece had fought successfully for her independence from the Ottomans.[2] Bulgaria and the Balkan countries also threw off the Ottoman yoke. After five centuries of subjugating Christian peoples, was the Turkish Empire about to disintegrate? Would liberation for the Christian peoples in the east follow? Sultan Abdul-Aziz seemed receptive to reforms that the European countries proposed. He signed a constitution which guaranteed individual liberties. The first Ottoman Parliament met in March 1877. These hopeful developments seemed to answer the prayers of missionaries and the historical churches. Had the missionaries come to the kingdom for such a time as this?

However, a succession of Sultans returned the empire to the safeguards of Islamic law. Abdul-Aziz was deposed and committed suicide in prison. His successor, Murad V, an alcoholic and mentally unstable, was also deposed. The next in line was Abdul Hamid II, an unknown who had spent his life inside the palace walls. Abdul Hamid's acceded to the throne in 1876. He ordered harsh measures towards the Christian minorities.

---

2 In the fall of 1821 the revolutionary Greek Senate appealed to the United States in the name of liberty and Christianity to "purge Greece from the barbarians, who for four hundred years have polluted the soil" (Daniel 1970:1). News of the rebellion in Greece thrilled the Americans. "The Greeks rousing themselves from centuries of subservience to the Turks, seemed to be reasserting the values and virtues of their heroic forefathers. . . . Inevitably many regarded the struggle as a 'war of the crescent against the cross'" (Daniel 1970:2). Turks, of course, felt the same. Foreign policy on both sides wrapped itself in religion.

SULTAN ABDUL HAMID TURNS BACK THE CLOCK

The new Sultan shrewdly used constitutional reforms to "disarm" the European powers (Kinross 1977:517). In reality, all individual liberties disappeared. The Treaty of Berlin guaranteed the rights of Armenians. However, the Sultan's personal terrorists, the Hamidiye, raided at will in the east. His Parliament was "a puppet assembly, manufactured to give an appearance of legal validity and popular assent to such measures as [the Sultan] elected to impose" (Kinross 1977:529). Words of reform soothed the European powers, yet blood flowed from the wounds of the churches in the east. These churches needed a political ally; *American missionaries never wanted to understand this need.*

European powers hailed the Sultan's signature on the 1878 Treaty of Berlin as the guarantee of rights for Armenians. But Muslims saw it "as a stepping stone towards the emergence of an independent Armenian state" in eastern Turkey (McDowall 1996:56–57). The Kurdish chief Obeidullah asked, "What is this I hear, that the Armenians are going to have an independent state in Van, and that the Nestorians are going to hoist the British flag and declare themselves British subjects?" (McDowall 1996:57). Missionaries encouraged the Christians toward independence, yet did not understand the seditious nature of this encouragement.[3]

WHAT THE HISTORICAL CHURCHES MISUNDERSTOOD

The historical churches never agreed to the missionary plan of Muslim evangelism. The churches did not want to understand their duty to go into all the world to preach the gospel. Far from wanting Muslims in their churches, the churches wanted Muslims out of their land altogether. The ancient churches supposed that

---

[3] In *A Bright Shining Lie*, Neil Sheehan describes "the disastrous consequences to which make-believe leads" in another context, the U.S.-Vietnam War (Sheehan 1988:340). His book on the misunderstandings of that war offers parallels to the misunderstandings which kept the 19th century mission on an unchanging, unwinning course.

Americans would bring Bibles and rifles; this was Christianity for the tribal churches. They imagined that Americans were a powerful tribe coming to rescue their fellow Christians. There was some truth in this, as demonstrated by missionary attention lavished on the churches of the east. The churches refused to hear that their blessings were meant to pass on to the Muslim majority. When Nestorians lost hope that a western power would sponsor a homeland for them, they turned to another, or emigrated to the west. A fever still burns in the hearts of Christians from the ancient churches to leave the Middle East and begin their lives over in a Christian land.

WHAT THE KURDS MISUNDERSTOOD

Jesus Christ offered Himself and His benefits to all humankind. Kurds did not understand this; they did not understand that "in Christ we have redemption through his blood, the forgiveness of sins, in accordance with the riches of God's grace that He lavished on us" (Eph 1:7–8); the religion of Muhammad seemed to leave the Kurds "excluded from citizenship in Israel . . . without hope and without God" (Eph 2:12).

The Kurds misunderstood this universal redemption, and confirmed their depravity at several opportunities. Kurds wanted to raid the Christian villages, buy and sell Christian peasants, carry off the women, and loot travelers, as their fathers had done before them. What appeal could possibly make the Kurds want to become like the oppressed, miserable Christians? Missionaries, like government agents, wrote letters to their ambassadors in Constantinople or Tehoran. This foreign influence alarmed the Kurds who suspected that the missionaries had come to protect the subjected Nestorians. Missionaries fulfilled these suspicions. Van Bruinessen has stated the misunderstanding clearly:

> Kurds and local Christians had identical expectations of the presence of the missionaries. Armenian, Jacobite and Nestorian Christians who converted to the Roman Catholic or Protestant churches never made it a secret that they did so to obtain French or British (later American) protection. Many British missionaries and other agents complained that the Kurds "misunderstood"

their motives and invariably considered them as forerunners of [for example] British conquest (1992:262, italics mine).

Were missionaries the forerunners of British conquest? Ainsworth of the CMS records a conversation in which a Kurdish agha confronted him on the road:

> What do you do here; are you not aware that Franks are not allowed in this country? No dissimulation! I must know who you are, and what is your business. . . . You are the forerunners of those who come to take this country . . . (Joseph 1961:54).[4]

From the Turkish point of view, missionaries stirred up a hornet's nest with their human rights campaign:

> As late as 1870 the British Consul at Erzerum conveyed to his counterpart in Tabriz the charge by the Turkish governor that "the American missionaries were exciting the hopes of the mountain Nestorians respecting political aid from England" (Joseph 1961:92).

So a Gordion knot of misunderstanding existed between Muslims and missionaries and between Christians and missionaries. Each saw the other through a fog. *Each side needed to misunderstand the other* to pursue its own ambitions. It was, as Napoleon said of history, a fable agreed upon. Muslims supposed that missionaries acted as agents of foreign powers. Ethnic Christians supposed that missionaries would deliver them from the rule of Muslims. And missionaries supposed that by educating local Christians, the converts would rise to their privilege of bringing the good news to Kurds. These three—Muslims, Christians, and missionaries—persisted in their courses, like ships that could not be steered after their initial courses were set.

HOW MISSIONARIES SAW THE KURDS

Frederick Coan of the Presbyterian work in Urmiah visited Bitlis in 1874. The Kurds made trouble for him. Coan reports,

---

4   Nestorians, meanwhile, welcomed Westerners. When the Kurdish agha, above, asked who brought the "visiting Franks," their Nestorian guide answered "I," laying his hand upon his breast "in an undaunted manner" (Joseph 1961:54).

There was a splendid work in Bitlis, with large congregations of devoted Christians. Bitlis, then a city of some 25,000 inhabitants, lies in a deep and picturesque valley with an old castle in its center. The population was Armenian and Kurdish, and in no place have I seen more ugly, fanatical Kurds. Although the missionaries had been there for some years, they were frequently reviled, insulted, and even stoned when they went out. When we came down the valley above the city we met a wild and nasty bunch of men, and I have never seen as much concentrated hatred and malice as that with which they scowlingly swore to plunge their daggers into us. It was only the presence of my Turkish guards that prevented it (1939:86).

While Mrs. Joseph P. Cochran was touring some Christian villages of Tergawar in Persia, Kurds attempted to kidnap her daughter:

Emma, at that time eight years old, was with her in a tent pitched near the village of Umbi. One night Mrs. Cochran waked up to see the rug on which Emma lay near her bed slowly moving out of the tent. She jumped up and gave the alarm. After much noise and some firing, in which one of the Assyrian guards was wounded, the Kurds were frightened away. Their leader, known as Kurdu, had seen the little American girl and tried to abduct her as an addition to his harem. This same Kurdu was implicated in the murder of Benjamin W. Labaree in March 1904 (Coan 1939:60).

MORE TROUBLE WITH KURDS

Kurds say, "We have no friends." Here is why:

One day when I was the guest of one of our helpers, I was witness to something that made it hard to restrain myself. Our pastor had just bought eight fat sheep that were to be the winter's supply of meat, for the meat is cooked and put into jars covered with melted butter so that it keeps for months. Some lazy Kurds who had heard of the plan came and made him butcher the sheep and compelled his wife and daughters to bake bread. The Kurds then sat down to the feast and remained until every scrap was consumed (F. Coan 1939:124).

A portrayal of chaos and cruelty, rampage and rape, by Kurds toward one another and toward the missionary families is found in Coan's memoirs (1939:264). Indeed, the records bulge with references to plunders and terror brought upon Christians and missionaries by Kurds.

"PEOPLE WITH NO HEARTS, LIKE THE KURDS"

The Kurds who terrorized the country were a kind of bogey-man to missionary children. In his autobiography, Coan writes, "It is awful to live in constant terror of an attack, and when mothers wish to quiet an unruly child, they will say, 'Keep quiet or the Kurds will come'" (1939:58). One Cochran child, five years old, repeated to her mother a verse of "Hush, My Dear, Lie Still and Slumber." When her mother asked what "brutal creatures" were, the child replied, "People who have no hearts, like the Kurds" (Coan 1939:69). He describes how some Christians became Muslims out of fear for their lives:

> At times some of the Nestorians are driven from their own village owing to the meanness of the Kurds. The Kurds then settle themselves as unwelcome guests on the Christians, eating them out of house and home. No attractive girls are safe, and even the married women do not escape. *Many a Christian village is now Kurdish by this process.* It is awful to see these quiet, peaceful people, who pay their taxes and are loyal to the government, gradually crushed in this way. Of course the Kurd is armed, while the Christian has no weapon and knows it is useless to resist (1939:70, italics mine).

"HIGHWAY ROBBERY IN A POLITE FORM"

Anglicans witnessed Kurdish cruelty. Missionaries came upon Assyrian refugees in 1897:

> It was really a heartrending scene. We counted one hundred and twenty-three persons, without reckoning babies, all in the greatest destitution, footsore to the last degree, many moreover shoeless, with scarce enough clothing for common decency, and sadly insufficient for the sharp nights of approaching winter. Some of the children ran along bravely, and even seemed in good spirits; but some cried piteously. Mothers, fathers, brothers and sisters, were burdened with swaddled little ones, slung across their backs; others had bundles containing their few remaining possessions. One boy was leading a solitary black goat by a string.
>
> We went safely on till we reached a spot where the river is crossed close by a small fortified village inhabited by Mussulmans and Kurds. Here four Bagzadi made their appearance—fierce-looking, well-built fellows, armed to the teeth—and roughly demanded toll of the poor refugees. At first we took a high hand with them,

but other Kurds appeared, watching from a little distance, evidently ready to come to their companions' assistance if needed, and we saw that it was necessary to parley. Mr. Neesan's knowledge of Kurdish was invaluable. "Are you not ashamed," he asked, "to oppress these poor people and even under our very eyes?" They replied, "We are guards of the road, and must have our toll; but if you will give us a present we will be content." This was of course pure imposition, and only highway robbery in a polite form. We gave them six *qrans*, about half-a-crown. They took the money ungraciously, and insolently threw it on the ground at our horses' hoofs. We, however, firmly refused to give more, and after further parley they consented to accept it, but said they must also have the goat belonging to the party. This we told them was "shame" to them, and that we would on no account allow it. Eventually they went sullenly away; and we passed on and reached Urmi without any further molestation (Heazell 1913:127–8).

Appalled by such persecution, missionaries moved to protect their Christian flocks. The missionaries wrote letters to their boards and to their governments listing the crimes of the Kurds and asked for justice on behalf of Christians. Converts became either Protestant, Anglican, Catholic, or even Russian Orthodox, depending on who seemed to offer a shield or sword. Thus did mission churches grow.

All the factors that comprise the problem of missionary work in Kurdistan can be seen in one event; the conversion of Nestorians and Armenians to Russian Orthodoxy in 1897. The factors are: governments offer weapons to restless minorities in exchange for loyalty; Christians (or, in a later day, Kurds) accept weapons and the proffered foreign protection; betrayal of the minorities in the end. The Middle East has turned around many times since Smith and Dwight first set out from Beirut for Persia. However, scripted roles between minorities and foreign powers are acted repeatedly on the ancient stage and everyone must play his or her part.

HOW KURDS SAW THE MISSIONARIES

Newshirwan Mustefa, a Kurdish writer in Erbil, charges the missions with preparing the way for European domination of the

region. "One of the tactics of the European countries to get a foothold in the [Assyrian] areas was to send religious missionaries"
(Newshirwan 1992:260). Newshirwan reviews the history of missions in the region, and blames the French, Americans, British
and Russian missionaries for operating on behalf of their governments. Consciously or not, Newshirwan says, missionaries
gathered information and established a presence in behalf of
their national interests:

> Among the missionaries were a lot of people seeking goodness,
> sacrificing themselves and worshipping God. Maybe most of them
> came with pure motives to bring the Holy Message of Jesus and
> the progress of Europe, to help the oppressed, persecuted, under-
> developed Christian nations of the area.... However, all the
> good attempts of these people in the final evaluation, was part of
> the strategy of European imperialist countries who were looking
> to control and occupy the region. In this, the missionaries became
> pawns, and the Christians of the area the victims without any
> gains (1992:264).

Missionaries will deny that they were pawns of western governments, or that Christians in Kurdistan were victims of mission
power. However, Kurds saw it so, and in this case, perceptions
made a new reality.

HOW MUSLIM GOVERNMENTS
SAW THE MISSIONARIES

The Ottomans ruled over Greeks, Slavs, Serbs, Bulgars,
Armenians, Kurds, Circassians, Arabs, and Alevis. It appeared
to the Sultan that the missionaries assisted the Christians
among these *vilayats* to organize against him.[5]

---

5   The Ottoman government, while indifferent to the internal fric-
tions within the Christian communities, looked with dismay at
the rending of the political and social fabric of the State....
Consequently when the Gregorians and Orthodox vented their
spleen in attacks on ... American missionaries and teachers, the
Turks manifested their frustrations by biding their time in bringing the malefactors to justice (Daniel 1970:51).

Americans promoted among the Armenians and Arabs an awareness of their distinctive cultures. Armenians who had been assimi-
lated by the Turks to the degree that they spoke only Turkish
began to learn and use their native tongue. The standardization
of the Armenian vernacular promoted by the American mission
press permitted Armenians in all parts of Ottoman Turkey—Constantinople, the Caucasus, or Cilicia—to communicate more easily
with one another. The American contribution to Armenian and
Arab nationalism was cultural, not political, but it was no less
effective in making these persons less receptive to the Ottomani-
zation desired. . . as a means of uniting the disparate subjects of
the Sultan (Daniel 1970:111).

WHAT THE 19TH CENTURY
MISSION TEACHES US TODAY

ABCFM missionaries evangelized Christians, not Kurds. The
missionaries taught, lived with, and befriended Christians, not
Kurds. No one put their nets into the deep. Why not? If the missionaries could speak here, they might suggest that the Holy
Spirit did not open a way to the Kurds. He seemed to say "not
yet." Direct work with Kurds was illegal and dangerous. Moreover, Christians in Kurdistan opposed any mixing of Christians
with Muslims.

The first stage of the Great Experiment—revival of the historical churches—was coming about. Hospitals and schools and
churches operated in every major city of the target area. Democratic principles, by which an individual could make up one's own
mind as to the meaning of the Bible, permeated their teaching.
The kingdom of our Lord was coming to the Christians of Persia
and Turkey.

However, missionaries no longer wrote about a second stage of
mission to the Kurdish majority. The time for Muslim mission
was not yet.

THE GREAT EXPERIMENT AT THE CLOSE
OF THE 19TH CENTURY

Missionary men and women held fast their hope of shaping
the historical churches and clergy in the Protestant image. Mis-

sionaries built Christian schools and churches, brick by brick, while the Kurds were left to themselves. Barnum, the missionary who worked forty years in Harput, remembered the Great Experiment at the close of the 19th century, when he wrote,

> In the early years we missionaries expected to complete our share of the work here, pass it over to native hands, and move on to some other field long before the present time. There has not been the ability and the readiness to accept responsibility on the part of the people that we had hoped for (ABCFM 1899a:402).

A Bridge Too Far?

The world has turned around many times since the 19th century mission heroes sacrificed their health and their lives to evangelize the Christians of Turkey, Mesopotamia, and Persia. We salute these courageous and resolute men and women of faith. Their goal,[6] however, eluded them. Kurds did not hear the gospel from the lips of Nestorians; neither did Armenians pity their unevangelized Muslim neighbors. Perhaps it was a bridge too far.

---

[6] The purpose of missions was to "enable the Nestorian Church through the grace of God, to exert a commanding influence in the spiritual regeneration of Asia" (Elder 1936:1–2).

HARRIET CUMBERLAND IN KURDISH DRESS, 20TH CENTURY
(FROM THE COLLECTION OF JANET CUMBERLAND SHAFRAN)

ROGER CUMBERLAND IN DAHOUK, IRAQ, 20TH CENTURY
(FROM THE COLLECTION OF JANET CUMBERLAND SHAFRAN)

Chapter 4

20th Century Mission
in Kurdistan, 1900-1990

Mission work in Kurdistan teetered precariously as the 20th century opened. Debris from the Armenian massacres of 1895–6 littered the landscape. Young Turks took a secret oath to overthrow the Sultan by placing their hands on a pistol resting on the Qur'an (Fromkin 1989:40). In 1909 the Russian army, eager for its warm water port, lunged into northern Persia. In Urmiah a missionary was martyred.

MISSION LEADER MURDERED IN PERSIA

Benjamin Labaree of the Presbyterian mission was murdered in 1904:

A fanatic dervish, or Moslem holy man, who had a hatred for all Christians, would go from house to house, village to village, begging food and clothing. One day he went to the threshing floor near a village, and asked the man there for some wheat. The man refused and the dervish shot and killed him. The victim was an Assyrian (Nestorian) who was a naturalized British subject. During those years Father [Joseph Cochran] had assumed the unofficial duty of being a sort of go-between for the Nestorians, bringing their grievances before the local authorities. In this case he urged the authorities to arrest the murderer and bring him to trial. It became evident later that the Moslem chief priest in the city of Urumia was in collusion with the murderer. The fanatic dervish learned that one of the missionary men in the mission station was accompanying Miss Margaret Dean to the Russian border. This man was the Rev. Benjamin Labaree, whom the dervish mistook for my father. In a desolate place among the hills near the village of Gavilan, Mr. Labaree was murdered (Cochran 1983:5–6).

Labaree had served as a doctor for 46 years in Kurdistan of Persia. He had revised the Modern Syrian translation of the Bible. Labaree's grave is in Urmiah, the city he loved. The United States government intervened on account of his murder.

POLITICAL REPERCUSSIONS OF LABAREE'S MURDER

Secretary of State Hay reported that President Theodore Roosevelt was "greatly disturbed" by Labaree's death and would bring the matter before Congress unless the Persian government gave immediate satisfaction. The Persian government caught the murderer, known to us simply as Kurdu, and imprisoned him for life. Mrs. Labaree received $30,000 instead of the $16,000 she had asked for. The missionaries, however, refused to consider the case closed and insisted on the death penalty for Kurdu. This the Persian government would not agree to. The murderer died in prison three years later without a resolution of the case.[1]

1913—HIGHWATER MARK FOR MISSIONARY WORK

However, by 1913 the situation looked stable. David Eddy of the ABCFM wrote a promising book called, *What Next in Turkey?* Here was the highwater mark for missionaries in Kurdistan. The past would be swept aside, the future would be bright with schools and hospitals and democratic ideals. At last the great work to revive the ancient churches would bring results. Following the massacres of 1895, the mission in Mardin recovered, such that "a sunrise prayer meeting, held each Tuesday morning increased in numbers from a dozen attendants to over 150" (ABCFM 1899b). According to Eddy there were

378 schools in Turkey, 33,000 enrolled in Sunday Schools, 54,000 adherents in churches, 25,000 in schools, 10 million pages a year from the Bible House in Constantinople which sounds the knell of bigotry and stirs within us *a vision of the Dawn that is spreading from Kurdistan to Albania* (1913:79, italics mine).

---

[1]   Shedd latter admitted that the missionaries were blamed by Kurds and by the Persian government for aggravating the Labaree case (Joseph 1961:126–127).

TABLE 6
SCHOOLS SUPPORTED BY THE WOMEN'S BOARD
(EDDY 1913)

Station	Name of Institution	Pupils
Samokor	Girls' Boarding school	100
Monastir	Girls' Boarding school	68
Kortcha	Girls' Boarding school	76
Sofia	kindergarten	50
Smyrna	American Collegiate Institute	301
Marsovan	Anatolia Girls' school	250
Sivas	Girls' High school	726
Adabazar	Girls' High school	293
Brousa	Girls' High school	169
Constantinople	Gedik Pasha school	268
Talas	Girls' Boarding school	147
Marash	Central Turkey College for Girls	118
Aintab	Girls' seminary	156
Adana	Girls' seminary	180
Hadjin	Hadjin Home school	267
Harput	Euphrates College—Girls' Dept.	395
Van	Girls' High and Boarding school	410
Erzroom	Girls' High and Boarding school	200
Bitlis	Girls' Boarding school	41
Mardin	Girls' High school	39

HIGH HOPES FOR MISSION SCHOOLS IN TURKEY

The ABCFM in Turkey operated a constellation of girls' school, supported by the Women's Board. In 1913 the future looked brighter than ever (*see* Table 5 above).

HIGH HOPES FOR MISSION HOSPITALS IN TURKEY

The ABCFM medical missionaries started the 20th century with enthusiasm. Equipment was modernized. The hospital recorded a rising number of patients.

HIGH HOPES FOR THE ANGLICAN
MISSION IN AMADIA

Headquarters for the Anglican Mission to the Assyrians relocated from Urmiah to Van in 1907. Anglicans purchased six acres outside of town, on which stood "a fine orchard with good old fruit trees" (Heazell 1913:167). Anglicans worked solely among the Assyrians, and left the Armenian mission to the ABCFM. Under that mission Dr. and Mrs. Raynolds operated an orphanage in Van.

But following the Young Turk revolt in 1909, harassment of foreigners by the Turkish government was unrelenting. Anglicans closed their mission in Van and moved south to Amadia, near Dohouk in modern-day Iraq. As was their custom, Anglicans limited their mission to the wishes of Assyrian church leaders. William Ainger Wigram asked for prayers to guide the mission aright "in all the great developments that the next few years may bring about in the Churches of the East" (Heazell 1913:212).

High Hopes for the Mission in Persia

Robert Speer of the Presbyterian Board of Foreign Missions wrote with optimism just before World War I: "The conditions of the evangelical Church and the economic situation of the Assyrians as a whole were probably better than they had ever been" (Joseph 1961:129). Speer numbered 3,000 Assyrian communicants and another 3,000 adherents. The mission provided higher education at Urmiah College and Fiske Seminary. In addition, "the mission hospital . . . was influencing the whole of western Persia and eastern Kurdistan" (1961:129).

Mission Was, Again, to the Ethnic Christians

Presbyterian policy in Persia remained the same: strengthen the historic churches that they in turn might be a light to their neighbors. Missions continued to the already-Christianized. One historian wrote: "In spite of obstacles, a Presbyterian missionary passed year by year through the wilderness of Kurdish mountains, *seeking in the most remote corners of the land the little companies of Christians*" (Richter 1910:316, italics mine). No mission evangelized Kurds.

MISSION WAS, AGAIN, A COMPETITION AMONG MISSIONS

In the 20th century, the Protestants again competed with Roman Catholics and Anglicans. The Protestants worried over the zeal of Catholic missionaries:

> The Roman Catholic missionaries, who have their headquarters in Mosul, seem to be gaining ground in the midst of the general confusion, and are advancing up the river Zab. They have even won over some of the members of the Patriarch's family (Richter 1910:317).

New missions gained a foothold in Urmiah, including the United Lutheran Church of America, German Orientmission, English Plymouth Brethren, American Dunkards, Holiness Methodists, American Southern Baptists and Northern Baptists, and English Congregationalists. *All these missions carved their portion from the Nestorian church.* Observed John Joseph:

> There was perhaps no missionary field in the world where there were so many rival "Christian" forces at work as were found in Urmiyah at the beginning of this century, *all struggling to get predominance among these few people* (1961:123, italics mine).[2]

Will not one mission evangelize the majority people?

---

2   In the late 1870s, the Herrmannsburger Mission had entered Persian Kurdistan. Like the Catholics, Anglicans, and ABCFM workers who already crowded the city, the Herrmannsburger Mission worked to reform the historical church, "that they might become a light in the midst of their Kurdish neighbors" (Waldburger 1983:8). In 1886 the Herrmannsburger mission supported an evangelical Assyrian, Pera Johannes, to work in Kotschannes in Kurdistan, "and he worked there among his fellow-Assyrians" (Waldburger 1983:8). Between 1879–1908 three Assyrians were trained in theology in Herrmannsburg, Germany. Two of them returned to Persia and ministered in the church and in schools. (Indeed, the Protestant mission to the Assyrians proved a great benefit to the church in Iran in the 20th century.)

WORLD WAR I: A CENTURY
OF MISSIONARY ENDEAVOR DESTROYED

When Eddy wrote *What Next in Turkey?*, he hoped the unrest that threatened ethnic Christians lay in the past; however, just as Eddy's book reached circulation, the First World War engulfed the region. Twenty-eight centuries of Armenian culture was pulled up from its roots.

THE LIGHTS ARE EXTINGUISHED IN TURKEY

Until 1914 some 86,000 Armenians lived in the Marash region of southern Turkey; by 1923 none of them remained (Kerr 1973:preface). The Armenian population of the Bitlis region, 150 families, was reduced to zero. In Van, Harput, Diyarbakir, Aintab, Bitlis, Urfa, everywhere in the east, the Armenian population perished. Turks and Kurds nailed horseshoes into the feet of Armenians and ordered them to walk into the Syrian desert. Reverend E. A. Allen of the American Board wrote, "One hundred sixty-one persons, buried by me, came to their death in the most cruel manner possible, at the hands of regular Turkish troops in company with Kurds under their command" (Yacoub 1986:102). In all, two of every three Armenians perished during World War I. The number of Armenian dead has been put between 750,000 and 1,000,000.

Not only Armenians, but Nestorians in Turkey suffered as well. The number of Assyrian dead was put at 250,000 (1986:121). For example:

All the inhabitants of Gavar [Rhea's Gawar?] district were gathered together. Some were pressed into the houses and the houses were set on fire; others were thrown into wells and ditches and were buried alive. All the Nestorians of Gavar and the adjoining plain country were totally exterminated, including the Christians of Albak and Barvar and of Qoodchanis (Werda 1924:9).

Reverend F. N. Jessup said, "This is the most awful calamity which has befallen the Nestorian people in the ninety years of our mission work among them" (Yacoub 1986:64). Sadly, Kurds perpetrated this evil as others would do unto them in the 20th century.

War, plunder, starvation, massacre annihilated Nestorian villages. Kurds and Turks "fell upon them, especially in the mountains between Mesopotamia and Persia, killed many, and drove others out. Numbers took refuge in Persia" (Latourette 1975:269). It was a pitiful sight. Turkish and Kurdish raiders swept thousands of Christians from their villages. Homeless, hungry, and crazed with fear, Christians walked up frozen mountain passes, and there made decisions too awful to imagine; they left behind their weak and elderly and walked on. Across the border in Persia some found refuge at the mission compounds in Urmiah. The story of the relief effort is told in the section on Persia that follows shortly.

American missionaries died with their friends. Dr. and Mrs. George Raynolds had worked with Armenians in Van since 1874. Mrs. Raynolds succumbed in the forced march, along with many others. Raynolds ended his days in California (F. Coan 1939:83). Other missionaries (Henry Atkinson, Fred Shepard, Daniel Thom) died of typhus in the 1915 epidemic (Shepard 1970:4).

ENVER PASHA MAKES AN OFFER

Czar Nicholas II hoped to enlist the Armenians when war broke out with Turkey. However, Enver Pasha of Turkey quickly offered to establish an autonomous Armenian state within the Ottoman Empire in areas populated by Armenians. The task of these Armenians would be to persuade their brothers in the Russian armies to join with Muslims in a revolt against Russia.

Negotiations between Enver Pasha and the Armenians took place at Erzerum. The Armenian representatives pledged support to Enver Pasha's government. Then the Armenians heard Russia's counteroffer of an autonomous state, which included a seaport on the Mediterranean. So it happened that Armenians threw in their lot with the Russians. [3]

---

[3] Turks enlisted some Armenians to fight against fellow Armenians. One Antone Pasha fought for the Turks. As a reward the Turks gave Antone Pasha a large tract of land between Sumeil and Zakhu in present-day northern Iraq. Today Armenians regard Antone Pasha as a traitor.

ARMENIANS FOUGHT ALONGSIDE RUSSIANS

Thousands of Armenians enlisted in the Russian army. They wore Russian uniforms and accepted Russian military awards. When the Russian armies invaded Turkey after the Sarikamish disaster of 1914, their columns "were preceded by battalions of irregular Armenian volunteers, both from the Caucasus and from Turkey" (Arfa 1966:26).

ARMENIANS MASSACRED KURDS

Diane Darke states that not only were Armenians massacred in World War I, but Armenians similarly put the Kurds to the sword. She writes,

> Armenian volunteers on the Russian side, when Turkey collapsed, also took their revenge. More than 600,000 Kurds are said to have been killed in eastern Anatolia between 1915 and 1918 (1987:256).

In December of 1914 an Armenian regiment, wearing Russian uniforms, massacred Kurdish women and children on the Plain of Alashkert-Bayazid. The men of those villages were away, having joined the Turkish Army (Kerr 1973:12). That same month, Enver Pasha led a Turkish army north into Russia. Russians and Armenians joined to destroy the invaders at Sarikamish in the Caucasus. Only a tenth of Enver Pasha's one hundred thousand soldiers came home. "The participation of the Armenian legions in his defeat at Sarikamish undoubtedly influenced his decision to take revenge on the Armenians" (1973:12). Hassan Arfa writes that

> Armenian volunteers, in order to avenge their compatriots who had been massacred by the Kurds, committed all kinds of excesses, more than six hundred thousand Kurds being killed between 1915 and 1918 in the eastern vilayets of Turkey. In this way the region became seriously depopulated, as more than seven hundred thousand Armenians had been deported in 1915–16 (1966:26).

THE YOUNG TURKS' PLAN
DOOMED THE ARMENIANS

Strange as it sounds today, Armenians had at first participated in the Young Turk movement. Early in the 20th century the Young Turk movement had included middle-class Greeks as well. This party

> campaigned for a liberal Turkey under British protection, where power would be held by the most competent without discrimination on grounds of race or creed. This would have amounted to acceptance of the [prevailing] dominance exercised by the essentially non-Muslim cosmopolitan bourgeoisie (Chaliand et al. 1993:12).

YOUNG TURKS INITIALLY OFFERED
HOPE FOR REFORM

The revolt of the Young Turks against the Sultan brought constitutional reform in 1908 and with it the ostensible guarantee of religious toleration. Armenians and Muslims rejoiced together. In mosques and churches fraternity and cooperation were publicly extolled. Enver Bey proclaimed, "Henceforth we are all brothers. There are no longer Bulgars, Greeks, Roumans, Jews, Moslems; under the same blue sky we are all equal, we glory in being Ottomans" (Kinross 1977:574).[4] In Constantinople, processions the Turkish mullahs, Jewish rabbis, and prelates of the discordant Christian faiths sat side by side in horse-drawn carriages: "Halting before the crowds at points en route, Moslem and Christian in succession would rise with hands outstretched in prayer, calling upon the One God to preserve the constitution and praising Him for its blessings of liberty" (Kinross 1977:574).[5]

---

[4] Just seven years later Enver Bey would order the massacre of the entire Christian population in the east.

[5] In Turkey's east, missionaries and Christians rejoiced to see that day. Wrote Wigram,

> We returned [to Van] in August to find ourselves in Utopia; Turks walking the streets arm in arm with Armenians, and all classes heartily celebrating the Sultan's birthday. . . . What will be the outcome of this peaceful revolution? Good must come of it, not least for our Mission. Suspicion of missionaries should disappear, and our Syrians ought to benefit, for they have always been loyal subjects of the Sultan (Heazell 1913:173).

THE YOUNG TURK MOVEMENT
DIVIDED ALONG ETHNIC LINES

But the Young Turk movement was unable to contain so many diverse interests. The Greeks and Armenians spun off in 1902; they formed the Freedom and Conciliation Party. With the Greeks and Armenians out, the Young Turks' platform was in the hands of narrower men who defined their aspirations in anti-foreign, anti-minority terms. They "categorically rejected all foreign intervention" (Chaliand et al. 1993:12). The Young Turks, known then as the Unionists, came to power in 1908. Within a year they implemented their beliefs in law:

> All non-Turkish associations, publications, and schools were banned. Now made up exclusively of Turkish nationalists, the Unionists proclaimed pan-Turanism as their official ideology. . . . This tendency sought to found a great Turanian Empire stretching from European Turkey to the steppes of Central Asia. The pan-Turanian Empire which the Turkish nationalists dreamt of— and still dream of—was in no way ethnically homogeneous: between Turkey and Turania (Azerbaijan, Uzbekistan, Turkmenistan, Kirghizia, etc.) there lay Armenia and Kurdistan, populated by non-Turks. On the eve of the First World War, the Unionist leaders had found their own solution to this problem; *to use the war in order to destroy these national entities,* by physical liquidation if possible; and, if not, then by massive deportation geared to thinning them out as much as possible. *The Armenians who, as Christians, were considered to be inassimilable would be exterminated.* The Kurds, on the other hand, were to be dispersed, deported or liquidated as required (Chaliand et al. 1993:13–14, italics mine).

Therefore, the Armenians' fate was probably sealed, like other scapegoat peoples of 20th century totalitarian states, whether they resisted or not. A calculated racism provoked the Turks to mow down the minorities:[6]

---

6   The Armenians, even before the Adana Massacre of 1909, set up revolutionary branch councils in Russia, Switzerland and London. Armenian terrorist bands became active in Constantinople and in the east. Both sides—Armenian and Turk—saw the war in 1914 as an opportunity to force a solution in their own favor.

Within less than a year, in April 1909, the great Adana Massacre took place. In his *Memories of a Turkish Statesman*, Jamal Pasha reports that seventeen thousand Armenians and eighteen hundred fifty Turks were killed in this massacre (Kerr 1973:7). Race was the bedrock on which Young Turks founded modern Turkey. Today Turkish school children pledge allegiance to Kemalism, with its "intense pride combined with an acute inferiority complex, a deep xenophobia with an overwhelming hospitality to strangers" (Darke 1987:11). Time and again in the 20th century the Turks have concocted "Pan-Islamic and chauvinistic propaganda which makes use of the Armenian bogey" (McDowall 1996:127).

THE LIGHTS ARE EXTINGUISHED IN PERSIA

Not only Turkey's Christians were put to the sword; World War I brought starvation, disease and massacre to the Assyrian people of northern Persia. We hear of thousands of Christians in the Urmiah area who perished as the war swept back and forth across northern Iran:

> The Nestorians in Persia in the vicinity of Urmiah, including the Aissors, those who in the preceding twenty years had become affiliated with the Russian Orthodox Church, were decimated by attacks by their enemies as they were in the neighboring mountains in the then Turkish Empire. The withdrawal early in the war of the Russian troops which had been defending them left them exposed to the Kurds and the Moslem Persians. Many took refuge in the compounds of the Roman Catholic and Protestant missions in Urmiah, but hundreds of Nestorians, Orthodox Aissors, and Armenians were slaughtered. (Latourette 1945:270)

Approximately a third of the Chaldean Uniates perished (Latourette 1975:269). About 3,000 fled to the French Catholic mission in Urmiah. Fully 17,000 Nestorians squeezed into the American Mission compound on Urmiah, over which flew the flag of the (neutral) United States of America. Many who started for the mission compound never arrived:

> Copies of the proclamation of the Holy War [jihad] were instantly posted in the streets of the city. Messengers were sent to all the Mohammedan villages, with the joyous news that the day of revenges and massacre had come!

As [Christians] emerged from their homes and villages, they found all their ways intercepted and blocked! Friends had become foes; they had come out for revenge, both to kill and to plunder. It was a wintry day, with temperature not far from zero. The fleeing throngs were literally stripped of their entire clothing. Naked women and little girls, eight to ten years of age, were subjected to the most revolting outrages. Many of these refugees fled back and sought the shelter of church edifices, thinking perhaps Islam's passion might balk at the sight of the sacred shrines. But the malignant flood of crime knew no bounds. The Christians' Holy Bibles were opened on the pulpits, and their pages desecrated by the committal of unmentionable deeds. They entered then the homes of the Christians for a richer haul of plunder. They emptied every home of its entire contents and set the buildings on fire.

Some men tried to bargain with gold for their lives, but after the victims had given up all they possessed, they were so brutally murdered that many of them could not be recognized by their wailing relatives. On the heels of this fearful wave, there came another, equally as fiendish, when the invading Kurds arrived. So far as the plunder was concerned, the latter had come for the gleanings only. But as for the perpetration of the atrocious deeds, there was enough left for them also to quench their thirst for blood. The Christian villages became a heap of ruins. This was the hour of the jihad! The proclamation of the holy war! And the brute who committed more and blacker crimes, believed that he was listed for special favors in his prophet's paradise of sensual pleasures (Werda 1924:31–36, selected).

THE RELIEF EFFORT IN URMIAH

Missionaries in Urmiah performed one of the heroic achievements of the war:

They proved to be the real saviors of the Christian Persians and during the long war years fed thousands of starving Kurds and Persian Muslims from their meager stores. . . . They won the affection and respect of all, and among the Nestorians this feeling became deep and lasting (Joseph 1961:133).

The missionary who carried the chief responsibility during the relief effort was William A. Shedd. Shedd was born in Urmiah where his father had been a missionary before him. He contracted with Muslim bakers in town to buy and transport about five tons of bread a day. Thousands of Christians were confined in the mission compound, in safety, for the next five months.

After the Turkish defeat at Sarikamish, the Christian population in Urmiah breathed a little easier.[7] Then came the Russian advance, and Christian men excitedly joined them in arms. Russians then committed some of the worst offenses of the war, and in these crimes the Assyrian Christians joined:

> Wherever they went they left the innocent Muslim population impoverished and hostile. Plundered of all the food they possessed, deprived of their cattle, flocks and transport animals, thousands died of famine. When Baratoff's Cossacks captured Rawanduz, not more than twenty per cent of the Kurdish population survived to recall the day (Joseph 1961:136).

However, Russia exited the war in 1917 when it signed a separate peace with Turkey. Turkey moved into Persia as Russian troops retreated. Assyrians fled from Urmiah. The mission compounds of the Americans and the French were destroyed (Guest 1993:180).[8]

HASSAN ARFA'S CONSPIRACY THEORY

Hassan Arfa, an Iranian intelligence officer, wrote a conspiracy theory, in which he argued that the United States used its missionaries to push the Assyrians toward Russia. In Arfa's view,

---

7   Persia remained neutral in the First World War, but its location between Russia and Turkey caused it to become a war zone.

8   Assyrians in Persia planned to set up a separate government in northern Persia, taking advantage of the instability brought on by the First World War. The Assyrian patriarch, Mar Shimun, planned this with a Christian warrior from Turkey, Agha Petros. However, Mar Shimun was betrayed by Ismail Simko, a Kurdish raider, on February 25, 1918; Simko assassinated Mar Shimun (along with 45 of his escorts) under a flag of truce: "Simko had invited the latter for a friendly conference. He received [Mar Shimun] cordially, and kissed him when leaving; then the patriarch and his men were pierced with bullets" (Joseph 1961:141). It was an act of unrestrained cruelty. This act in turn enraged the Assyrians, who took revenge on the helpless Azeri Muslim population of Rezaiyeh [Urmiah], killing hundreds of men, women and children without discrimination and looting their homes.

The Turks had tried to remain on good terms with the Assyrians, but Russian and American propaganda, conducted through the missionaries (who even before the entry of the United States into the war on the Allies' side were violently anti-Turkish), and induced them to throw in their lot with the Russians (1966:51).

Arfa criticized William A. Shedd of Urmiah, for showing "great partiality towards the Christians, [encouraging] the Assyrians in their hostile attitude towards the Iranian authorities and people" (1966:51). Arfa's criticism, unfortunately, stands on known facts:

> During the summer of 1918 Urumia was caught between a British expeditionary force moving up the Tigris River and Turkish troops to the west of the city. A British officer was busy in the area recruiting an army of refugees to assist the British against the Turks, and indiscreet American missionaries diverted some $100,000 in relief funds to support this "Christian army." One of the missionary-relief workers, William Shedd, also the American vice consul at Urumia, seriously compromised the American government by signing in his capacity as vice consul an offer to pay the bills of the Christian army. He also issued orders summoning "every young man who has a rifle" to join the Christian army "without any delay or excuse," an action which Shedd admitted was "directly in contravention" of orders of the State Department (Daniel 1970:158).[9]

---

[9] One missionary was related to President Woodrow Wilson's family. Another missionary acted as U.S. consul in Tabriz. From the Middle Eastern viewpoint, the bond between Christian missionary and his or her government was strong. Probably this deterred the indigenization of the gospel in Iran.

Margaret Kahn writes that the persecution of the church was partly due to the suspicion aroused when the western powers came to help the minorities:

> The college where we taught [Iran] had been built originally as a hospital by the American missionaries who came to help the poor Christians (Assyrians) clinging to their ancient faith in the midst of the Muslim onslaught. *Partially because this attention from Westerners roused the suspicion and envy of their Muslim neighbors,* the Assyrians were subsequently massacred in large numbers by both Turks and Kurds in the early twentieth century (1980:16); italics mine.

TABLE 7
STUDENT ENROLLMENT IN ABCFM SCHOOLS, TURKEY

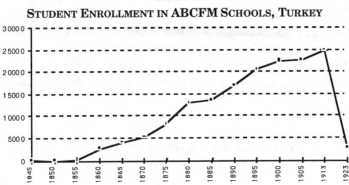

THE NEAR EAST RELIEF MISSION

Following the Great War, homeless multitudes envied the dead. Starving, disease-racked masses wandered and fell across the wounded land. James L. Barton, foreign secretary of the ABCFM, and Cleveland H. Dodge from the mission in Beirut organized a rescue mission. At their first meeting they voted to raise $100,000. Thus began the Near East Relief mission. More than a hundred million dollars was eventually contributed, "the largest volunteer relief project to that date" (Shepard 1970:5). Volunteers arrived from American and worked without pay. Missionaries who had left Turkey before the war eagerly joined the Near East Relief in order to be among the first to return in 1919 (1970:5). Herbert Hoover, then head of the American Relief Commission, arranged to contribute goods equal in value to about half a million dollars per month, for nearly a year.

> Funds were needed for refugees in Anatolia, but also in the Caucasus, Syria, Lebanon, Persia, and Greece.... Nearly a thousand Americans served overseas. They displayed wonderful heroism, even martyrdom. Twenty-one of these workers and five missionaries died in the field from typhus, pneumonia, and other diseases (Kerr 1973: forward).

The Near East Relief mission ended the 19th century era of mission to the Armenians and Nestorians.[10] "Nearly all the mis-

---

[10] The American Board and the Presbyterians maintained their missions in newly-formed Lebanon and Syria. In 1920 Margaret

sion schools, churches and hospitals were closed" (Glover 1928:223). A few schools in western Turkey re-opened. Although the subject of Christianity was not allowed,[11] these schools influenced many Turkish students in the 20th century.

Meanwhile, Lutherans began the first-ever Protestant mission to Kurds. We turn now to the history of the Lutheran Orient Mission Society.

THE LUTHERAN MISSION TO THE KURDS

The only sustained mission to Kurds in either the 19th or 20th centuries was borne by the Lutheran Orient Mission Society (LOMS) of the United States. Lutherans familiarized themselves with the Great Experiment (of working to reform the ethnic churches) which had cast a spell over the mission in 19th century

---

McGilvary wrote a book with the hopeful title, *The Dawn of a New Era in Syria*. In it the Great Experiment recurred: reform the ethnic churches to reach the Muslim masses. McGilvary wrote: "The Oriental Church is the canker at the heart of Christianity, and insamuch as it is the chief point of contact with Islam, it behooves the Christian world to renovate the system which so unworthily represents its cause in the Near East" (Kaplan 1993:22).

As in Turkey and Persia, missionaries in Lebanon and Syria were shown the door, this time by the Greek Orthodox and Maronites. Again, missionaries founded separate congregations. Again, missionaries tried to remain free from politics. Again, missionary schools created a national consciousness and the aspriation for self-rule. Arabs, they said, differed from Turks: democracy and concern for the public good would grow in Damascus, Aleppo, and Beirut where it had failed in Turkey and Persia.

[11] Some of the older missionaries found it difficult to accept the new pattern. When Miss Edith Sanderson, a teacher in the American Board school at Brusa [sic], persisted in having Moslem children read the Bible, she and two of her colleagues were arrested, and the school was closed. . . . Thereafter American educators were careful to observe the letter of Turkish law, and there were no further disagreements of major import between the mission schools and the Turkish government (Daniel 1970:173).

Kurdistan. Lutherans wanted to break the spell by trying a new experiment.

THE BEGINNING OF THE LUTHERAN MISSION

In 1899 the American Norwegian Lutheran Committee sent Reverend M. O. Wee to consider a work among the Nestorians and Armenians of Turkey. However, Wee saw that many other missions already working in this field, while none worked with Kurds.

On his trip he met several influential Kurds, among them Sultan Salmamin. Upon returning to the United States, Wee filed a most unusual report: he advised the Norwegian Lutherans *not to take up work among the Syrians and Armenians* (Lohre 1918:284, italics mine).

This remarkable advice would result in the Lutheran commitment to Kurdish work, made in 1910 at the Edinburgh Conference.

The Lepsius Society

Johannes Lepsius had founded the Lepsius Society in 1895, "with the aim to do evangelistic work among the Muslims" (Waldburger 1983:9). The son of a famous Egyptologist in Berlin, Johannes Lepsius stirred European Christians to evangelism in the Middle East. However, the day after he founded his mission, the massacres of 1895 began in Constantinople! Lepsius changed his mission to a relief organization for Armenians. He made public in Europe the plight of the Armenians.

In 1909 Turks again massacred Armenians, and again in 1915, so relief work continued to define the Lepsius mission. However, Lepsius did send missionaries in 1907 "to take up work among the Kurds" (Lohre 1918:284). His workers served under the German Orient Society for five years.

The German Orient Society

In 1902 Detwig von Oertzen began an orphanage in Khoi, Persia. Von Oertzen trekked through Persian Kurdistan in 1903–4, reaching Urmiah in November of that year. "He almost died on the journey, suffering from pneumonia and typhoid, but in Urmiah an American missionary and medical doctor took care of him" (Waldburger 1983:9). He took a furlough in Germany, then returned to Persia in 1905 with his bride, Juliette Huguenin-Virchaux:

> In May 1905 they settled in at Soujbulakh being the first resident missionaries there. Because it was too dangerous to live in the Kurdish quarter they stayed in the Jewish one. Though he started Bible studies for the Christians there *they deliberately didn't want to reach the Kurds through a revitalized church of Syrians, Nestorians, Armenians and the like but through personal contacts* (Waldburger 1983:9, italics mine).

Von Oertzen began studying the Kurdish language. His teacher was a Kurd named Mirza. Mirza translated some Bible verses, and the Gospel of Mark was begun in seriousness. This was in the Mukri dialect with Arabic script.

> Of course, von Oertzen was accused of turning Mirza away from the truth of Islam, but he was successful in explaining that if Islam was the truth he wouldn't be able to do that. To have more contacts with Kurds he started to organize forums and lectures with discussions on various themes like geography, the alcohol problem, the status of women, etc. (Waldburger 1983:9–10).

In these practical ways the first missionary to the Kurds showed his concern to improve their social conditions.

Immanuel Damman Arrives, But Is Martyred

The Lepsius Society took over the work of the German Orient Society in 1906 or 1907. Lepsius re-appointed the von Oertzens to the field. Immanuel Damman joined them in the summer of 1906. Damman began doctoral work on Kurdish grammar, but after only a few weeks he contracted a case of encephalitis and remained an invalid for several months. Then,

> on the night of February 15 he [Damman] was murdered in Soujbulakh instead of von Oertzen by Kurds who wanted to bring the local governor into troubles. Von Oertzen was seriously wounded in that attack but was able to lead the funeral service the next day (Waldburger 1983:10).

Now protected by soldiers, the von Oertzens continued in Souj-bulakh a few more months, but then returned to Germany.[12] There they printed Mark's Gospel. They never returned to the field, and no one replaced them.[13] The German Orient Mission ended its work, although the mission did not disband until 1965. The German Herrmannsburger mission had been active among the Assyrians since the 1870s. It now decided to enter direct work with the Kurds. Professor Carl Roebblen, head of the mission, also attended the 1910 World Mission conference in Edinburgh. He evidently played a part in meetings there that assigned the Kurdish mission to the Lutherans.

In 1913 a new mission society was founded in Germany with the aim "to spread the Gospel among the Muslims in northwestern Iran, especially among the Kurds living there" (Waldburger 1983:8). The first missionary was sent out in 1914, but immediately World War I broke out; he returned to Germany even before he had reached Kurdistan (Waldburger 1983:8).

The Edinburgh Conference became a mainspring for mission in new places, and new ways, around the globe. The conference and its task became the basis of ecumenism in the 20th century. The denominations of the world came together at Edinburgh.

EDINBURGH CONFERENCE ASSIGNS KURDISTAN
TO THE LUTHERANS

During the 1910 Edinburgh Conference a committee consisting of Robert Speer of New York, Lepsius of Germany, Detwig von Oertzen and John Newton Wright met with L. O. Fossum. Fossum had just returned from Kurdistan. Wright was a Presbyterian missionary in Persia. The committee recommended that the Kurdish people be assigned to Lutherans and to the

---

12 David McDowall writes that "one Kurdish faction" murdered Damman "for no other reason than to secure the removal of the Mukri chief whose appointment as district governor was bitterly resented. It worked; the Iranian authorities were sufficiently embarrassed to remove him" (1996:75).

13 Lepsius and von Oertzen would be present in 1910 at the Edinburgh World Mission Conference, at which the Lutherans took responsibility for a mission to Kurds.

Herrmannsburgers of Hanover, Germany. They recommended Fossum as the leader.

Fossum Enters the Field

Fossum was not new to the Middle East when the committee chose him to lead the Lutheran work in Kurdistan. In 1905, Norwegian Lutherans in America had sent Fossum to the Nestorians west of Lake Urmiah. He worked among the Christians there five years. However

> Fossum's attention had been drawn to the Kurds. But he was forced to return [to the United States] in 1909, and the work among the Syrians and Armenians was abandoned. He succeeded in enlisting the interest of individuals, selected from several Lutheran synods, who constituted a board, which adopted the name, The Inter-synodical Evangelical Lutheran Orient Mission Society (Lohre 1918:284).

Fossum felt convinced that God wanted him, and Lutherans, to evangelize Kurds, without the eastern churches as intermediary. He attended the 1910 Edinburgh world mission conference. There "the Mohammedan Kurds" were assigned to "the Lutheran Church." Of course, the Lutherans were divided enough to ask, "where and what is this evasive thing called the 'Lutheran Church'?" (Jensen and Oberg 1985:11). Lutheran mission work needed a Lutheran mission structure. *It was this structure that provided the Lutherans with the means* to begin and sustain their work in Kurdistan.

Fossum Forms a Mission Society

After Edinburgh, Fossum spoke of the Lutheran mandate to various congregations. However, the Lutheran Church could take no action, because it had no mechanism for cross-cultural mission. "Finally he [Fossum] called a conference to survey the foreign mission situation. A meeting was held at Berwyn, Illinois, September 8–10, 1910" (Jensen and Oberg 1985:11). Individuals from several Lutheran synods were invited, and they constituted a board (Lohre 1918:284). Thus was formed the Lutheran Orient Mission Society (LOMS).

A Mission Society Was the Vehicle
for Lutheran Mission

Fossum engineered the means for Lutherans to go to Kurdistan. Martin Luther had dismantled the sails of mission when he decreed that Protestants should have no monastic orders. For more than three centuries Lutherans had no "means" (William Carey's term for mission societies) to organize and send missionaries. Lutherans owe to L. O. Fossum and his Orient Mission Society a practical model for sending Lutheran missionaries.

FOSSUM'S PLAN TO EVANGELIZE KURDS

Fossum became the first editor of *The Kurdistan Missionary*, which first appeared in October 1910. In its first issue, Fossum wrote down the reasons that Kurds should come to faith in Christ:

> Why should the evangelization of Kurdistan be hastened? The reasons are the same as pertain to the rest of the unevangelized places of the world. But there are a few particular reasons as a Moslem country in its relation to the Moslem world, why a definite systematic attempt should be made right now to reach effectually the whole of Kurdistan (Jensen and Oberg 1985:7).

Fossum suggested four reasons that workers among the Kurds might have good hope:

1. First of all, the character of the people. For the most part warm-hearted, quick to make friends, usually loyal in friendship,[14] the love, the friendliness of Jesus would appeal to them; democratic, freedom-loving, the freedom wherewith Christ maketh free would attract them; strong, brave, hardy, the manliness of Christian character would compel them.

2. Social conditions in Kurdistan place men and women on a recognized equality, working together for the common living, holding property with equal rights and administering their affairs with equal honors, a type of character has long been produced to which the appeal of the pure and holy life pressing forward to a holy and happy heaven can be made much more hopeful than it

---

14 Contrast Fossum's cheerful disposition toward Kurds with the perspective of missionaries who allied their efforts with the historical Christians.

can be to the ordinary Moslem, who gives to woman no honor in this life and no place of her own in the next.

3. Then there is the political situation of the people. They have no sovereignty to maintain and it is a mere matter of convenience whether they are subject to any central ruling power or not. Their souls are their own and they can do what they like with them. Married and intermarried, related and double-related throughout the tribe and into the adjoining tribes, the petty persecution that would arise because of a change of faith would be quickly extinguished by mutual friends (Jensen and Oberg 1985:7).

4. [The Lutherans claimed that] among the Kurds there is a "constant passing from one to another of these sects—Sunni, Shi'ah, Ali Illahi—through social relationships," so that "there may also be the adoption of Christianity without much stir being made among those who are satisfied to remain with the sect into which birth introduced them" (Jensen and Oberg 1985:8).[15]

Fossum offered twenty conversions as proof that the time to evangelize the Kurds had come at last:

In a certain village the first baptism stirred up a petty persecution, but nineteen more [baptisms] within a year were passed over with little adverse comment. And in another part of the mountains a young man after having first given himself to Christ brought one by one all the five members of his own immediate family and four more distant relatives. In both these cases the converts remained in their own villages going on with their ordinary occupations (Jensen and Oberg 1985:19).

Presbyterians Endorse the Lutheran Mission to the Kurds

Upon learning of the new Lutheran Orient Mission Society, Reverend John Newton Wright, D.D., of the Presbyterian Mission in Tabriz sent the following letter of welcome to Fossum:

Dear Sir and Brother in Christ,

You can be sure that I was much interested in the plan for the Evangelical Lutheran Conference to be held in Berwyn, Illinois, September 6–8, in reference to the organization of mission work

---

[15] Fossum probably erred in number 4. Kurds do not constantly pass from one religious loyalty to another.

for Mohammedans. For my own work the past 32 years has been largely for the Moslem in Persia and Trans Caucasia.

The need in Persia is work for the Moslem races, and the real, genuine mission work that seeks to meet the need, will *send workers for the vast and almost untouched Mohammedan field*. There are nearly 2,000,000 Kurds of various tribes of the Sunni sect of Islam, who live south and west of Urumia in Persia and Turkey.

As yet, no church has undertaken work for these Kurds by organizing a mission for them.

While at the [Edinburgh] World Conference, I [and several others mentioned here] had a conference with Dr. Robert E. Speer about entering the Kurdish field. I had instruction from the West Persia Mission of the Presbyterian Church to act for them. The outcome of the conference was this: The Germans all agreed with us that the work in the Syrian field, and especially the Urumia part of it, *was being greatly injured by keeping there the representatives of so many denominations.* We also agreed that there was an urgent need for the organization for the vast Kurdish field which lies south and west of Urmia in Western Persia and Eastern Turkey; and it was further agreed that this Kurdish field which is virtually unoccupied and which contains, it has been estimated, some two million souls to be set apart for the work of the Lutheran Mission, or mission there represented.

There are in all, it is estimated, some four million Kurds, and this would give you and the Evangelical Lutherans of Germany a grand field to conquer for Christ (Jensen and Oberg 1985:11, italics mine).

"Combine Evangelistic with Medical Work"

Wright suggested a strategy for evangelism among the Kurds. Fossum printed it in the first issue of *The Kurdestan Missionary*:

1. Combine evangelistic with medical work. This was Christ's method. He everywhere taught the people spiritual truth and healed the sick. Moreover, when His disciples were sent forth it was to preach the Gospel and to heal the sick. Paul, the Apostle to the Gentiles, had Luke, the beloved physician, as his constant companion.

2. Be careful not to let these two forms of service get divorced the one from the other. Do not send out men or women who are simply "Faith healers," on the one hand and do not send out phy-

sicians and surgeons who are not men of faith and of the Holy Spirit on the other. Have a hospital manned with a good surgeon and physician; and where the ordained Missionary can hold private and public spiritual service with patients and their friends. The whole personnel and atmosphere of the hospital must be strongly spiritual, and steeped in prayer. This is the more necessary because very few of the Kurds can read and they have next to no literature.

3. Make work from the very start, *as largely self-supporting as possible.*

4. Leave educational work for converts to develop later on. Let it follow rather than precede the development of the native church. Then when you have a Christian community, where the children need education, begin it; but with the view of training up Christian workers in the home and the church. No class of people are so hard to reach with the Gospel as those who have been educated by us in the schools where the atmosphere is non-Christian, or even nominally Christian. Subordinate secular education then till there is a Christian environment for it to develop in.

5. Require all the missionaries sent out to give up the first year almost wholly to *language study. Our mission has a message to deliver, and it must be given to the people in their own tongue where they are born.* The one who goes to work before acquiring a thorough equipment in languages will be handicapped all his life, and can render only a very defective service. Learn the language from Kurds—not Syrians, Turks, or Persians. None of these latter will pronounce the Kurdish correctly, or speak it idiomatically. Our missionaries have at times made a great mistake in hiring a Syrian or Armenian teacher for the Turkish.

—John Newton Wright, 1910 (Jensen and Oberg 1985:12, italics mine)

Presbyterians Compare Kurdish Tribes to Scottish Clans

It was popular for Presbyterians to compare the Kurds to Scottish Highlanders. In 1911 John Newton Wright said,

> The Kurds are to Turkey and Persia what the Scotch were to England and Ireland. They are a brave, manly vigorous race of Indo-European stock, but wild, uneducated, uncivilized and without Christ and His Spirit. But a finer race, by nature, I have not

seen in Asia. Their need is great. I shall rejoice to know that you hear the Macedonian cry and go to help. And I am sure that you will find it an ample field and worthy of your best efforts to save for Christ (Jensen and Oberg 1985:12–13).

Roger Cumberland, another Presbyterian, writes similarly,

It is not many centuries since the canny Scot was a rough and ready freebooter, much like the Kurd of today. Both countries are rugged and breed rugged men. And Scotsmen today are occupying many of the most important positions in the English-speaking world. A like leadership in the Orient is open to the Kurdish, if they have a like power working through them. *The day of the Kurdish Knox seems far distant, but it will come* (1926:153, italics mine).

N. J. Lohre, used the analogy to Scottish tribes in his article, "The Highlanders of Kurdistan," in *The Muslim World*, in 1918. Lohre was a member of the LOMS board.

Blanche Wilson Stead's **Kurdistan for Christ** *Appeal*

Blanche Wilson Stead, a Presbyterian medical missionary in Kermanshah, wrote a paper, *Kurdistan for Christ*. It appeared in *The Moslem World* and as a pamphlet published by the LOMS. In her plea for a mission to the Kurds, Stead refers to the failure of the Great Experiment:

No adequate attempt has been made to take the Gospel to the Kurds. Both on the Turkish and Persian sides, mission stations have been located in places where population is largely Christian, partly for greater security and partly because it is only natural to hope that in the reviving or reconverting of the old dead churches a living influence will be exerted in all the regions round about and a force of Christian workers raised up who, being conversant with the customs, character, and language of their neighbor Moslems, can reach them with the Gospel to better advantage and with greater expedition.

The contrary has proved to be the case. Hereditary enemies, accustomed for centuries to give and take alternately in matters of plunder, rapine and massacre, ever on the watch for opportunity for retaliation, the Armenians and Assyrians have as little desire to be the bearers of the Gospel to their Moslem neighbors as the Moslems have to receive it of them, and the location of mission in a district occupied by Christians is a barrier to its success in work for Moslems (1920:147, italics mine).

FOSSUM ARRIVES IN KURDISTAN A SECOND TIME

The first LOMS missionaries arrived September 6, 1911, in Soujbulakh. They were L. O. Fossum and E. Edman, a medical doctor, who with his wife, Augustana, had served previously in India. In their company were two nurses, Miss Augusta Gudhart of Russia and Miss Meta von der Schulenburg of Germany. The Herrmannsburger Mission of Hanover helped the mission financially.

Fossum and his party took up their abode in the same house where Damman, in 1907, had been murdered. From their arrival in 1911 until forced to leave in the early part of 1916, the missionaries had built up a Kurdish congregation, established an orphanage and medical dispensary.

During part of 1915, the Board was unable to reach the missionaries with funds. During all that time, the native Kurds supplied the missionaries with the needed funds for the work, and when they were obliged to depart, Kurds also supplied them with the funds needed for travel (Lohre 1918).

War Plagues Fossum's Mission

Kurdish inter-tribal warfare plagued Fossum from the first. Kurds fought one another continuously. Moreover, Russia continued to occupy northern Persia; the threat from Russia and the need for Persia to fortify its border would cause the LOMS grief more than once in the 20th century.

The First World War brought armed incursion from Russia into neutral Persia. Missionaries abandoned Soujboulak in January 1916. The hospital, dispensary, and orphanage and church were completely destroyed. Fossum and the others moved in with the Presbyterians in Tabriz. In 1916 the Lutherans returned to the United States.

Yet Fossum had cause to rejoice. The blessing of "thousands of human beings who had experienced the power of a skilled and consecrated physician," and thousands more who "had heard some part of the Gospel story" (Jensen and Oberg 1985:20) was a beginning. Nothing like it among the Kurds had happened in the history of modern mission.

Fossum Returns to America with Manuscripts

Fossum brought home his literary productions: a Kurdish grammar, the four Gospels in the Kurdish language, Luther's *Smaller Catechism*, a hymnbook containing 100 hymns and a Lutheran liturgy, and an English-Kurdish Lexicon. All these Fossum would print, and take back when he returned to Kurdistan in 1919.

THE MISSION BEGINS AGAIN, BUT FOSSUM DIES

After the First World War, Fossum and other missionaries set sail again. This was Fossum's third journey to Kurdistan. But he never arrived; Fossum died November 10, 1920, on a mountain journey up "Little Ararat" near present day Van. He reportedly suffered a nervous breakdown and died of exhaustion. He was 41 years old.

Much was said of Fossum's accomplishments: "He laid the foundation for all missionary work and all other civilizing agencies in Kurdistan for all time to come" (Jensen and Oberg 1985:21). He was survived by his wife and two children, who had remained in Minneapolis.

The Lutheran Orient Mission would send other missionaries to replace Fossum, but the death of the founder proved a great loss. Fossum had done it all: awakened the Lutheran Church, formed a mission vehicle to take Lutherans to the field, published the society's magazine, translated the scriptures, written a catechism, and returned twice to the "dreadfully wicked conditions" which Judith Grant had seen in Kurdistan a century earlier.

Fossum's Followers Carry On

Other Lutherans took Fossum's place. They included Fossum's sister, Alma Fossum (a nurse), and Miss Hanna Schonhood (a teacher). Reverend G. H. and Mrs. Bachimont of the Herrmannsburger Mission joined them. They arrived in Soujbulakh in May 1921. One complaint from Hanna Schonhood, a single woman, was the "shallow conversation" in which Kurdish women engaged her:

> They are interested in knowing if you are married—if you are, how many children you have—if you are not, why are you not, etc. They are fond of pretty clothes and load themselves down with jewelry, bracelets, as many as eight or nine on one wrist (Jensen and Oberg 1985:25).

The Orphanage Work

In 1921 the missionaries re-opened an orphanage. It took in young girls whose hair was "alive with bugs," and had to be cut (Jensen and Oberg 1985:26). Sometimes a girl would not allow her hair to be cut, and would leave. Sometimes a woman would come, claiming this or that child as her own, and take it away. The missionaries could not be sure if the child was actually an orphan, and had simply worked as a servant for the woman.

Martyrdom: All is Lost a Second Time

On October 7, 1921 the notorious Kurdish chief, Ismail Simko, overran Soujbulakh and the mission station. Simko and his 2,000 raiders, from the Shikkak tribe,[16] killed most of the 800 Persian soldiers who guarded the town. Hanna Schonhood described the scene:

> Looting began immediately. They took practically everything in the house, even to the clothing we had on, leaving us enough to partly cover our bodies; and the cruel treatment was too horrible to describe, hitting with their guns, kicking, pulling hair, etc. (Jensen and Oberg 1985:28).

In the raid, Kurds shot and killed the male member of the mission, Bachimont:

> Mrs. Bachimont saw her husband coming slowly down the stairs with three men following. By the pallor on his face she knew something serious had happened. When she spoke to him he was unable to answer, but turning to her he carefully seated himself then lay down on the floor. The blood began to flow from a wound in the region of the heart. Closing his eyes he continued breath-

---

[16] Glenn Fleming and others claim that Shikkak Kurds were once Christian (Fleming 1981:10).

ing for about five minutes and he passed away. He often expressed the wish that if he should be killed that he might not be tortured, but go quick, and his wish was certainly granted. A short time before the mob entered the house, Mr. Bachimont came in from the office saying, "I just came across this pamphlet of Fossum's." It contained two stanzas of "Jesus lover of my soul," which he wished us to sing together. He brought in the big Bible, opened it with the hope of finding an appropriate scripture passage. When he came to Isaiah 43:1, "Fear not, for I have redeemed thee, I have called they by name, thou art mine," he closed the book with a look of relief and satisfaction. This large Bible was the first thing to be flung on the floor [when the raiders entered] (Jensen and Oberg 1985:28).

The Sunday before his death, Bachimont had preached his first Kurdish sermon, a liturgy in Kurdish having been written for the occasion.

Escape to Tabriz

Bachimont's wife and the three single missionary women escaped from Soujbulakh. They arrived at Tabriz, where Hanna Schonhood wrote that the Presbyterian missionaries

are of the opinion that it would be unsafe to go back to Soujbulakh for some time. The country is in a very unsettled condition and it is impossible to know what one ought to do. We will simply have to trust to Providence to show us through this season of unexplainable discouragements, until the mists have rolled away and we shall again be able to praise Him for His wonderful guidance (Jensen and Oberg 1985:26–27).

Mistaken Identity?

Someone suggested to the LOMS that Simko's raiders mistook Bachimont for a Kurdish chief. "The killing was a case of mistaken identity" (Jensen and Oberg 1985:28). This seems a bit far-fetched; sometimes shameful acts prompt far-fetched explanations in Kurdistan.

Bachimont's bones were found later under a public lavatory with a hole in the vertebra; he was re-buried in the churchyard in Tabriz. Later his relatives arrived and reburied Bachimont in a suitable place near the mission station in Soujbulakh (now Mahabad) he had helped to found (Gardiner 1982:9).

Missionary Nurse Marries a Muslim

Richard Gardiner says that one LOMS missionary nurse

> caused consternation by marrying a Kurdish Moslem and they had
> a son. When her husband died she moved back to Mahabad. . . .
> She was the only missionary of an era who became truly inte-
> grated, though [comments Gardiner] unwisely with a Moslem, and
> spent her life with her adopted people (1982:9).

A THIRD BEGINNING FOR THE LOMS WORK

The LOMS Board prepared to return to the field. The *Kurdistan Missionary* had six thousand four hundred subscribers in
1925. Each issue reminded its readers of the unfinished work
among the Kurds. True, the missionaries had twice abandoned
Soujbulakh. However, the work resumed in 1924. Three veteran
women returned to the field—Miss Augusta Gudhard, Miss Alma
Fossum, and Miss Hanna C. Schonhood. The new mission leader
was Herman Schalk from Danzig, Germany (now Poland).

Schalk directed the mission for three years. The missionaries
were involved in medicine, education, and evangelism. Children of
Persian, Armenian, Syriac, and Kurdish background attended
the mission school (Jensen and Oberg 1985:35).

On furlough in 1927, Hanna Schonhood, the teacher, took ill
and was unable to return to the field. She wrote a book, *Bible
History in Kurdish*. Samuel Zwemer commented,

> It seems to me to be admirably suited for the work of students and
> general circulation. I am glad that on page 135 you have not been
> ashamed of the offense of the Cross. I believe we have been too
> timid in putting the issue of Christ crucified before the Moslems
> (Jensen and Oberg 1985:55).

Hanna Schonhood died in 1938. The Herrmannsburger Mission
worked with the LOMS until the year 1931, when the
Herrmannsburger Mission closed.

LOMS Work in the Depression Years and World War II

The years of the Depression and World War II were difficult
for the LOMS. Uprisings and government reprisals made movement difficult. Reverend Henry Mueller served from 1929 to 1936

in Soujbulakh as an evangelist. In 1934 Mueller reported that his ministry increased as his language ability improved:

Last winter and spring we were very largely confined to activities in the city, consisting of personal visiting among the merchants in the bazaar and with their friends in their houses at night. In turn I had more callers and visitors last winter than ever before. It is so much more interesting now and fascinating to know their tongue, rather than to be relying upon an interpreter. *There is a great satisfaction in being able to sit with these mountain people, to converse quietly and confidentially, to know them heart to heart, and not as the outside world loves to brand them as a cruel and fierce people.* It is vastly more general to find in all that universal craving, the hunger that centuries of Islam has failed to still. Almost unwillingly at times they are drawn by the wonderful parables so numerous in our Bible. It's the message, the Gospel, that ever elicits attention (Jensen and Oberg 1985:87, italics mine).

Henry Mueller is *the first missionary in Kurdistan* to write that he knew the Kurds "heart to heart"; what a proof that language learning unlocks the secrets of friendship and knowledge! Mueller goes on to describe the interest of Kurds in the gospel:

One villager and his son, kettle cleaners by trade, came down from a village about twenty miles distant, by foot, to learn more of Christianity. Dr. Cochran and I had met them on our tour last summer and their first contact with Christianity stirred them deeply.

In my house they felt free to unburden themselves, stayed almost a week, and the time never passed so quickly before. We talked before breakfast, for hours during the day, and several times it was midnight before we got to bed. It surprised me with what readiness he accepted the doctrine of the Trinity. The doctrine of the Trinity is one of the greatest offenses to Islam and woe to him who strays so far as to accept it. No Nicodemus was more attentive than this father and son.

Those illiterate villagers fully grasped what many of the most learned teachers of Islam cannot understand. "Blessed are they which do hunger and thirst after righteousness, for they shall be filled." St. Paul says: "The natural man receiveth not the things of the Spirit of God, for they are foolishness unto him." Jesus quotes from Isaiah: "The Spirit of the Lord is upon me, because He hath anointed me to preach the Gospel to the poor" (Jensen and Oberg 1985:37).

Of Augusta Gudhard the record says:

Miss Gudhard told the story of Jesus and His love to many Kurds in Soujbulakh and for many miles in the surrounding towns, visited the sick and conducted cottage gospel meetings. In this way she had often been able to reach people who would not come and hear the Gospel at the mission station (Jensen and Oberg 1985:33).

1934—All Urumia Missions Close

Reza Shah faced the dual challenge of Russian aggression from without and separatist movements from within. In 1934 he reinforced the northern region of Iran. He also removed the missionaries.[17] Presbyterian work in Urumia closed after exactly 100 years of mission work. Robert Speer described this loss as a "grievous course for the missionaries and their friends in the Board and the home church . . . but there appeared no alternative . . ." (Joseph 1961:226). Then a farewell to the Christians, object of 100 years of mission effort:

The Mission [should] make the whole situation clear to the Christian people and with full sympathy to aid them to adjust themselves wisely to the present conditions and to go forth as loyal citizens of Persia in full fidelity to the Christian spirit and to their Christian faith (Joseph 1961:226).

Speer wrote no farewell to the Kurds, since neither the mission nor local churches had relations with them.

LOMS MOVES TO IRAQ

The Shah offered Teheran as a site for the LOMS, but "the mission, faithful to its original commission to preach the Gospel only to the Kurds," decided to move to northern Iraq, closer to the center of Kurdistan (Gardiner 1982:9).

By 1937 the LOMS had re-located to the city of Arbil (Gardiner says the LOMS went to Mosul first, but this is an error). Arbil is

the ancient Arbela, which is the only Assyrian settlement which has been continuously occupied since its foundation, and has retained its original name. To the west of Arbil, on the banks of the Greater Zab, was fought the Battle of Arbela [Gaugemala],

---

[17] As Gardiner put it, "Reza Shah came along and said he would not have a foreign mission near the border in Kurdistan" (1982:9).

where Alexander the Great dealt the final death blow to the Persian Empire on the 2nd of October 331 B.C. The citadel where Darius left his treasures before the great battle, and where Alexander afterwards fixed his headquarters, is represented by the tell, on which most of the present village of Arbil lies (Jensen and Oberg 1985:31).

Twenty Years of Mission Work in Arbil

Miss Augusta Gudhard returned to America when the mission in Iran closed. Henry Mueller and his wife, Margaret, also returned to the United States. The LOMS had difficulty getting workers to stay in the field. For instance, one family sent a telegram, saying, "Mrs. Agerstrand and I are leaving Iraq," just eight months after the couple arrived. The sending board was deeply disappointed (Jensen and Oberg 1985:52).

However, one Philip Muller and his wife, Regina, arrived. They had five children who grew up learning Kurdish the natural way. Another family, Earl Erickson and his wife, Jean, arrived with their children. Gardiner writes later, "My wife and I met them all and had hours with them reminiscing and we could see that they were genuinely all out to win Kurdish souls for Christ" (1982:9). The work expanded to include a mission station in Shaqlawa,[18] north of Arbil.

Yezidi Converts

In a letter dated January 4, 1944, Mr. Clarence Mueller (no relation to Henry Mueller) reports that Sadiq Shammi and two other young Yezidi converts were baptized in Baghdad. "We thank God for this manifestation of the power of the Spirit among the Moslems"[19] (Jensen and Oberg 1985:47). This Sadiq would figure centrally in LOMS work, after the western missionaries were forced to leave Iraq.

---

[18] Shaqlawa is a resort village in the mountains north of Arbil. Presbyterians conducted summer camps in Shaqlawa in the 1950s. Seventh Day Adventists bought property there in the 1970s and still come from Baghdad to enjoy a change from the summer heat.

[19] The Yezidis would feel astonished that a missionary board in the United States considers them Muslims.

Outside Evaluation

The LOMS board asked for an outside evaluation of its work. Accordingly, in 1945 Paul W. Harrison of the Reformed Church of America and the United Mission in Mesopotamia (UMM) made a month-long investigation of the work in Arbil. Harrison reported to the LOMS home office:

> It will be well to put three couples in that field just as soon as possible. One of the three might be better out in the district somewhere. They must learn Kurdish and learn it well" (Jensen and Oberg 1985:60).

Harrison also said that "Iraqi government persons assured me that the Iraq government would welcome an American hospital in the Arbil area" (Jensen and Oberg 1985:60).

In 1950 the LOMS commissioned two couples to go the field. This followed a season of despair in the Board. Their names were Klein and Schlossin, but they are not mentioned again.

The newsletter, now called *The Lutheran Orient Mission*, had a circulation of 3,000. "We have no statistics of conversions, but there have been confessions and baptisms" (Jensen and Oberg 1985:62).

LOMS WORK AFTER 1950

Clarence Mueller returned to Iraq from furlough in 1952. During his absence Sadiq Shammi had held the work together. Sadiq had conducted baptisms and preached since 1947. However, Clarence Mueller managed to offend Sadiq Shammi upon his return; Mr. Mueller "practiced the concept that the natives were never to be given the feeling of being on an equal footing; they were to be servants and do as told" (Jensen and Oberg 1985:63). Mueller had another interesting principle: It was not necessary for a missionary to speak the Kurdish language. Clarence Mueller worked in Kurdistan for nine years but never learned to speak Kurdish. This was quite opposite from the attitude of Fossum and other early LOMS missionaries.

Iraq in Revolution—1958

The Iraqi army revolted in 1958 and killed King Faisal II and the royal family. The monarchy ended. All LOMS work was lost in this revolution. Writes an LOMS missionary of that time:

God is witness, we did not leave our post until the Iraqi revolutionary government (without charges against us) expelled us from her borders. The expulsion of peaceful missionary families, the violence and bloodshed among the peoples of the Middle East, are but outward symptoms of the desperate floundering about for the higher things in life which bankrupt Islam and empty nationalism cannot supply. The blind cannot lead the blind (Jensen and Oberg 1985:66).

This footnote follows: "Unofficially, in the eyes of the Iraq Revolutionary Government, we foreigners are guilty of having lived among and befriended the Kurds. The movement for an independent Kurdistan is much feared [by the Arabs]" (1985:66). That comment is valuable now, just as then. What Jensen says next is also valuable:

It is absolutely essential to keep in mind that the whole Near and Middle East is aflame, politically. Like it or not, we cannot ignore it: visas depend on it, also permission, goodwill, safety or person and property. And every foreigner is potentially suspect, especially Americans.

It would be quite naive and immature in matters relating to relationships of existing Christian mission under Moslem governments if we should be so bold as to ask, "Will this government permit us to do Christian mission work among Moslems?" *Officially the answer could only be a flat "no," but unofficially, missions are "tolerated"* even if prominent Moslem friends have to "cover up" and point out the wonderful social programs of these foreign missions. Persia has had over 125 years of this good work (1985:67, italics mine).

Sadiq Shammi Continued the LOMS Work

Sadiq Shammi continued the LOMS work in northern Iraq during the 1950s and 1960s. After the Revolution of 1958 when government closed its doors to western missionaries, Sadiq continued to evangelize Kurds in Iraq.

Having left Iran in 1934 and Iraq in 1958, where could the Lutherans re-locate? Turkish law did not permit Kurds even to speak their language; Lutherans could not work in Turkey. The Lutherans set their sails for Lebanon, home to several thousand impoverished Kurds.

Lutherans Remove to Lebanon

Lutheran missionaries felt welcomed and encouraged by the missionaries in Lebanon:

> By sheer good fortune we find ourselves here among men of missions who are sympathetic and conservative. Let me mention several. Foremost is: Dr. Park Johnson, Field Representative in the Middle East for the Presbyterian Board of Foreign Missions. And Dr. Harry Dorman, Chairman of the Near East Christian Council (Jensen and Oberg 1985:70).

Return to Iran Considered

LOMS representatives visited Iran in 1960, to consider returning to the land where they had begun work in 1911. William Miller and Fred Wilson, of the Presbyterian church, "gave their cordial support" (Jensen and Oberg 1985:71). There were hospitals to re-open in Hamadan; in fact, "Rev. Miller explained that the authorities were imploring him to re-open" (1985:71). Acting on the suggestion of Miller and Wilson, the LOMS re-entered Iran in 1961 after an absence of twenty-eight years.

RETURN TO IRAN—HOSPITAL AT GHORVEH

The LOMS returned to the familiar ground of northern Iran. Richard Gardiner, a British surgeon and former army officer, was granted permission to build and operate a Christian hospital at Ghorveh in 1963.[20] His work is recorded below.

THE WORK OF RICHARD GARDINER

Gardiner did his Kurdish studies at London University with Major C. J. Edmonds (Edmonds, who wrote *Kurds, Turks and Arabs*, had been political officer for the British in the early days of the new Iraq.)

With his wife alongside, Gardiner worked full-throttle for many years. For years they had no help and no furlough. One year, a male nurse, Ray Scattlebury, worked for Gardiner. Scattlebury still remembers the fast pace that never let up. Gardiner

---

[20] Gardiner wrote a helpful summary of his sixteen years in Iran, and I am indebted for his records.

would often answer the door in the middle of the night and see patients.

THE INTERNATIONAL MISSION IN PERSIA

The International Mission worked in Iran for most of the 20th century. In Kurdish Iran, the International Mission maintained the orphanage in Kermanshah that Blanche Wilson Stead[21] had begun.

Blanche Wilson was born January 24, 1870 in Nova Scotia. She ran the Presbyterian hospital in Kermanshah. Her husband, Reverend Stead, was hospital chaplain and directed the church work and did evangelism (Gardiner 1982:11). During the First World War, orphans massed in Kermanshah, driven from their homes in Urumia. A terrible cholera epidemic created as many orphans as did the war. Dozens of these orphans became the wards of Mr. and Mrs. Stead. This situation drove them to open the orphanage.

Blanch Wilson Stead died on the field February 21, 1922. Her husband remarried, "hoping to get a wife's help but when she saw it all she returned to the U.S. and never came back" (Gardiner 1982:11). Stead resigned from the hospital when the Presbyterian mission board refused to permit his work among the Kurdish orphans. He opened a public appeal fund in the U.S. and so built up the orphanage. This orphanage continued, under International Missions, into the 1980s, and was directed for years by Omer and Harriet Burris.[22]

Meanwhile, an accomplished doctor, R. D. Bussdicker ran the hospital in Kermanshah for next 35 years. Bussdicker "had many Kurdish patients and staff and faithfully told them about Christ as he healed their illnesses and wounds" (Gardiner 1982:11).

THE UNITED MISSION IN MESOPOTAMIA

In 1924 three American churches formed a single mission:

---

[21] Tony Estaidi and Dawood Estaidi, Kurdish followers of Jesus, and other orphans took their last names in honor of Stead, the founder of the orphanage.

[22] Harriet Wilson Burris' brother, Fred Wilson, was a Presbyterian missionary in Iran until 1979.

Three somewhat closely related American bodies, the Reformed Church in the United States (German) the Reformed Church in America (Dutch), and the (Northern) Presbyterian Church in the United States of America, organized, in 1924, the United Mission in Mesopotamia, with an approach to Moslems as an avowed objective. The missions were facilitated by legal provision for religious liberty and for freedom for the individual to change his religion even if that should be from Islam to Christianity. Social pressure might make such a step next to impossible, but the legal obstacles had been removed (Latourette 1975:270).

"Provision for religious liberty" to which Latourette refers was one reason that hopes were high for the new mission among the Muslims in the Middle East. John R. Mott, Chairman of the International Missionary Council, said that,

> while formerly indirect methods of approach were necessary on account of government restrictions and Moslem opposition and fanaticism . . . in many lands today the way is open to widespread and direct evangelization (Joseph 1961:223).

THE APPRAISAL COMMISSION
REDEFINES THE MISSIONARY TASK

The new wine of post World War missions seemed to require new wineskins. What was the missionary task in the newly-formed Middle East?[23] Failure to convert the native populations, in a trial of a century, evinced in the UMM a new humility. The 1928 world missionary conference in Jerusalem recommended that Christians approach Islam in a spirit of openness; it also recognized "certain spiritual values in the Muslim faith" (Joseph 1961:227). Then, in 1931, the Appraisal Commission of seven Protestant denominations redefined mission into social and educational, but no longer evangelical, objectives. It declared that Christians should "look forward to the continued co-existence of other religions with Christianity, each stimulating the other in growth toward the ultimate goal—unity in the completest relig-

---

[23] In 1902, Alfred Thayer Mahan, an American naval officer and historian, coined the compelling phrase, "The Middle East," to designate the area between Arabia and India. Mark Sykes gave it currency in the summer of 1916 in a series of speeches (Fromkin 1989:224).

ious truth" (Joseph 1961:227). The term "missionary" was abandoned for the most part; the term "fraternal worker" defined the approach of the UMM (1961:228).[24]

"WESTERN GUILT COMPLEX"

During the 1930s the purpose of the mission was further confused by theological liberalism; John Mackay, president of Princeton seminary said that "christological uncertainties" caused the crisis in mission. Lamin Sanneh of Ghana, Yale Professor of Mission History, traces this uncertainty to what he calls the "western guilt complex" (1987:1).

The UMM was confronted by liberalism from within, by the nationalism of Turks and Arabs and Persians from without, and by a guilt complex from its past. However, the UMM also made room for two Presbyterians who evangelized the Kurds: veteran missionary Edmund McDowell and a newcomer, Roger Cumberland.

PRESBYTERIAN MISSION IN IRAQ

In 1924 the Presbyterian church re-established its mission in Mosul after an absence of four decades. A missionary couple with thirty years' work in Kurdistan, Dr. and Mrs. Edmund McDowell, opened a girls' school in Mosul in that year. Two of the boarders were children of the respected Yezidi leader, Ismail Beg (Guest 1993:183).

Presbyterians had mission stations in five cities of the newly-formed Iraq: Mosul, Hillah (Babylon), Dohouk, Baghdad, and Kirkuk. One of these cities, Dohouk, was Kurdish and two others, Kirkuk and Mosul, had large Kurdish populations. One Presbyterian missionary worked among the Kurds in Dohouk for twelve years. No other missionary has worked so long with the Kurds. He was Roger Cumberland.

---

[24] Fraternal workers enter church work alongside existing congregations. If "missionary work" refers to church-planting in new locations or among unreached peoples, then most missionaries in the Middle East have been fraternal workers.

ROGER CUMBERLAND AMONG THE KURDS

Roger Cumberland was born in La Verne, California, east of Los Angeles, on November 16, 1894. Cumberland graduated from Occidental College in 1919, following military service. In 1922 he finished McCormick Theological Seminary in Chicago. His home church was Highland Park Presbyterian in Los Angeles.

Cumberland writes that his years at home and college were "permeated" with missionary interest. He was active in Christian Endeavor and the Young Men's Christian Association. Of his parents, Cumberland writes, "My mother was always actively interested in the missionary society, and my father a liberal contributor" (Young 1939:4). Cumberland's own desire would only be satisfied if he could go where no one else wished to go; for Cumberland, that appeared to be Afghanistan, because, he said, "it was the hardest place I could see" (1939:5). However, the mission assigned Cumberland to Kurdistan, Iraq.

Cumberland Explores Kurdistan

Cumberland arrived in Mosul in 1923. Very soon he undertook a grueling three month expedition through Kurdistan with another missionary who had arrived the year before, Edwin Wright. Wright comments:

> We were tramping on foot the perpendicular mountains which were to be Roger's home the rest of his life. There was nothing soft about Roger's nerves or physique. As soon as he arrived, I led him for three months in Kurdistan where neither of us had a bed, a shave, a chair to sit on, nor a table. Though laid up with jaundice on this first trip, he was so enthusiastic that he was looking around for a place to start (Young 1939:7).

Cumberland began to regard Kurdistan as his particular field of effort. One can feel the enthusiasm with which the 31 year old missionary approached his work:

> He made long trips among their villages, living with the people, eating their food, sleeping under their roofs, learning their language, winning their confidence, and establishing Christian centers among them wherever possible (Young 1939:8–9).

The reference to "Christian centers" may refer to his purchase of an Assyrian village.

Cumberland Buys a Village

Roger Cumberland planned to "demonstrate the Christian way of life" by improving the agriculture of the region. He had seen the benefits of scientific farming in his own native desert California. He dreamed of proving that Kurds could similarly profit. In 1924, Cumberland tried to buy an Assyrian village, Babillu, located in the mountains about 10 miles east of Dohouk. The owner did not respond at the time. However, in 1925 Cumberland wrote,

> He came to me and offered to sell. We agreed on the price, and I sent for the money. About a year later (such is Oriental speed) negotiations began to get through the mazes of red tape; and unless there is a very unexpected slip "twixt the cup and the lip," I shall be the proud possessor of a village in Kurdistan by the time this reaches you. . . . To be sure, I have given away so much during this famine year that I don't have enough left to pay for the village—what else could a man do? But I'll get it from some-where. And I expect it to be for me an excellent "hobby" and an actual aid in the work of winning men to the Master as well (Young 1939:9).

Old Kurdish men today remember Cumberland's Babillu. The village was Cumberland's experiment in Christian community living. He started a school there, and employed an Assyrian teacher.

Cumberland Marries

In 1927 Roger Cumberland traveled to Manila to marry Harriet Gilbert Gunn. Harriet was the daughter of missionaries serving in the Philippines. Harriet, like Roger, had been active in Christian Endeavor.

In 1928 the newlyweds returned to northern Iraq. After some months in Mosul, the Board recognized the Cumberlands' wish to live in Dohouk. They bought a two acre property near the edge of the town. Roger Cumberland wrote, "It was government property; I secured it, in keen competition with the local Chaldean (Catholic) priest, who really has no use for it except to keep us out" (Young 1939:12). In this house, just before Christmas of 1929, their first son, David, died after only eleven days of life. Their second child, a girl named Marion, also died as a baby. The Cumberlands later had two healthy daughters, Wendela (Wendy)

Graeme born August 3, 1935 in Los Angeles, and Janet, born October 18, 1937 in Beirut.

Cumberland Describes His Surroundings

Roger Cumberland wrote an article in *The Muslim World*, describing the people and land of Iraqi Kurdistan:

> The scenery in these mountains is magnificent. I, who come from California, admit it! And the people live about as close to nature as one can get, tilling the narrow fields that, during countless generations, have been terraced above the streams, and pasturing their flocks of goat and fat-tailed sheep on the steeper slopes above (1926:151).

Cumberland Describes the Kurdish People

Cumberland was acquainted with the Kurds "north of Mosul as far as Zakhu and Amadia" (1926:152). He wrote,

> The men generally do the ploughing and harvesting, but such work as weeding rice and tobacco is done, or at least shared, by the women, who do also the household work, and bring the water from the village spring, and clean the stables, and take care of the ever-present baby. The men are champion sitters; some of them get up often enough to say their prayers. And that is about all there is to life. They have no incentive, and no equipment for mental adventure, and their totally ritualistic Mohammedanism furnishes no spiritual urge. So they have been century after century, and will continue to be until some new power enters their lives (1926:153).

> To like is to put everything at the disposal of the one liked; not to like is to set all against him. The Kurds are reputed to be violent haters; but it is interesting to note that they themselves have no word for hate. To be sure, the man of whom they say, "*Az has zhwi nakem*" (I don't like him) is in danger of his life (1926:152).

Cumberland Describes the Religion of the Kurds

Cumberland wrote of the chasm separating Muslim Kurds from Yezidi Kurds: "To be sure, the Yezidis speak Kurdish, but neither would acknowledge the other to be better than a dog" (1926:154).

Cumberland mentioned a Nestorian holy day, honoring a saint, which the Kurds celebrated well. Kurds would dance and sing and smoke and make merry on the special day, to get a blessing. Cumberland described the Kurdish world of charms and amulets, and he then made this telling observation:

> The point I am trying to clear up is this: *the religion of the mountain people whether nominally Christian or Moslem, is essentially the same*: powers of magic working through charms and amulets and incantations, and imposing certain taboos. It is difficult to distinguish between them by their daily manner of life (1926:156, italics mine).

As to evangelism, Cumberland wrote:

> There is no Macedonian call here. . . . But the one in the deepest darkness is the one that most needs the light. . . . To me, simply living among them and showing them something better than what they have that can be had "without money and without price," perhaps helping them in methods of cultivating their crops, and certainly speaking the Word in due season, seems the best approach. But "approaches" and "methods" will never save them; here, as in all things, our confidence must be in Him who said, "Other sheep I have, which are not of this fold; them also must I bring, and there shall be one fold, one shepherd." He must bring them, for He alone can. And in His fold there is a place also for these wild mountaineers (1926:157).

Religious Hostility in Dohouk

It was Cumberland's observation that Christian groups in his city, as well as Muslims, Yezidis, and Jews, were "each hostile to all the rest . . . , making an integrated cooperative community impossible" (Young 1939:14). Cumberland goes on to write,

> The various Christian sects, remnants of ancient churches, consign one another to hell with great gusto; but they join the Moslem majority in despising the Jews; and all unite in cursing the Yezidis, commonly known as Devil Worshipers. If we, as foreigners, appear especially friendly with any one of these groups, it is assumed that we are unfriendly to all the rest. The idea of standing for the right, irrespective of party or group, is beyond the comprehension of the local mind, of whatever millet. . . . We pray, and hope you will pray with us, for divine wisdom in living this essential ideal (Young 1939:14).

In his report to the Presbyterian Board of Foreign Missions in 1934, Cumberland referred to the Assyrians as "a special problem in our field."

Cumberland Brings Water to Dohouk

A mile from the Cumberland home was a small spring of water. Cumberland bought the spring in 1930 and laid a pipeline to the city. Until that time, stated Cumberland, the city depended on a "filthy little stream that meanders along beside it" (Young 1939:12). He laid about 4000 feet of inch pipe in two days:

> The people of the town were interested; many were skeptical about the possibility of making water run up-hill to our house. But it came—enough for us and a quarter of the town. The people gladly use all that is available. . . . We did not invent the Water of Life, any more than we made the spring at the foot of the Kurdish mountains. And we do not force it down the people's throats, any more than we made our neighbor's drink pure water. No compulsion is needed, nor even advertising; pure water, physical or spiritual, is its own advocate. The need is to make it available; and that is the job of the missionary (1939:12).

"The Rather Primitive Conditions Here"

In 1934–35 the Cumberlands furloughed in the United States. Upon returning to northern Iraq, they must have felt the miseries as fresh as ever, perhaps more so since his wife now cared for a baby. Cumberland was asking himself the question,

> What is the right balance between our inherited manner of life and the rather primitive conditions here? We make a certain contribution to the life of the community in demonstrating what a decent, hygienic life is; but I often find myself begrudging the time it takes, because too much of it has to be improvised here where we are the only foreign residents. Please pray that we may be constantly guided in seeing these various elements of our life in their true perspective "in the aspect of eternity" and have the strength of body and of character to keep the balance that will be most helpful to the community rather than the most comfortable and convenient for us (Young 1939:13–14).

Before his marriage, Roger Cumberland had lived as ruggedly as any foreigner ever has among the Kurds. But Cumberland as a family man faced the same stress as have others since then: living as Kurds live, yet desiring a more healthful, comfortable home.

Cumberland Baptizes "Blind Aboud"

Roger Cumberland baptized a teacher, an Arab named Aboud. Aboud had become a Christian through another missionary, James Willoughby. Aboud was the brother of the assistant police chief in Dohouk. When Aboud was assigned to teach Islam, he refused, and announced that he was a Christian. Soon afterwards, the Dohouk government jailed him for three years in under the pretense that he had taken money from the government school.

Aboud's wife was ordered to divorce him on the grounds that he was no longer a Muslim. Later, when Aboud wanted to change his identification card to read "Christian," the court said this was impossible. But Aboud argued that the court had already called him a Christian in the divorce case. In this way he was permitted to change his identification card.

While he served time in jail, his two children were taken from him. They died of neglect.

After three years Aboud was released. He remarried and moved to Baghdad. There he became blind, and from that time was known as "Blind Aboud." He sold Bibles for years in Baghdad for the Bible Society (Cochran 1996).

Muslim Leaders Turn against Cumberland

Success brought danger. In 1937 a Kurdish man and wife in Dohouk declared themselves to be Christians. They were teachers in the Government schools. After that, Moslem leaders strongly opposed Cumberland's work (Young 1939:14). In a letter less than a month before his death Mr. Cumberland wrote of this opposition and of the boycott placed against him. He wrote, "People were forbidden to come to us, not openly (for that would be contrary to the law that guarantees religious liberty) but secretly" (Young 1939:14).

The growing hostility troubled Cumberland; he wondered whether he should continue in Dohouk. He inquired repeatedly of the Government as to any objections to his work, so that "we might mend our ways." However, "we were always informed that there is no objection to us or our activities" (Young 1939:15). Then Cumberland noted, "Any official who might undertake to enforce the law of religious liberty would find himself in no end of trouble from the large majority. The temper of the people is quite contrary to that law"(Young 1939:15). The situation was about to become dangerous; Cumberland wrote that "the promises of God are for those who endure; and I'd like to try it" (1939:66).

Cumberland's Inner Thoughts before His Death

In May 1938, Cumberland attended a meeting of the Near East Christian Council in Syria. From there Cumberland wrote to his board in New York that the boycott against him was continuing:

> We are perplexed about what to do; more specifically, if the present situation continues, it is hard to see the point in staying in Dohouk. For more than a year now, since the declaration of Tofiq, the teacher, that he was a Christian, the lid has been clamped on tight. Most people do not dare come near us.
>
> Naturally, I don't care to be a stubborn fool. No one wants to spend his life banging his head on a stone wall. Neither does one want to be a quitter (Young 1939:15).

Cumberland was warned by a Muslim friend that "he was approached by a group and asked to help them get me." Cumberland comments,

> This [warning] is good Moslem practice. This may have been just to scare me, and it may be that they intend violence. . . . But that would be no reason for leaving. Ever since the world began people have been called cowards if they did not risk everything for tribe and nation, and today how many thousands are daily in danger just as a simple matter of duty, without any heroics about it. The church might make more progress if it would get the same attitude (Young 1939:16).

Cumberland Dies a Martyr

The end came suddenly on June 12, 1938. Cumberland was killed in Dohouk. According to Samuel Zwemer,

Two fanatical Kurds from outside of Dohuk, his station in Iraq, shot him as he was giving them Christian literature in his home. A servant tried to help him but was also shot. British government friends in Mosul sent an airplane to bring them to the hospital there. But the care was in vain, and both victims of the attack died within a few hours (1941:210).

Richard Cochran says that Cumberland knew one of the murderers and that Harriet had even cared for his children (1996). One was Salim Mustafa, son of Sa'eed Agha of the Mizurî tribe, who lived in a village about two hours' distant. Cumberland received them in the upstairs sitting room, which was also his library. They had passed an hour of time in conversation with Cumberland, whose servant had brought fruit drinks and then water. One of the men asked for scripture portions.[25] When Cumberland stood and turned to get them, one of the young men pulled a pistol and shot several times. They ran downstairs and out the door, still shooting. One of these last bullets reached Musa, the dear family servant, whose lung was hit. A British military plane flew Cumberland and Musa to Mosul. Musa died on the way to the hospital. Cumberland lived 12 hours. Harriet was at his side when he died. Cumberland and Musa were laid to rest in the mission cemetery in Mosul.[26]

Book-Burning Preceded the Murder

Harriet Cumberland later told of a book-burning prior to the murder. Looking back, one can see how dangerous their situation had become. She writes,

> There may have been some connection between the sad events of June 12 and a very successful campaign about May 26 and the following days during which many Bibles and portions were sold in villages and in Dohouk itself. In this Mr. Cumberland was not active because he had not been permitted in recent months to make evangelistic trips to the villages. The work in Dohouk was particularly good and the feeling evidently favorable. Mr. Glessner had an illustrated lecture and the demand for it was such

---

[25] In Roger's library was a tall trolley ladder on wheels.

[26] Later, the murderer himself was killed by his Kurdish accomplice in the office of the governor in Mosul (Cochran 1996).

that it was given in the large meeting room of the Cumberland house, which was crowded by a seemingly appreciative audience. On the Friday before June 12 the Mullahs had gathered a number of the books which people had purchased, and had staged a public burning of them (Young 1939:19).

"Few If Any Envy Me"

All who knew Roger Cumberland admired his strength of character.[27] He was a rugged pioneer, the kind of person who loved an exceedingly great challenge. Of his own work in Kurdistan Cumberland wrote,

Here is a job that . . . demands all one's knowledge, both rational and intuitive, the exercise of every ability that the entire personality can muster. . . . Whatever position I might hold in the U.S.A. there would be a constant awareness that I should not really be needed; there would be hundreds of men, just as competent and worthy as I, who would be glad to take my place. Here I fill a niche peculiarly my own, and few if any envy me (1939:105).

MISSION TO THE YEZIDIS

The Swedish Mission to the Yezidis organized a work in Bashîqa, northern Iraq. It was run by Swedish women who were not resident there. They hired an Assyrian, named Rabi Nestorus di Kolaita, as manager and teacher and evangelist. His descendants now live in the United States. For a while he ran a boys school. Several Yezidis, including Sadiq Shammi, became Christians in that school. Elias Hamo was another Yezidi who was converted in that school. Elias' older brother, Badeel, and their father also became Christians (Cochran 1996).

Sadiq Shammi and Elias Hamo became ministers of the gospel. The UPCUSA minutes of 1953 note that:

A most effective co-worker [in Iraq] is a Yezidie convert who uses a reading room as a base of operations for Bible classes and personal interviews. The Yezidis are a people whose religion centers in appeasement of a demonic deity who is conceived to be supreme (UPCUSA 1953:57).

---

[27] I know a pastor's wife, now a widow in Eugene, Oregon, whose husband entered the ministry sixty years ago after hearing Cumberland speak while home on furlough.

Revolution of 1958: Most Missionaries Deported

Iraq's King Faisal II and his family and advisors were murdered in 1958. Arab nationalism swelled, and the new government took offense at all things western. The new government expelled all but four of more than fifty Protestant missionaries by the middle of 1959. However, the new government also improved the conditions of Iraqi Christians; in all, the Chaldeans and Assyrians gained a more favorable position than they had under Faisal.

Ba'ath Party Comes to Power: Iraq Mission Abandoned

After a short time, some western missionaries were permitted to return to Iraq. They worked until 1968, when the Ba'ath party closed the American missions; all missionaries left. Early in 1970 the Iraqi Government seized the two schools (in Baghdad and Mosul) of the Presbyterian mission. On June 30, 1970 the United Mission in Iraq and its governing body were formally dissolved.

The LOMS missionaries also left. In Arbil Sadiq Shammi of the LOMS kept the religious services going. He also wrote often to the LOMS board for a increase in salary:

The concept of local support is what should always be the goal. Shammi's problem was compounded because a congregation was never organized. Why this happened is a puzzle that was never solved. [But] since the group was in all reality basically only children and a few adults, perhaps the puzzle is not so difficult (Jensen and Oberg 1985:77).

Sadiq Shammi was a Yezidi Kurd, not from a Muslim background. And he had married an Assyrian; Moslem Kurds in Arbil would have viewed him as a stranger. This partially explains why Sadiq Shammi never organized a congregation. Marvin Palmquist of the LOMS visited Arbil in October 1993. Palmquist discovered that Sadiq Shammi had moved that summer to Mosul and retired. Nothing in Arbil was found of his work.

MISSION TO KURDS IN SYRIA

Following World War I, a Kurdish medical doctor in Syria, Bedr Khan, became a Christian. Bedr Khan lived in Damascus.

He put his hand to translating the gospels into Kurdish (See Appendix C for a history of translation attempts).

The only other reference to mission work in Syria comes from Gardiner; he knew of French Protestant missionaries and pastors working under the Action Christian Orient. They worked among Kurds in northwest Syria. (Gardiner 1982:7).

Since 1962 an Arabization program has eroded the Kurdish identity in Syria; the government sought to resettle Kurds in Turkey and replace them with Arabs. This strategy comes under the "Arab Cordon Plan." Since Hafez al-Assad took control in 1970 the Armenians and Kurds have not posed a security problem to the government. The large Armenian population in Aleppo is well-known, but it has not evangelized the Kurds who live in that city and in Afrin to the north.

MISSION TO KURDS IN ARMENIA AND GEORGIA

What about working among Kurds of the old Soviet Union? What seemed impossible during the 1980s becomes imaginable today. About twenty-five percent of the Kurds in the old Soviet Union live in the Caucasus Republics of Armenia and Georgia; the remainder reside in Central Asian Republics of Azerbaijan, Kazakhstan, Kirghizstan, Turkmenistan, and Uzbekistan. Joseph Stalin deported Kurds to Central Asia in the late 1930s; today many of them wish to return home.

MISSION TO KURDS IN TURKEY

Following World War I, the American Board of Commissioners for Foreign Mission in Turkey continued as the American Board. It appointed a full-time Medical Secretary, Mark Ward, in 1925. From 1914 to 1955 the number of hospitals reduced from twelve to two. Most hospitals and schools were turned over to the Turkish government. However, the American Board continues to operate schools in Istanbul, Adana and Izmir.

The policies of Ataturk and successive Turkish governments to disenfranchise minorities in Turkey has made any recent mission work among Kurds undisclosable.

KURDS WHO BECAME CHRISTIANS IN IRAN

In Chapter two we detailed the conversion and life of Dr. Sa'eed Kurdistani; his life and witness spread across the 19th and the 20th centuries. Other Persian Kurds followed Christ as well.

THE WITNESS OF AVONI

Gardiner records the witness of a Kurd named Avoni. Gardiner's account is printed here in full, from his personal correspondence.

Avoni was born of Kurdish parents and brought up a strict Moslem. But in common with so many he had no schooling hardly and had to work from early years in his father's business. He heard about Jesus Christ from Christians, maybe at the Christian Hospital but was persuaded to stick to Islam in which he found no help. He developed a crippling rheumatic disease and was able only to hobble with the help of a stick. One day when he was about 23 he was driven out to a ruin from Biblical times called Take Bustan where we used to go for picnics and hobbled off into the desert. Coming to a pool of water he lay down exhausted in great pain, and slept. Before dawn he had a vision. Christ himself stood in the pool and spoke to him. Christ said to him that he should go and tell people that He was the Son of God and that in order to do this He would heal Avoni. When dawn broke and the vision vanished Avoni got up completely healed and free of pain. (He often re-lived that joyful moment with us). On returning to Kermanshah Avoni fulfilled the Scripture command to confess Christ with his lips and from then on in one degree or another suffered persecution for the rest of his life as a renegade from Islam. This he said was nothing compared with the joy of life with Christ and in the end many who persecuted stopped when they saw such a Christ-like life lived in just about as much simplicity and poverty. Never an angry word and always turning the other cheek (Gardiner 1982:16–17).

Avoni Takes Christian Instruction

Pastor William welcomed Avoni warmly as a Christian brother and at once set about instructing him in the faith. Daily for two years he taught him first to read and write and then to study the Scriptures and learn Christian doctrine. Avoni compiled a book containing selected passages from the Bible, some illustrated by small pictures, and these he learned almost by heart and used frequently in his ministry to avoid stumbling over random Scriptures which, because of the difficulty of Arabic script and it not being in his mother tongue might not have come out clearly (Gardiner 1982:16–17).

Avoni Begins a Life of Witness

Avoni's conversion came straight from Christ Himself so there could not have been any accusation that he had professed conversion under a mission or Church with the ultimate object of obtaining financial help or employment from them. Avoni set to work to be independent and took a shop in one of the main streets of Kermanshah where he installed a loom and made money for his bare living expenses much like Paul in weaving the heavy cloth for tents, curtains or saddle bags. The shop was open to all comers and there was nearly always someone who had come to hear more about Jesus Christ and His word or to argue or discuss His passion and resurrection which Moslems do not believe in. No one failed to be impressed with the love and sincerity and obvious personal conviction with which Avoni testified for His master. He used to tell me of his frequent summonses to appear before the Governor or Chief of Police but even the Mullahs could not make any charges stick and their hate melted before the love and lifestyle which so closely resembled that of the Savior. They even put the washing facilities of the mosque in the corner at his disposal. They even gave him their protection so long as he restricted his evangelism in the town to his shop (Gardiner 1982:16–17).

Avoni Suffers Beatings

Several times per year, having made enough money for expenses, Avoni would be off on a missionary journey to Kurdish towns and villages. He went as the Spirit led him. Sometimes he would be treated kindly and given traditional Kurdish hospitality and other times once his message was seen to be in conflict with the Koran fanatics would stir up the people against him and he would be chased off with sticks and stones. Often he would end one of his journeys at our hospital. Sometimes he would come sick from rough living or bruised from ill treatment. He would recover in his special room in the hospital and then spend two or three weeks going around the wards and out-patients with the Gospel, taking our open morning worship and taking part in our services and prayer meetings for the Christians. Staff and patients loved him and considered him a prophet. Some of my sweetest memories were of him on his knees praying in the corner while I struggled with limited medical facilities to save someone desperately ill or wounded. The Lord sent him to make our burdens more bearable. He also used to visit the Christian orphanage in Faraman [Kermanshah] and encourage the workers there (Gardiner 1982:16–17).

Avoni Bears Witness to Iranian Soldiers

On his last visit but one to us he arrived covered with blood but in a great state of spiritual joy. It seems that he had been to a Kurdish village where some fanatics had stirred up the people but while they were dragging him out of town a detachment of Gendarmes came up and at once arrested the trouble makers and took them with Avoni to their nearby Gendarmerie Post according to custom. There their officer investigated the trouble and suggested that Avoni bring charges against those who had attacked him so that they could be punished. Avoni refused saying that they had acted in ignorance before hearing him out. The officer suggested that there and then Avoni should give his message; tea, the symbol of hospitality, was brought. When he had read God's word and explained his message the officer was delighted and expressed his surprise that he should have been ill-treated for it and dismissed them all. Avoni was taken back to the village and given food while he gave out gospels. In our hospital he recovered but his chest had now become worse. He stayed a month and set off for his shop. Later on his next journey he was walking along the road when he was knocked down by one of a convoy of army lorries. The soldiers were very concerned and put him on a stretcher and took him to their barracks. He was treated in the sick bay and the colonel came daily to visit him and showed great interest in Avoni's way of life and message he proclaimed. His clothes were torn and old so that colonel brought him one of his own best suits. When he was convalescent he asked the colonel's permission to tour the barracks and speak to the men and give out his small stock of Gospels. The colonel was happy that others as well as himself should hear the message so for three days Avoni testified to these young men. He was astonished how kind and receptive they were. Never could he have got within miles of them in the ordinary way. They said good-bye to him and sent him on his way to our hospital (Gardiner 1982:16–17).

Avoni's Final Journey

He was full of joy but it was clear that the Lord had given Avoni this special joy to sustain him in the last journey with the visible Lord to greet him at the end of it. I hurriedly called Pastor William and we had a happy time of prayer and fellowship before the pastor left for Teheran. Our staff visited Avoni and he used every energy to remind them of Jesus. When night came and the patients settled down we were alone. As the Lord called him he gathered his last breath to say "Masih zendeh ust," Christ is alive (Gardiner 1982:16–17).

Gardiner's mission in Iran saw other Kurds come to Christ as well. Some are listed here.

ALLAHIAR

Allahiar was raised at the International Mission orphanage in Kermanshah. At different times the Presbyterians and International Missions employed him as evangelist, administrator, and teacher and interpreter. Allahiar moved to Teheran, where he worked at the Presbyterian headquarters. After the 1979 Revolution, he moved to the West and helped make gospel recordings. Later a Christian radio broadcasting company hired Allahiar to teach Christianity in the Sorani Kurdish language.

SAYARDI

Sayardi is the brother of Allahiar. He worked for Gardiner as an evangelist and chaplain at the Christian Hospital at Ghorveh. His whole family took part in Sunday worship.

AZIZI

Gardiner introduces Azizi, who was

the Kurdish wife of Mehdi, a Persian who was a salaried Evangelist at the Christian Hospital. She was brought up at the Kermanshah Orphanage. She used to go round the hospital and speak to the Kurdish women in Kurdish about Christ as she was very much one of them. She also entertained Kurdish women at home. They eventually founded a small Church by the Caspian (1982:18).

KHALIL

Gardiner calls Khalil "a Kurdish miracle of grace":

He was born blind as were three of his brothers and although he never had physical sight yet he could testify "although I was blind now I see" spiritually. Indeed the Lord used his blindness as a testimony that Christ can use and give joy in His service to those who up till then in Iraq were usually exploited for begging. He was a student of a pioneer missionary worker among the blind, Pastor Christofel with his Blindenheim, first in Tabriz, then moved after the war to Isfahan where it was eventually incorporated with the existing Diocesan Girls Blind School. Khalil had a full and strict Christian upbringing and gave his heart to Jesus Christ. He was one of the first to study at Teheran University and obtained his degree in Philosophy. He then became the first blind teacher to sighted pupils in Iran as he taught his subject at the Bu-Ali (a medieval Moslem medical philosopher) High School in Sanandaj, capital of Kurdistan, which I frequently visited for administration. He was highly regarded by his pupils one of whom was the Christian son of one of our staff members.

Khalil used to come regularly to our hospital for fellowship and the prayer room was always packed out when he preached there and he did a lot of personal work. Khalil opened a small evening school for the blind in Sanandaj and for the first time blind Kurds were able to learn to read and write and undertake other skills. Eventually it became so successful that the government took it over and put it in a proper building with a Moslem sighted principal. Khalil remained its principle teacher for some time but found Moslem standards and pressure too much for him. He is now studying for a further degree under Christian sponsorship in Sri Lanka (1982:18).

MARZAKI

Marzaki was a Christian Kurd who worked in the Oil Company in Iran. Later he worked in the administration of the Presbyterian Church in Teheran.

ONE HUNDRED MUSLIM CONVERTS
IN KERMANSHAH?

John Elder, a Presbyterian missionary in Kermanshah, reported a Muslim convert community of over 100 in the city in 1963. By 1969 it had dwindled to a dozen or so. David Cashin asks, "What happened to over 100 members of a Muslim convert community?" (McCurry 1978:306). Perhaps a sizable number in this congregation were related to the orphanage in Kermanshah.

David Shaad, with International Missions, moved to Kermanshah in 1975. No believers were to be found. Two or three elderly Kurds came to a new fellowship that began during his time in that city. It was a fellowship of mixed Kurds and Assyrians. They met on Friday. One Kurd named Mash'allah R. showed great promise. Mash'allah would go to teahouses and recite the Persian poets. He would come to parts of the poetry that allowed for the gospel or part of the Bible to be emphasized. By these points of contact, Mash'allah taught the Three in One God and other concepts (Shaad 1997).

Customers in the teahouses would give coins to Mash'allah, as reciting from the Persian poets was an honorable profession. In this way God's message of redemption came in accustomed form.

ISLAMIC REVOLUTION: IRAN WORK ABANDONED

Foreign mission work in Iran ended with Khomeini's Revolution in 1979. The Ayatollah returned a to thunderous welcome by the Persian people; Iranian Kurds hailed him as well. So did the Armenians and Assyrians, at least in public. Writes Gardiner:

> The Archbishop of the Armenian Church in full regalia had been in the party of VIPs at the airport to welcome the Ayatollah. The large Armenian and smaller Assyrian Christian minorities were not molested other than to enforce Islamic morality on them, making it as difficult as possible to transfer themselves or funds abroad and of course there was no exemption for their sons being called up to the army (1982:3).

The Ayatollah's Wrath Descends on the Converts

The Islamic Revolutionaries had no quarrel with those who were "born Christian." But woe to the Muslim who had become a Christian:

> Their wrath descended on those who had renegaded [sic] from Islam by being Born Again. . . . The (Anglican) Episcopal Church was picked out for special terrorism and plunder because its Bishop, half his clergy and some of his congregations, including a very fine Christian Kurd were on this category. There was also a

Kurdish convert and family in the Presbyterian Church, and a few other Kurdish and Persian converts (1982:3). The Presbyterian work in Kermanshah was all destroyed. Similarly the government closed a Pentecostal church in Kermanshah. The membership was Pentecostal, all converts from Islam; they suffered a terrible persecution under Khomeini. A couple of Iranian Christian workers went to begin work in Sanandaj, but the Iranian Government expelled them; any attempt to help the Kurds is viewed with suspicion. Fruit from the Presbyterians in Urumia remains until today. Some of the families have moved to Teheran where they continue the evangelical work (1982:3).

GARDINER EXITS IRAN

Gardiner and his wife were probably the last western missionaries to work among Kurds in Iran. Official word arrived that the Iranian Ministry of Health would take over the Ghorveh Hospital. The date was March 21, 1980. He writes of the end:

As the storm clouds of revolution came up and the missionaries had left the area I preached my last sermon at this little Church to the little crowd of faithful Kurdish believers. As the evening fell after the service I went with them to a bluff overlooking the river where the Rev. Stead and his first wife lay buried, while in front of them were the graves of orphans and staff members who had died in the half century of the orphanage's life. . . . But we also remembered the other orphans, scattered all over the country and even abroad who had as a result of this work had a thoroughly Christian upbringing. Some we know are in active Christian service, some are themselves founders of families where Christ is honoured. Others are quiet believers while others are struggling among thorns. All have heard the Gospel and if they have not accepted it yet who knows whether some day the Holy Spirit will use His Word or some experience to lead them to give their hearts to Him (1982:12).

When Rick Clewis exited Iran after the fall of the Shah, he counted fifteen known Kurdish believers in the country. Five lived in Kermanshah and were active with the IMI (International Missions). Other Kurdish believers from Kermanshah have moved to Teheran and other cities. M. F., a convert from Islam, reported to me that many Ininan Kurds have kneeled before Christ in the 1990s.

Some Armenian and Assyrian pastors have worked fearlessly to evangelize and baptize Kurd and Persians. These men are under considerable pressure from their bishops, and under threat of death from the Revolutionary government, to quit the outreach. Accordingly, many ministers work secretly. Some have been martyred, but others continue.

MISSION WORK AMONG KURDS IN PERSIA MORE SUCCESSFUL—WHY?

Testimonies of 20th century Christian Kurds come from Persia, while almost none (before 1990) come from Turkey or Syria or Iraq. Any reasons? From the records of the western mission in all these countries, one finds:

1. In Persia, missionaries spoke Persian, the language of Muslims; in Turkey and Iraq missionaries spoke Armenian or neo-Aramaic, the language of the historical churches.

2. Persia recognized the right of Kurds to speak Kurdish; Turkey denied this right. In addition, the Shah allowed mission work among Kurds (until 1934 and again after the Second World War). The Shah did not view Christian missionaries as a threat to his westernizing policy. This tolerance was unique among the four governments where Kurds reside.

3. Missionary work in Kurdistan of Turkey became more difficult following World War I. Turkish nationalists suppressed minorities. Missionaries had to delay their hope to work in Kurdistan until the winds changed. Robert Glover wrote, "Many Kurds are already favorably disposed toward Christianity, and under better political conditions these people would offer a promising field for missionary effort" (1928:206). It was "not yet" God's time for evangelizing the Kurds.

4. In Syria there was no missionary effort in the 20th century, at least until 1990; Bedr Khan of Damascus is the sole Kurdish believer reported.

5. In Iraq, Clarence Mueller of the LOMS did not regard the learning of the Kurdish language as important. This carelessness compares poorly with the measured steps that the LOMS took at its beginning in Iran.

Chapter 5

The Historical Churches
Since World War I

Since World War I thousands of Middle Eastern Christian families have moved to the United States and to Canada, Australia, and Europe. Today, Father Patros of the Virgin Mary Chaldean church in Zakhu reasons with his congregation to stay. They listen politely; however, they have caught a fever to emigrate. Christians in northern Iraq pay thousands of dollars for false passports; Kurds, Arabs and Turks conspire to take the last money from these very desperate people.

ASSYRIAN PETITION
FOR NATIONHOOD DENIED

Assyrians hoped that the League of Nations would grant them a nation following the First World War. They proposed Mosul as their capital city. In 1932, at the end of the British mandate in Iraq, the Assyrian patriarch traveled to Geneva to plead his case to the League of Nations.

But it was not to be. All measures to gain Assyrian statehood failed. Britain co-opted the oil fields of Mesopotamia, and the League of Nations granted Britain the mandate to govern a newly minted country called Iraq. Assyrians felt betrayed by the British, for whose cause the Assyrians had fought against the Turks in the First World War. Comments Gardiner:

I have spoken to and lived with many of the hierarchy of the Assyrian nation including the Royal Family and they are certainly under the impression that the British promised them at least a secure homeland from of the dangers of massacre only to be bitterly disillusioned in 1932 when the British handed over their mandate to Iraq to the Arabs in spite of the Assyrian protests taken even to the League of Nations. Massacre of Assyrians by the Arabs in the Mosul area followed in spite of protection [for the Assyrians] given by the Kurds in some areas (1982:1).

Following the denial of nationhood, Assyrian resistance to the Iraqi government intensified. Patriarch Mar Shimun refused to cooperate with the new Iraqi government, and in June 1933 he was "detained" in Baghdad (Marr 1985:57). He left for Chicago, and his successor still makes his headquarters there.

BRITISH ALLIANCE WITH THE ASSYRIAN POPULATION IN IRAQ

Iraqi Assyrians enjoyed a privileged status during the British Mandate:

[The British] settled about 20,000 Assyrians in northern areas of Iraq around Zakhu and Dohouk. . . . Their uninvited intrusion into the country through the *intervention of a foreign power was deeply resented by the Muslims, and especially by the Kurds in whose areas they were settled* (Marr 1985:11, italics mine).

Christians in northern Iraq estimate that Zakhu and Amadia were seventy percent Christian before the mandate ended, and the persecutions began, in 1933. Villages near Zakhu have been occupied in the 20th century at various times by Kurds, Turks, Christians, Arabs, and Yezidis. In previous centuries the armies of Mongols, Byzantines, Persians, and Greeks, Medes, and Assyrians rolled along the Silk Road and crossed the Habur River. Even the Jews settled there in the Captivity.[1] How shall the land be justly occupied by its true owners in this situation? The British chose one group—the Assyrians—and armed them. However, when the British mandate ran out, Kurds took revenge on the interlopers.

---

[1] "In the ninth year of Hoshea the king of Assyria captured Samaria and deported the Israelites to Assyria. He settled them in Halah, in Guzan on the Habur River and in the towns of the Medes" (2 Kg 17:6).

ASSYRIAN MARTYRDOM IN THE 20TH CENTURY

Kurds massacred about 100 Assyrian villagers in Dohouk and Zakhu in early August 1933. Panic and bloodlust spread out of control. Then, on August 11, the Iraqi police ordered the Assyrian men to the police station in Sumeil between Dohouk and Zakhu, supposedly for their protection. But an Iraqi army company, under the command of Ismail Tuhalla, an aide of Bakr Sidqi, entered the buildings and fired on the unarmed Assyrians. Some 315 Assyrian men perished at Sumeil. Forty or fifty nearby villages were looted and partially destroyed (Marr 1985:58). For carrying out this action, Bakr Sidqi rose in rank.

CHRISTIANS IN KURDISTAN
REMAIN DISADVANTAGED

William Masters found a number of Christians among the government workers in Rowanduz, Iraq in the early 1950s. These Christians minded their steps in relation to the Muslims:

For example, the postmaster and several teachers profess to be Christian. Because of their religion, these men are at some disadvantage among their colleagues. At a gathering to which one or more Christians has been invited, they may be embarrassed whenever religious matters are discussed and are generally limited in the forcefulness of their words, for they are unable to argue with the fluency of expression permissible between fellow Muslims. A Christian teacher cannot castigate his pupils with the freedom of some other teacher, often to his chagrin, for *the students are aware of his social inferiority* (Masters 1953:202, italics mine).

PERSECUTION OF NESTORIANS
DURING THE BA'ATH YEARS

The Ba'ath regime gained power in Iraq in 1968. Persecution of Nestorians began immediately:

The first crime of the Ba'ath government against our people was in the Assyrian village (Soria, near Qarawilla) late in 1969, when the regime forces forced the people of this peaceful village into a cave. Women, children, old people and even the priest of the village were ordered into the cave and the gate was locked and kerosene was poured into the cave and they were burned alive. The priest's name was Hanna (Assyrian Democratic Movement 1992:1).

Ba'ath "revolutionaries" destroyed seven churches along the road between Zakhu and Faysh Xabur, a distance of 25 miles. In northern Iraq, 200 Christian villages have been destroyed during the Ba'ath years (Assyrian Democratic Movement 1992:1).

Since A.D. 360 three Assyrian churches had existed near Amadia. The Ba'ath government dynamited them. One sanctuary was reconstructed in 1983 and again in 1988; both times the government destroyed this building.

In 1988 a priest near Amadia refused to fight in the Iran-Iraq war. He was executed. He was 28 years old, with a wife and two children.

CHURCH BROUGHT UNDER GOVERNMENT CONTROL

Following the Kurdish uprising in 1991, Assyrians in northern Iraq printed a history of recent atrocities carried out by the Ba'ath regime.

The regime used to bury these springs of water with reinforced concrete to make them useless for the people. After the immigration of our people from villages to towns, the regime's operation started in an organized way to deny the Assyrian nation identity by interfering in internal affairs of the churches and trying to divide the church by creating arguments among the communicants. Also, the church was "nationalized" and came under the authority of the Ministry of Religion (Assyrian Democratic Movement 1992:2).

The Iraqi secret police made a prison of the Assyrian church in Dohouk; they offered no compensation to the church. The police used the church buildings to interrogate and torture and imprison suspects. The police told the priest, Father Daniel, not to come there anymore. Father Daniel went to see Saddam Hussein to apply for promised compensation. However, the appointment was canceled. His congregation now worships in a basement of an unfinished church.

CHURCH STATISTICS REVEAL DECLINE

The declining number of Christians in Kurdistan is steep and unrelenting. From van Bruinessen's *Agha, Shaikh and State* (1992:201), the following comparison can be made.

TABLE 8
POPULATION OF BITLIS IN 1870 AND IN 1992

Bitlis population census c1870

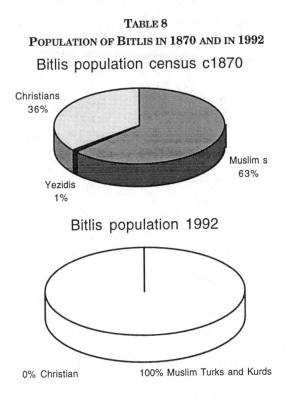

Christians
36%

Muslim s
63%

Yezidis
1%

Bitlis population 1992

0% Christian   100% Muslim Turks and Kurds

THE POPE MAKES A PLEA

In 1993 Reuters news agency reported the following plea by
Pope John Paul II:

> An emotional message from Pope John Paul expressing his hope
> that Iraqi Christians remain in their country was read out at a
> Sunday mass in Iraq.
>
> Thousands of Christians have left Iraq, hit by U.N. trade sanc-
> tions after its 1990 invasion of Kuwait, and many are waiting on
> the Mediterranean island of Malta for other countries to consider
> their requests for asylum.
>
> Dr. Yousif Habbi, Iraq's church historian, told Reuters that
> more than 100,000 Christians have left since the start of the cri-
> sis in the Gulf.
>
> "Now we have about 200,000 Iraqi Christians in foreign coun-
> tries," Dr. Habbi said.

The number of Christians in Iraq has dropped to about 600,000. They are served by two patriarchs, 15 bishops and 160 priests (1993).

TABLE 9

EMIGRATION TO THE WEST, ST. MARY'S
CHURCH, DOHOUK, IRAQ

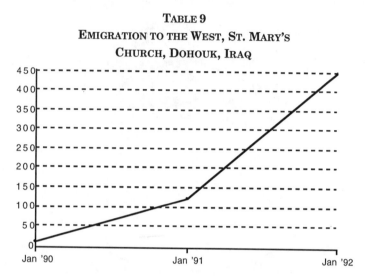

Concerning the diminishing number of Christians, Izady writes,

> Far fewer non-Kurds live in Kurdistan today than did only a century ago. Then, vast numbers of Armenians, Assyrians, Turks, Turkmens, Arabs, and Azeris lived within the territories of Kurdistan proper. World War I changed all this. By 1925, the Armenians had all either been killed or had fled, leaving behind a tiny community of about 10,000 people where there had been nearly half a million at the turn of the century. The Assyrians . . . who once resided in much larger numbers in Kurdistan from the environs of Mosul to the shores of Lake Vân and Lake Urmiâ, fled the region after the massacres of the late 19th and early 20th centuries. They now reside only on the peripheries of Kurdistan, near Salmâs and Urmiâ in Iran, near Dohouk Arbil, and Mosul in Iraq, and Qamishli, Mardin, and Siirt in Syria and Turkey (1992:126–7).

CHURCHES IN TURKISH KURDISTAN:
AN ENDANGERED SPECIES

Since the 1950s, Protestant churches in Turkish Kurdistan have nearly all closed. They are like scattered embers from a fire for which no more wood for fuel exists. The Protestant church in Diyarbakir closed in about 1965, all the families having emigrated. The Roman Catholic church in Diyarbakir closed in 1992. The Syrian Orthodox church in Diyarbakir now numbers five families, and seems on its way to extinction. The historical churches have dispersed, and the trend seems irreversible.

RECENT CLOSURE OF THE CHURCH IN HASSANA

In the 19th century, the villagers in Hassana converted to Protestant Christianity from Syrian Orthodoxy. We have said that Hassana, renamed Kösreli, is possibly the oldest Protestant Church in the Middle East. In the fall of 1993, the agha of Shernak went on government television; he falsely accused the Christians[2] of being Armenians who aided the PKK. The Turkish army surrounded the village, forced the citizens from their homes, and set the village on fire. Hassana fell victim to the Turkish government's war against the Kurds. Along with hundreds of other villagers from southeastern Turkey, the Christians of Hassana scattered to large cities.

The pastor of the evangelical church in Hassana, Matté Eksan, emigrated to Germany in 1992. The pastorate had been in his family for three generations. Some say that his "great-grandfather" was Yosip, the bishop who became a Protestant through the witness of (it seems) Samuel Rhea. After Matté Eksan left, Protestant members worshipped with a Syrian Orthodox congregation in the same village. I was present on the final Easter Sunday worship service, in 1993. The number of families in Hassana had declined from 700 in the 1960s to seventy before the Persian Gulf War in 1991, to thirty in 1993, and finally to zero.

---

2 This accusation is in contrast to the goodwill shown in 1895, when the agha of Shernak spared the village of Hassana during the general massacre that year. That agha was "very friendly to the Christians" and when he could no longer protect them, he helped them escape to Persia (Coan 1939:125). A century ago, Christian minorities in the Shernak province had more protection than today!

TURKISH GOVERNMENT FORCED
OUT THE LAST ARMENIANS

As recently as the 1980s Armenians lived in the southeastern Turkey province of Sirnak, around the town of Silopi. They spoke Kurdish.[3] All 250 Armenian families moved first to Istanbul and then to Marseilles, France.

PERSIAN CHRISTIANS
WHO EVANGELIZED KURDS

Mentioned below are some Christians from the Middle East who bore Christian witness to the Kurds. We are indebted to Gardiner for his private record. Names of workers who are now active have been omitted.

PASTOR KHAN

Khan was instrumental in bringing Dr. Sa'eed Kurdistani to Christ in 1879. He traveled around with two fellow Assyrian colporteurs.

PASTOR MOOSHI

Mooshi came from Kermanshah. "His ministry saw a remarkable revival and his thirst for the souls of Moslems brought many [to attempt] to seal his testimony with his blood" (Gardiner 1982:14). Gardiner goes on to write,

Pastor Kasha Mooshi made trips into Kurdistan villages and discovered the strange Kurdish sect the Alialiars [sic], who while paying lip service to Islam have their own worship including a kind of Lord's supper. Some say that they were originally Christian and to avoid massacre became nominally Moslem but secretly changed the name of Christ to Ali so that when they said Ali they meant Christ. The International Missions rediscovered them fifty years later and found them receptive to the Gospel more than others (1982:14).

PASTOR WILLIAM

William also came from Kermanshah. He spoke Farsi as well as Assyrian. It was Pastor William who instructed Avoni (in Chapter Four) in the Christian faith.

---

[3] Sometimes Kurds and Turks refer to these Armenians, and other Christians in Turkey who speak Kurdish as "Kurdish Christians."

CHRISTIAN BOOKSHOP MOBILE UNIT IN IRAN

The Mobile Book Unit came north from Teheran to Faraman (Kermanshah) Hospital two or three times per year, and when conditions were favorable it made incursions from the Christian Hospital deeper into Kurdistan.

> They used to do things thoroughly and fearlessly, doing open colportage in the bazaar and offices with the Word of God. When our town later started up a Police force they barely tolerated our evangelism and pulled me in for interrogation twice. Three times they arrested the colportage group and sent them out of town, but in the direction they wanted to go! (Gardiner 1982:18).

KENAN ARAZ

Kenan Araz is the only Turk on our list of Christians who evangelized Kurds. Kenan was born in Midyat, a town in southeastern Turkey with a monastery and a large Christian population. When he moved to Istanbul for schooling, Kenan changed his name from Emmanuel. Kenan overcame the pressure of his Assyrian boundaries to share the love of Christ with Muslims. Bruce Farnham tells Kenan's story in *My Big Father* (1985).

Other Middle Eastern Christians speak to Kurds of Christ. They are bold in their witness. A very few ethnic Christians from the Middle East evangelize in the Kurdish language.

WHO ARE THE "KURDISH CHRISTIANS?"

Christian publications sometimes refer to "Kurdish Christians." In addition, Kurds in Turkey describe the ethnic Christians who once lived among them by this phrase. I believe there are three types of Christians to whom Kurds refer as "Kurdish Christians" today.[4]

---

4   In the 10th century, the Arab geographer al-Masudi referred to Christian Kurds. At that time, "Christians were clearly included in the term 'Kurd'. . . . A substantial proportion of Assyrian and Syrian Orthodox may well be of the same racial stock as their Muslim neighbours" (McDowall 1996:13).

1. ORPHANS OF THE PERSECUTION

"Kurdish Christian" sometimes refers to orphaned Christians whose parents or grandparents perished in the persecutions; these orphans "became Kurds." Kurds adopted them into the Kurdish village. These children have grown up, and now have children of their own. Many are quick tell the visitor that their real fathers were Christian. Beyond this confession, the "Kurdish Christians" have no knowledge of their ancestral faith. In this way a legacy of the ethnic church in Kurdistan remains today.

2. CHRISTIANS WHO SUFFERED ALONGSIDE THE KURDS

In recent times the term "Christian Kurds" refers to Nestorians or Armenians in Kurdistan who, though not Kurdish, "identified themselves so much with the Kurdish cause that they did not protest when the Kurds called them 'Christian Kurds'" (van Bruinessen 1991:8). These Christians have become *honorary Kurds*. Christians and Kurds made common cause against oppressive governments in Turkey, Iraq, Iran, and Syria. In the United Nations safety zone in northern Iraq, armed Assyrian freedom fighters defend the territory alongside Kurds. Hence the honorary title, Christian Kurds.

3. CHRISTIANS WHO CONVERT TO ISLAM

Some Armenians and Nestorians converted to Islam. We quote van Bruinessen in full:

> The Armenian and Aramaic-speaking Christians who until the First World War lived throughout Kurdistan (after massacres, deportations and flight only a few small communities remain) were usually considered as the last representatives of the region's original population, forcefully subdued by the Kurdish and Turkish tribesmen arriving later. These minorities distinguished themselves from the Kurds by religion, language, and a superior technology, but not very clearly in physiology. Several travellers have observed that at any one place in Kurdistan the local Armenians and Kurds resembled one another more than they did the Armenians and Kurds of other regions. These physical similarities may in part be due to the not uncommon practice among the Kurdish tribesmen of abducting Christian women, but there are several observations of *large numbers of Christians in the process of*

kurdicizing, while in the past the reverse may also have taken place. Molyneux-Seel (1914) observed that large numbers of Armenians in Dersim had recently become Kurdish Alevis. I encountered in 1976 in the province of Siirt, in Turkish Kurdistan, small communities of former Armenians who had recently crossed the ethnic boundary. They spoke Kurdish and Turkish only, and had become Muslims. Some young members of the communities were then active Kurdish nationalists. They had, however, not yet become so Kurdish that they would refrain from telling me (usually within the first five minutes) that they had Armenian origins (1992:117–118, italics mine).

Kreyenbroek, an authority on Kurdish ethnology, writes of Christians in eastern Turkey who recently converted to Islam:

In Hakkari I came across Kurds who told me that "originally" they were Nestorians, and who spoke of the Christian dialect of Kumkapi in Istanbul as "ours." Such recent converts, some of whom should perhaps be called "crypto-Christians," are still recognized as different from the Kurds proper, but they are acceptable as marriage partners and those who wish can easily be integrated (1992:46).

In sum, the term "Christian Kurds" refers to traditional Christians in Kurdistan who either survived the massacres as orphans, or became *honorary Kurds* for suffering alongside the Kurds, or converted for reasons of social survival. In all three cases the designation "Christian Kurd" identifies ethnic Christians who became Kurds. In no case do we see a group of Muslim Kurds who convert to biblical Christianity. There is no chance for Kurds to become Christian in this same sense.

"DO YOU KNOW WHAT WE CHRISTIANS SAY?"

A Chaldean friend in Zakhu confided to me, "Do you know what we Christians ask in private?" I answered that I would like to know. My friend asked, "Why did the Allies rescue the Kurds in the mountains [in April 1991]? If the Allies had waited another month, all the Kurds would have died, and we would be finished with them." I was speechless; he wished that two million persons had perished. My friend filled the silence by saying, "Don't speak to me of loving our enemies. You have said that before. We have been hurt too badly to do that."

I have since confirmed that other Christians in Zakhu feel the same as my friend. With such a wall of contempt, how long shall one wait until the church rises to its privilege? It takes only one side to remove the dividing wall. Until now, the Christians in Kurdistan have not made the first move.

Why is there no Kurdish Bible? Some Middle Eastern Christians say that the Kurds do not want one. An Assyrian priest from Istanbul visited my home in northern Iraq. He said, "Isn't it wonderful that northern Iraq is free, and we can help our people. What do you think is the greatest need?" I answered, "I think you need to translate John 3:16 into Kurdish." He paused, then said, "I think you should do that instead of us." The Christians live in one test tube, the Kurds in another. One Ark carries ethnic Christians; who will build another to carry the Kurds?[5] Former Middle East Council of Churches Secretary General Gabriel Habib suggests that missionaries link themselves to the ethnic churches, so as not to be "alien to the local spiritual and cultural ethos" (1988). However, we know that missionaries must choose *which cultural ethos* they will enter; they will remain alien either to the Christian tribes or the Kurdish tribes.

Ethnic Christians were disappointed that I chose to learn Kurdish. Christians laughed at my children, because Kurdish is all that my children can speak. Christians ask me "point blank" whether I am a *falah*, a Christian of their understanding; it seems as though they are asking whether I am "one of them." I answer, absurdly, "No, I'm not a *falah*."[6] Christians wish that I would live in their neighborhood. "We can take care of all your

---

5 Mehmet Iskender, a Turk, writes,

> This segregation of life and language certainly did not make easier the transmission of ideas, which were in any case unlikely to be well-received when put forward by a subject race whose religion belonged to the corrupt and conquered Byzantine Empire. . . . It is very doubtful whether people from minority Christian backgrounds can act as a bridgehead for the formation of Muslim convert churches in which a Turk would really feel accepted and at home. . . . Hence the need is for truly Turkish church-life and forms which are not tied to a minority ghetto-mentality with all its overtones of "foreigness" and "intrigue" (McCurry 1978:291).

6 This term is not the same as the Arabic word for peasant, *fellah*. Kurds have a different word for peasant, *djutiyar*.

needs," said one priest, "and you will never have to go out among Kurds."

CULTURAL FENCES SEPARATE KURDS
FROM THE HISTORICAL CHURCHES

Cultural barriers separate Kurds from *falah*. *Falahi* persons (Christians) are born into the *falah* community; *falah* is a language, a history, a pride, a religion, a shared suffering; in short, the *falah* community is a nation with boundaries; a fence separates insiders from outsiders. To live in the *falah* community is to live on a submarine with hatches closed; no one gets on, no one gets off. Were a Kurd to become a *falah*, he would no longer be considered a Kurd by his community. He would break his father's heart; he would betray his people. A Kurd in northern Iraq would no more consider becoming a *falah* than he would consider having a sex change.

"WHAT ABOUT WITNESS AMONG THE SIOUX?"

Mission as usual in the Middle East would bring all mission resources to bear on the tiny historical church, and leave none for work among the majority people. Kenneth Bailey offers a parable:

> Let us imagine that America was not Christian and Japan was. The Japanese then come to the United States and establish a church among the Navajo Indians. After one hundred years it is perceived that the Japanese have too much control over the destiny of the Navajo church. The Japanese church leaders then say to the Navajo church leaders, "We are dissolving our Japanese organization in America and turning everything over to you—we will do nothing within the fifty states except at your specific request and under your direct authority."
>
> After a period of time the following dialogue occurs:
>
> "What about witness and service to the Sioux?" ask the Japanese.
>
> "The Sioux are our traditional enemies, " comes the answer.
>
> "Well, then, we can start work in white America?" say the Japanese.
>
> "White America?" the Navajos reply. "White Americans took our land, killed our grandfathers and shamelessly broke the treaties they made with us. White America is not on our agenda!"

"Very well." continue the Japanese. "Perhaps we can do something for the Eskimos."

"Eskimos," counter the Navajos, "are also native Americans. But our people look on them as inferiors. Our people will not be able to understand why resources available for the Navajos are being spent on the Eskimos."

The deeper question then must be put to the Japanese. Is it fair to the Navajo churches leaders to place on them the burden of providing the vision for witness and ministry for all of America? Vision for all Navajos, yes! But the Navajos also have a constituency that they must take with them. They also live in an ambiguous world and realistically only a certain range of possibilities is open to them. Is it right to say to the Navajo church council, "We the Japanese will not work with the Eskimos unless you, the Navajo church council, decide that teaching Eskimo children is more important than teaching Navajo children."

Would we want a similar burden placed upon us? (1989:10)

Chapter 6

A Brief Missiology
for Workers

A book on the history of mission to the Kurds would be slender indeed. But a history of mission in Kurdistan is twenty times larger. The difference illuminates our thesis: missionaries continued for a hundred years to "pass through the wilderness of Kurdish mountains, seeking in the most remote corners of the land the little companies of Christians" (Richter 1910:316).

Sift through the record, like a prospector panning for gold, and the occasional reference to evangelizing Kurds jumps off the pages. I fear that concentrating these references in one place, in this book, may dull the readers' feelings to how rare these nuggets are.

We must think about the failure to establish churches among the Kurds. We do not judge any missionary for his or her work; the reward for faithful service is not seen in this world. However, the mission in Kurdistan failed, as measured against Eli Smith's inaugural words, to find "the lever which would overturn the whole system of Mohammedan delusion" (Joseph 1961:44).

THREE REASONS FOR THE
FAILURE OF THE MISSION

For three reasons Protestant missions—our main subject here—failed to evangelize Kurds. First, missions continued to invest almost exclusively in historical churches. By this, missionaries washed out any bridges to the Kurds. Second, missionaries among Kurds died. Third, missionaries believed that the time of mission work among Kurds had not yet arrived; perhaps in a later day, God would bring multiplied numbers of Kurds into His church. We will develop these reasons in the pages that follow.

1. THE CHURCHES OF THE EAST DID NOT EVANGELIZE THE KURDS

What happened to the hope that Armenians and Nestorians would evangelize the Kurds? The ABCFM had "commenced with the expectation that the revival of gospel light and influence among the Nestorians 'would rekindle their ancient missionary spirit'" (Joseph 1961:44). The mission followed a logical plan: local Christians would more naturally, more numerically, and more economically preach to their Kurdish neighbors than would foreigners from across the sea. However, the experiment failed. It failed after ten years; it failed after 50 years; after a hundred years of Protestant mission, the Great Experiment proved only that it could not be done. To be sure, a Protestant church was carved from the soft belly of the historical church. William Miller, missionary to Iran, tells what happened next:

> Foreign missionaries then became totally occupied serving these new churches they produced. Occasionally, one of these Protestants became a zealous and courageous evangelist to the Muslims. But, *for the vast majority of believers, the walls of dialect, custom, prejudice and fear which have existed between Christians and Muslims for more than a thousand years were too high to scale and too ponderous to move.* The "evangelical" churches have done little more than the Catholic or Orthodox churches had done to confront Muslims with the claims of Christ (Miller 1971:232, italics mine).

Mission leaders might reply that Ottoman and Persian laws prevented work among the Muslims. This is fair enough. The Ottoman and Persian Empires granted official permission to the Protestants to work among the Armenians and Syriac Orthodox and the Nestorians (Assyrians). All the Christian communities, however, were united by a common opposition to any mission to the Kurds. Protestant and Catholics continued to devote every missionary dollar and every brick school house and every hour of language study to the Kurd's "hereditary enemies," the Christians, who had "as little desire to be the bearers of the Gospel to the Moslem neighbors as the Moslems have to receive it of them" (Stead 1920:147).

The Historic Churches Opposed a Mission to the Kurds

Evangelism of Muslims failed because the historical churches opposed it.[1] Armenians, Assyrians, and Chaldeans were happy when missionaries learned their language, educated their children, employed their graduates, and defended their rights. However, a mission to Kurds was not on the church's agenda. When the Catholic mission in Aleppo gained quick success among Yezidi Kurds, Armenians became jealous; they opposed the mission to Yezidis. As a result, Yezidis stopped coming to worship. Catholic mission among Kurds ended. Catholics never again worked in Kurdistan except to convert the historical Christians. Never did the historical church envision what the missionaries intended, to love their enemies and offer them the Kingdom of God. What do Middle Eastern Christians say when allowed to speak for themselves?

[The Kurds] are a people without literature and without history. . . . It is amusing to notice them on their way to their work, dragging along their sluggish limbs as though they might drop asleep at any moment. They will waste two hours before they even start to work. After an hour of pretended labor, in which they have really accomplished nothing, they will have to sit down

---

1   David Barrett writes, "This failure to impact the non-Christian world has several causes. Chief among them are (1) the older foreign mission boards and societies of Europe and America no longer place missionaries among unevangelized peoples without an invitation to do so, having decided to engage in mission only in cooperation with their overseas partner churches; and (2) these agencies and their overseas partners respond in most cases exclusively, to formal requests for foreign mission resources submitted by church leaders, missionaries or local Christians. But among World A individuals there are no churches and no persons who are likely to request mission resources or church planters, so none get assigned to World A contexts (1997:24).

and smoke awhile. Poor creatures, they are good for nothing. . . . Robbing is their business, and they believe that God created them for this purpose only. I myself have conversed with many of them, and asked them why they steal. They answer that every man has some occupation. One is a judge, one a merchant, one a farmer, and "we are robbers." . . . Like Cain, their hand is against everybody, and everybody's hand is against them. (Yonan 1895:6–8).

Yonan bleeds for his Armenian people, but he feels steel-cold rage toward Kurds:

The Koords are profoundly ignorant and stupid, with neither books nor schools. Of the whole race, not one in ten thousand can read. . . . The name Koord is a terror to the Christians, who are treated by them as a wolf would treat a lamb, robbing them of their property, sometimes murdering them, and often burning their villages (1895:11, 12–13).

Missionaries worked alongside church leaders who referred to the Kurds as "profoundly ignorant and stupid, good for nothing, with sluggish limbs, without literature and without history." Nestorians demanded all the attention for themselves.

The Historic Churches Still Oppose a Mission to the Kurds

Protestants planned to evangelize Kurds by first revitalizing the Assyrian church; this was like trying to start a fire with wet matches. For example, a "brilliant future" for Euphrates College in Harput was threatened when missionaries tried to admit a few Kurds and Turks into the student body. Faculty members and well-to-do Armenians, who had begun to support the school, objected (Daniel 1970:107). Even today the historical church has no mission to Kurds. The church remembers every wound inflicted by the hands of Kurds. After I spoke at a church in San Mateo, California, a woman introduced herself as an Assyrian from northern Iraq. She admired the work we were doing. "But we could never do that," she said, "because the Kurds have hurt us too badly." She remembers Kurds as her enemy; her church does not imagine how it can co-exist with Kurds, so the members are emigrating to the West. Inviting Muslims into the Messianic feast is not on the to-do list for the church in Kurdistan.

"The Kurds Don't Want It"

Each Sunday for more than two years I visited Iraqi Christians living in a refugee camp in eastern Turkey. I transported a Chaldean priest who conducted Sunday mass. After worship one day, a Chaldean said to me, "You have to help me get to America." We knew each other quite well, so I answered, "You have to help me stay in Kurdistan." He said, "You don't understand; I am willing to sell my house, my car and give up my job if I can go to America." I answered, "You don't understand; I gave up my house, my car, and my job to get to Kurdistan." He asked, "Why?" I replied, "Because the Kurds all around us do not know the blessing of Jesus Christ, as you and I do." He did not know what to say, so he blurted out, "The Kurds don't want it." I didn't know what to say, so I answered, "Let the Kurds decide whether they want to know Jesus Christ."[2]

At the world missionary conference held at Madras in 1938 the church's opposition was described in more general terms: "Too often [these] churches seem indifferent to Muslim enquirers, or look upon them with suspicion as to their motive in becoming Christians" (Joseph 1961:230). When the Great Experiment failed, the missionaries had no Plan B.

2. MISSIONARIES TO THE KURDS DIED

The second reason that the mission to the Kurds failed is that its workers, and their wives and children, died. Grant, age thirty-seven succumbed to typhoid. Samuel Audley Rhea died of cholera, age thirty-nine. Kurds killed Immanuel Damman just a few months after he arrived. During the attack, Detwig von Oertzen was wounded and consequently left the field. L. O. Fossum died of exhaustion after the First World War. Kurdish raiders murdered Bachimont the week he preached his first sermon in Kurdish. Roger Cumberland was shot in the back. The Presbyterian Church did not replace Cumberland; as he said, few if any envied him. The Presbyterian mission returned to its regular work alongside the Assyrian evangelical church. The Lutheran Orient

---

2 That man got his wish; he lives near Detroit, with thousands of other Chaldean immigrants. Happily, I got my wish too, and stayed in Kurdistan another five years.

Mission Society never recovered from the loss of its early missionaries.

3. THE "TIME" OF MISSION
AMONG KURDS HAD NOT YET ARRIVED

The third reason that the mission to Kurds failed may have been that the right time had not yet come. Perhaps the missionaries knew instinctively that God's time for the Kurds was "not yet." John Joseph says that in Persia "the missionaries arrived at a difficult time for their spiritual campaign, for on this eastern front the Russo-Persian conflict had already intensified the religious animosities" (1961:45). In Turkey, successive Sultans and then Young Turks applied ever tighter bonds on the overburdened Christians. A mission to Kurds needed to wait for another time.

The lesson of God's timing, His *kairos*, has elsewhere helped the church to explain the failure of its mission. St. Francis explained his failure to win the Sultan of Egypt in terms of God's timing.

Saint Francis and the "Not Yet"
of Christ's Mission to Muslims

Francis lived while Europeans fought Muslims in the Fifth Crusade. Francis renounced the sword, and preached the refusal of power. He asked for an audience with the Sultan in 1219. To reach the Sultan, Francis crossed through the no-man's land separating the Christian army from the Muslim army. Francis and the Sultan met over a period of two weeks. When the Sultan bade farewell, he bestowed gifts upon Francis, who is said to have given away all but one (a prayer rug?). Francis worried that he did not see fruit. He viewed his mission as a failure. This troubled Francis and caused him to seek God for the reason. His followers came to believe that time (kairos) for Muslims had not yet come. The Franciscans who gathered at Assisi on the 8th centenary of Francis' death wrote:

> When Francis speaks of mission, he is primarily thinking about the Muslims (Saracens). . . . At the same time Francis writes in the rule of 1221 that his brothers explicitly proclaim the Gospel only when it pleases God.

We feel that, through the signs of the times, God is telling us that *the "when" of Francis' directive has not yet arrived.* In many countries the open preaching of the Gospel is not possible; Islam is renewing itself. Do these facts not show us that, as Francis waited for God's pleasure, we too have to place ourselves in God's hands? (Franciscan Mission 1982:1, 13, italics mine).

Missionaries to Kurdistan would agree with the Franciscans: open preaching of the gospel in Kurdistan was not yet possible. This predicament was partly due to the law in Turkey and Persia, and largely to the depravity of Kurds. Missionaries, including Franciscans, "waited for God's pleasure" to open the door to work among the Muslims. This waiting was an act of faith. They lived in hope that the "not yet" would give way to the "now" of mission to Kurds.

New Testament Examples of God's "Not Yet" in Mission

As recorded in the book of Acts, God's time for mission to some places is "not yet." Paul was prevented from preaching here and there (Ac 16:7); other times he was expelled from the region (Ac 13:50) and on occasion he fled for his life (Ac 14:6). In a similar way the missionaries had to wait, as Francis waited, "for God's pleasure." In some way, God Himself seems to have blocked the Kurdish mission for long seasons. How could the missionaries work among Kurds in the Ottoman Empire when the law forbade conversion to Christianity? Or in Iraq, where, though lawful, local sentiments endangered Cumberland? Paul went to where he could, that is, to where there was "an open door" (Ac 14:27) The missions in Kurdistan of the 19th and 20th centuries did the same.

We have tried to explain the reasons for the failure of the mission to the Kurds. We turn now to suggest some ground for new workers among the Kurds to cover.

THE MISSIONARY MUST PAY ATTENTION TO KURDISH DIVERSITY

Many kinds of Kurds exist; they are divided by terrain, by tribe, and by language. Wycliffe identifies at least four Kurdish languages that need a Bible translation. When Kurds evangelize other Kurds, they will encounter barriers of language, tribe, and class. These barriers define homogeneous groups in which the gospel will spread.

KURDS FROM EVERY TRIBE

To the outside world, Kurds present a common cause. However, narrower tribal loyalties bind Kurds more intimately, and fracture Kurds more obviously, than the slogans that cry for a unified homeland. Tribes separate Kurds into opposing politics. "The very fact that a certain chieftain *participated in the nationalist movement was often sufficient reason for his rivals to oppose it, and most commoners followed their chieftains without question*" (van Bruinessen 1992:7, italics mine). If one tribe would consider a movement to faith in Christ, a rival tribe may even more vehemently resist. When the gospel comes to the Kurds, it must come to Kurds who will reach Kurds in other tribes.

Tribal loyalties are pre-eminent.[3] This loyalty defines one's friends and the borders of those friendships. Bride and groom usually come from the same tribe. Political parties seem to spread through a tribe, but no further. From Turkish Kurdistan, van Bruinessen relates a story of tribal factionalism from the 1970s:

> Down to the smallest towns, branches were opened, political tracts read and discussed. *Ideological difference and in particular personal rivalries caused many splits in the organizations*; by the end of the decade there were about ten of them (1992:33, italics mine).

Even in large cities of Kurdish Iraq political loyalties run along tribal lines (Barzani, Surchi, Zêbari, Doski, Mizuri). The historian for the Lutheran Orient Mission Society was right: "The Kurds have little regard for any government further away than their own tribal chiefdoms" (Jensen and Oberg 1985:5). When the gos-

---

[3]　Less so in Turkey, home of half the Kurds. The 19th century Ottomans and 20th century Kemalists banished tribal leaders and replaced them with government agents. This has greatly diminished tribal awareness in Kurdistan of Turkey.

pel comes to the Kurds, it must cross the barriers that men have built. Kurds must accept the commission of taking the gospel to every tribe. Every tribe must confess that God upends the last to be first and the greatest to be servant of all.

KURDISH TRIBAL CHIEFS ARE LEADERS
IN COMMUNITY DECISIONS

Kurdish tribal chiefs are called *aghas* or *shaikhs* depending on the area. Martin van Bruinessen has definitively described their importance in his book, *Agha, Shaikh, and State*. In that book, the author describes the declining influence of the agha, as the modern states of Turkey, Iran, Iraq and Syria reward those tribal leaders which adhere to state policies, and replace rebellious aghas.

The village head man *(mukhtar)* acts as judge in disputes and representative of the village when visitors arrive. He is keeper of the peace. When the gospel comes to an entire village, it will likely come from discussions that take place in the house of the mukhtar.

KURDS MAKE GROUP DECISIONS

The decision-making process often takes place in the group, not as individuals. Kurds believe, "we are, therefore I am":

The concept of "I" hardly exists in the context of a tribal culture's value system: "we" (the tribe) predominates. Individuals define themselves entirely in terms of their tribe. They are first a member of this or that tribe, then a Muslim, a Yezidi, or a Christian (Chaliand et al. 1980:24).

Therefore, when the gospel comes to the Kurds, we try not to extract individual young men or women from their family roots; we should wait for multiplied conversions that will happen in extended families. In a 1938 statement freighted with western worldview, the Near East Christian Council mentioned as a hindrance to Muslim evangelism: "In the thought of the Muslim a change of religion is primarily a change of group-communication and group-loyalty" (Joseph 1961:230). This group-loyalty is normative, and need not be negativized. Muslims should normally become followers of Jesus in company with others in their group.

KURDS FROM EVERY CLASS

Kurds are class-conscious, ever aware of insiders and outsiders. Town-dwellers whose family moved from villages (*gund*) even forty years previously are considered outsiders (*gundee*). Look at the village or town and you will find wealthy Kurds and poor Kurds. Wealthy Kurds own land and animals. A landowner rents his land to peasants who work his land and tend his animals. The peasants retain half the crop or herd; the other half belongs to the owner.

Some Kurds have amassed a fortune by trading. They are absorbed in their wealth, more covetous by far than the poor peasants around them. When the gospel comes to the Kurds, it must require a repentance from these rich traders. Indeed, it would be better for some to "sell everything" to follow Jesus.

Most Kurds are poor, and do not know where their bread will come from tomorrow. They own a house and some animals, but that is all. Their sons cannot afford the dowry, so a marriage arrangement is made with the family of a poor girl. Roland Allen says that they poor make good church members: "Illiterate members often bring to the church a profound spiritual knowledge, and a sense of the practical application of Christian truth to daily life, which is hidden from the accomplished student" (1962:148). When the good news comes to poor Kurds, it must offer them Christ and His spiritual blessings. Followers of Christ must remember the poor in their charity.

Religious Leaders as Well as Known Sinners

Some Kurds are religious, and society respects their status. The religious family or even the religious tribe is proud of its reputation. If a Kurd makes the pilgrimage to Mecca, the title of *hajj* (pilgrim) is applied even to his sons for as long as they live. I know of no Kurdish women who have made the pilgrimage.

In some families, one young man or (more often) woman seems to take the role of keeper of the faith. (Other family members may feel no religious impulse.) He or she says the five prayers, reads the Qur'an, and preserves the family religion. When the gospel comes to the Kurds, it must face almost certain opposition from the conservators of Islam. They may even imagine they are friends of God if they persecute, or deceive, the followers of Jesus. Other Kurds are sinners, recognized as such by society. Some are prostitutes (never talked of in polite company). Some are men who visit prostitutes. One Kurdish woman in our knowledge was murdered by the men in her family for suspected adultery. Among Kurdish men are gamblers, drunkards, thieves, wife-beaters, and homosexuals. Among women are mothers-in-law who break their sons' wives through battering and contempt. There are traitors to their family or tribe, who have served the dictatorship for money, as surely as did the tax-collectors with whom Jesus broke bread. These are the outcasts, the public sinners. When the gospel comes to the Kurds, it must heal many sinners who know they need a Physician.

God-Fearing Kurds

Some Kurds worship God with fear and awe. They seek Him with their hearts. God has planted in their souls a longing to know Him. Other Kurds gather around a holy man, or they gather in his memory. Sufis feel the intimacy of God's love. God-fearing Kurds may recognize followers of Jesus as fellow pilgrims on a spiritual path. God-fearing Kurds want to read the Bible. They will more likely decide to follow Jesus apart from their family approval. When the gospel comes, it must soon attract many God-fearers whom God has prepared to belong to Himself.

Kurds who have come to faith have one quality in common; they were on a personal journey to find God. These few elect souls wanted to know God, and they had an extraordinary desire for the truth. They would understand an old hymn:

I sought the Lord and afterward I knew
He moved my soul to seek Him, seeking me.
It was not I that found O Savior true.
No, I was found by Thee (Hymns 1976)

Dr. Sa'eed says that his search for truth led him to Christian faith. He once regarded the food of Christians to be unclean (Rasooli and Allen 1957:26); later he accepted their food and their faith as clean, an act that Sa'eed's biographer described as a bomb exploding in his father's house. When the gospel comes to the God-fearing Kurds, they are first fruits of a harvest.

Nomadic Kurds

Mehrdad Izady estimates that two centuries ago a million Kurds lived as nomads, about thirty percent of their population. In the mid-nineteenth century Henry Layard called the Kurds a nomadic people. However, today less than three percent of the Kurds live as nomads (Izady 1992:229). Ismet Vanly writes, "The 'nomad tribes,' which are still equated with the Kurds in Western minds, do not in fact exist in Kurdistan" (Chaliand et al. 1993:144).

But Kurdish nomads in eastern Turkey still pitch their black wool tents in pasture land for a season and then move on. So we can still quote Freya Stark, who traveled a century ago and paid exquisite tribute to the Kurdish nomad:

> The life of insecurity is the nomad's achievement. He does not try, like our building world, to believe in a stability which is non-existent; and in his constant movement with the seasons, in the lightness of his hold, puts something right, about which we are constantly wrong. His is in fact the reality, to which the most solid of our structures are illusion; and the ramshackle tents in their crooked gaiety, with cooking-pots propped up before them and animals about, show what a current flows round all the stone erections of the ages. The finest ruin need only be lamented with moderation, since its living essence long ago entered the common stream. No thought of this kind is likely to come into the head of the Turkish nomads; they are happy to shelter their goats in the warmth or the shade that they find, whether the ruins be of Nineveh or Rome. Their women were cheerful and fierce, unlike the peasant, and dressed in brighter colours—equals of their men or of anyone, as one may be if one lives under the hardness of necessity and makes insecurity one's refuge (Darke 1987:268).

Besides nomads, semi-nomadic Kurds have two homes, one in the mountains where they live during the summer grazing. They return to villages when summer ends. Only the most determined Christian worker imagines himself or herself traveling with Kurdish nomads. It has never happened to my knowledge.

Mountain Kurds and City Kurds

Terrain divides Kurds between those whose home is in the mountains, and those who move to the plains (and thus to cities and towns). Distrust separates the two. Izady is the best source here. He cites Siaband (1988), that "the relation between a Kurd and his mountain habitat is like a farmer to his farm; one has no meaning without the other" (Izady 1992:188). And this description: "To a Kurd the mountain is no less than the embodiment of the deity: mountain is his mother, his refuge, his protector, his home, his farm, his market, his mate, and his only friend" (1992:188).

On the other hand, modern Kurds settle in the cities on the plains; they assimilate into the surrounding culture. The cities on the plain is the world of politics, and successful Kurds who go there may not be trusted to be the leaders of mountain Kurds:

> It is as if he has lost his virtue by leaving the apron of mother-mountain and living among the crafty plains people. . . . To know the secrets of the mountains, the passes, rivers, and caves; to know the tribal customs; and to be brave, are essential characteristics of Kurdish chiefs and leaders (Izady 1992:189).

This distrust of the society outside the mountain fastnesses figures in two ancient stories that Izady summarizes. In both tales, a warrior man from the mountains is tempted by, and then betrayed by, a woman from the plains. These stories, told around the evening fires, would teach a lesson to every mountain boy: Don't go down to the plain, or it will make a fool of you. Conversely, when mountain Kurds come to the big cities, they may appear as simpletons to street-smart urban Kurds.

The political rivalry between Kurds in northern Iraq can be divided between mountain Kurds (Barzani) and Kurds who moved to the big cities on the plain (Talabani). When the gospel comes to the Kurds, it must take root in the mountains and also on the plains. From its beginning, the gospel in Kurdistan must bless all the families of the earth, even those families that the fathers and grandfathers taught their children to avoid.

KURDISH WOMEN WILL HEAR AND BELIEVE

Mistreatment of women begins early: boys do little work, girls do all the work; a teenage girl is forced to live in her house and seldom goes out until she is transferred to the home of her husband. Teenage boys, on the other hand, do as they please; orders

206 *Ethnic Realities and the Church: Lessons from Kurdistan*

from a sister or mother carry no weight. A woman can carry as much firewood as a donkey and still make dinner in the evening; women suffer a lifetime sentence of chores and mothering and eating leftovers. They sit in the unheated back room while the men drink their tea and complain about the service. When the gospel comes, it must end the way men mistreat women.

Kurdish society seems patriarchal, but take another look. Women find ways to influence their families and to a lesser extent the society that oppresses them. Women are not left without power. They can make the home life pleasant or painful for the men. They have complete care of the children. Society expects women to preserve the family religion; wives remain faithful to Islam even when their husbands do not. Women also maintain the honor of the family, even when the men do not. Thus, women are a conservative influence; they are not change-agents. Henny Hansen, an anthropologist, says,

> In view of the great part that conformance with the rules of Islam plays in the life of Kurdish women, her positive attitude toward the five pillars of Islam, *any change in her life pattern in this quarter would involve a complete transformation*. It is not surprising that *the altered life of women in Turkey has had to proceed hand-in-hand with a sustained offensive on all things Arab* (1960:183, italics mine).

For some women, the practice of the five pillars *is* the religion of God. All else may fail her, but the woman of Islam can rely on the unshakable pillars. Should an outsider suggest that a woman give up her practice, she would cry, "Blasphemy!"

KURDISH WOMEN WHO ARE NOT MUSLIMS

In non-Muslim religions—Alevi,[4] Yezidi, and Jewish—Kurdish women and men mix more in the religious life of the community. Kurdish Jews allow more freedom for their women, and this "gave rise in the 17th century to the first woman rabbi, the famous Rabbi Asenath Bârzâni" (Izady 1992:195).

---

[4] Alevi is probably a form of Shi'ite Islam, but rejected as perfidious by Sunni Kurds.

MISSIONARIES SHOULD BEGIN
A MISSION ORDER

Missionaries usually think of gathering believers into congregations; however, *missionaries should start mission orders*. By mission orders, we mean groups of men or women who make a commitment to the task of evangelism and discipleship.

When they plant only congregations, missionaries neglect the *means* by which they themselves obeyed the Great Commission. The congregation invites like-minded people to join: children of members and culturally-near neighbors. However, the mission order blesses the strangers outside the homogeneous unit. This has been God's missionary plan since He blessed Abraham to be a blessing to all the families of the earth. Mission orders extended Christian faith through the Middle East and into Persia, Afghanistan and China.

Crucial to the missionary's task is his or her awareness that *there are two structures to God's redemptive mission*. Ralph Winter has described these as the warp and the woof:

> Just as it is impossible to make cloth without threads going both crosswise and lengthwise, it is crucially important to regard these two structures working together as the warp and the woof, the fabric being the Christian movement—the people of God, the *ecclesia* of the New Testament, the church of Jesus Christ. Therefore, to make either of the two structures central and the other secondary, as the term para-church seems to do, is probably unwise (1977:1).

So two structures comprise the church: the congregation and the missionary band. The *ministry* of the congregation was given to elders and deacons. However, the *work* of the church—going into all the world to make disciples of the ethné—was given to the apostolic order:

> While they were worshiping the Lord and fasting the Holy Spirit said, "Set apart for me Barnabas and Saul *for the work* to which I have called them." So after they had fasted and prayed, they placed their hands on them and sent them off (Ac 13:2–3, italics mine).

When the gospel comes to the Kurds, the Holy Spirit will set apart some to the work of the apostles. These join the missionary order described below.

THE MISSION ORDER IS A COMMITTED COMMUNITY

Christians with deeper aspirations for the apostolic work should form themselves into a separate structure—a committed community. These communities have taken many forms in the Middle East—ranging from contemplative monasteries to special groups in parishes dedicated to mission and service. When these structures exist, a tangible witness develops.

The Protestant Church had almost no missionary activities for the first two hundred years of its existence. Latourette, the church historian, cites *the lack of these structures for the spiritually committed as a reason* for the inability of Protestants to evangelize non-Christians (Teague 1992:112).

The order exists *not* to nurture a congregation, but to evangelize strangers *beyond* the reach of the congregation. John Buteyn, for years the General Director of the Reformed Church of America mission, was thinking about this when he said,

> A smaller group of workers, with special commitment, might be more able to do new things, in some of those sensitive places, to be accountable without the backing of such a broad group as comprises the Reformed Church of America (1989).

John Buchanan, 1996–1997 General Assembly Moderator of the PCUSA, said,

> Maybe we in the PCUSA should think of ourselves as a mission society. What if we float the idea of a mission order dedicated to the urban poor? Maybe I'm dreaming but if we challenged Christians to join for three years to live among the poor, we would have a multitude of volunteers (Feb. 1, 1997).

In summary, there are two structures in God's redemptive mission: the congregational life for nurture and the committed community for mission.

ISLAM INTRODUCED A MISSION ORDER IN KURDISTAN

Kurds already have a mission order. Hundreds of years ago the Naqshibandi order arrived from India. This order is now "indigenous," that is, regarded as fully Kurdish. Significantly, Kurds accepted the foreign order, while they rejected the Hanafi sect of Islam. The subject is worth clarifying.

The Ottoman denomination of Islam, called Hanafi, failed to make headway among the Kurds in a trial of 400 years. Hanafi

Islam is heavily freighted with Turkish culture; Kurds, proud of their own culture, would never yield to an alien (though still Sunni) Islamic denomination. However, a mystical Islamic *tarika* (way), the Naqshibandi, made large gains among the Kurds. Even today, leaders of the Barzani tribe maintain their leadership partly by their status in the Naqshibandi brotherhood.[5]

Rapid expansion of the Naqshibandi occurred when it arrived in Mesopotamia from India. It took root; it indigenized. Kurds followed the path of the Naqshibandi *as Kurds, and invite other Kurds to join as well.* The missionary should think about the implications of this people movement to an order as he/she considers which structures cause the Kurdish church to reproduce.

Membership in the Naqshibandi order attracted leaders. The order was a place for men to prove themselves spiritually. The order was an attainment of a certain spiritual and mental height. In addition, the members were accountable to the teacher for learning their lessons.

The Naqshibandi order was a committed community whose influence exceeded its numbers. Van Bruinessen underscores "the rapid rise of one order [the Naqshibandi] in the past century and the prominent role it has played in the Kurdish nationalism since then" (1992:8).

Another order, the Qadiri, was founded by a famous saint, Shaikh Abdul Qadir al-Gilani (1077–1166). The Qadiri is a second example of a *tarika* that came to be accepted as perfectly orthodox; a descendant of the founder has always held, and still holds, the office of Primate of the order and keeper of the tomb in Baghdad (C. Edmonds 1957:63)

THE ORDER IS A PROVEN MEANS OF DISCIPLING

There is power, beyond numbers, in a minority of dedicated believers. Leadership in the churches in the Middle East rose from the mission orders. Remove the monasteries from the history of the Middle East, and the Christian presence evaporates like morning clouds in the desert:

---

[5] The Naqshibandi order was founded by Muhammad Behaud-Din of Bukhara (1317–89).

On both sides of the frontier between the empires [Byzantine and Persian] the spiritual life of the Christian churches was invigorated by communities of monks and nuns who trained novices for the priesthood and copied and recopied the manuscripts of sacred books for future generations. Monasteries and convents stretched from Deir az-Zafaran outside Mardin, through the highlands to the east known as the Tur Abdin—the mountain of the servants (of God)—to Mar Behnam, Mar Jonah (the prophet's reputed grave) and Mar Mattai on the left bank of the Tigris (Guest 1993:7).

Missionaries to Kurds should set up a teaching order. This order will have two levels of membership, the novitiate and the regular member. A teacher is responsible for the novitiates, who may be called *readers*. The Readers read the scriptures and memorize a catechism. After a time of testing, the Reader takes his or her place as a regular member. A *regula* or rule of the order must be obeyed. From the regular membership some are chosen as teachers.

All members of the order must work with their hands. Some will work to free the teachers to prepare lessons. The goal of the order is to make disciples. New disciples become Readers, and from this group some are chosen as regular members. All members, whether novitiates or regular members, are accountable to a person for matters of faith and practice. They are formed into cell groups of not more than ten members. This cell group meets every week; in addition, the cell group leader, a teacher from the regular membership, meets every month with each individual and will teach and pray for his or her cell group. For Christmas and Easter and certain occasions, the entire order meets for worship and festivities. Accountability to the rules of the order is in the cell group. Teachers meet together to discuss the problems in each cell group and to pray for their disciples. Congregations minister to the believers; mission orders work to evangelize the world.

Missionaries Should Make Disciples

The mission order is the place where the foreign worker does his or her main work, the work for which the Holy Spirit has set him apart. The foreign worker disciples faithful men and women to win others. This Biblical principle (2 Ti 2:2) will keep the worker on the right course. How many Kurds can the foreign worker expect to bring to faith in Jesus Christ? Precious few; the social distance is too great to cross for most Kurds. A few Kurds *will* come to faith through the missionary's work, and God *will enable these few to continue* in discipleship. Readers should be gathered into cell groups of the mission order. The medical doctor trains his apprentice in the discipline of the healing profession. The apprentice becomes a doctor. Likewise, the missionary must train the Readers. The medical mission in Kurdistan offers an example of this principle:

> By the middle of the 19th century it became evident that the foreign doctors alone could never meet the medical needs of the region. They had to share their expertise. Solitary doctors began to train assistants. At Sivas, during the 1860s and '70s, Dr. Henry West alone trained nineteen physicians and the Ottoman government asked him to judge the qualifications of other physicians in the area (Shepard 1970:2).

In the same way, the foreign workers must disciple local workers. The means of discipleship is the missionary order.

Prune the Branch That Bears No Fruit

The foreign worker whose mind is cleared to begin a mission order is not a minister to a congregation. The ministry to the congregation must be left to others. The congregation welcomes all manner of infirmed believers, many of whom do not have the inclination to read the scriptures, learn the catechism, obey the *regula*, and teach others. The ministry to all who come in the church doors must be left to pastors. Pastors have a calling to the congregational ministry.

To begin a mission order, the worker must forsake the believers who want to emigrate to the West. He must forsake the believers who are lazy or unteachable. The worker must be careful lest barren seed take his or her attention. He should work most closely with the ones who evangelize and disciple others.

Fruit that does not remain must not occupy the worker's time. The worker is not a minister to a congregation; he or she is an apostle, set apart for the work of church-planting. He teaches faithful men, and she, faithful women, who will then teach others. It will be necessary to push past some early friendships which demand one's time and energy, yet bear no fruit. The worker must concentrate on Kurds who continue as Readers, despite initial setbacks.

CHURCH-PLANTING MUST
MEAN MISSION-PLANTING

What is *church-planting*? Many missions affirm church-planting now. However, in using this term, we do not all mean the same thing. It is not enough to speak of *congregation*-planting. Church-planting missionaries should be *mission-planting* missionaries. A mission-planting missionary will begin a mission order that will have as its object the training of Kurdish missionaries. The order requires discipleship and accountability of its members; this will attract the finest men or women in the church. They will give themselves to the most important task in the world, the making of disciples. *The primary task of the missionary to Kurds is to teach disciples who will in turn teach other disciples.* This kind of reproduction occurs in the mission order.

THE MAKING OF GOOD MISSIONARIES
AMONG THE KURDS

Suppose that the missionary is freer to work in Kurdistan than were his or her predecessors a century ago, or even a decade ago. Might we suggest a certain level of preparation? I refer to the preparation of the mind. The heart devotion to Christ is a recognized requirement. But in addition, if one is free to work in Kurdistan among the Kurds, perhaps a thoughtful preparation could bring about an impossible dream: seeing the wonderful Kurdish people gathered as groups of believers, following the way of Jesus Christ their Lord. We may suggest that the worker consciously "put on" four articles of preparation: language learning, hospitality, Kurdish culture, and the sufferings of Christ.

PUT ON LANGUAGE LEARNING

Phil Parshall wrote, "It is the ultimate compliment to the Muslim to learn his language well" (1980:107). When the gospel comes to the Kurds, it must come in their own words. No mission task demands more energy than language learning.

Language Learning Takes a Plan

The worker will want a book, yet until now few resources exist for learning Kurdish. A basic course for learning Sorani is available from the University of Michigan (Abdulla and McCarus 1967). Programs for learning Turkish Kurdish are available in Germany.[6] The worker could learn through *Language Aptitude Made Practical* (LAMP) by Thomas and Betty Sue Brewster (1976); or Baran Rizgar's *Dersen Kurdi* (1996); also the *Ni Roj Language Learning Series* by Shireen (1996).

It Takes a Partner

Language learning requires a partner who will stay with you. Pay this person. You will attract many friends who are amazed that you want to learn their language, but volunteers will drift away. The language helper will come and force you to a certain level of study.

It Takes a Push

Language learning requires accountability to another person. When the worker plateaus, when he or she is tired, when he feels guilty, when he feels lazy, then he or she needs a push. Who can do such a job without being held accountable? Set goals and report to your "accountant" each week. Inch by inch, the language learner will progress.

It Takes Planned Neglect

The learner must plan to neglect other "priorities" which seem to demand his or her attention. Let them fail to succeed at language learning.

The reward for study and for practice is access to the heart: the student proves his or her love to the Kurds. Do other outsiders learn the Kurdish language? Not the Turks, nor the Persians, nor the Arabs in a thousand years. The United Nations worker

---

6   Orientdienst, Postfach 45 46, 65035 Wiesbaden, Germany.

does not learn Kurdish. Language learning is an act of love and understanding. The person who feels understood feels loved. The outsider who loves and understand is rare enough to be noticed.

Kurds speak of "linguicide" to describe the attempt by powers (Turkey, Iraq, Iran, Syria) to smother their language. Is it not for the sake of love that we should learn the language of oppressed peoples?

Lamin Sanneh of Ghana tells a story on himself, regarding the power of a missionary who learned the native language:

> After completing my Islamic studies in the Middle East in 1969 I went to Yorubaland in Nigeria as a lay worker with the Methodist Church. I was immediately taken to the local market to purchase some bare essentials for my flat. My companion was a senior English missionary who had spent many years in Ibadan and knew his way around. He translated for me as we did the round of market stalls, with the stallkeepers' curiosity naturally aroused by the missionary, in their eyes a stranger from beyond the stars.
>
> Before we had picked our way through the market, a small crowd had gathered to marvel at the sight of a white man translating for an African in an African language. It was as if we had got our arrangement wrong and put the Western cart before the African horse. *The image of "total stranger" the stallkeepers had of the Western missionary was completely belied by this exposure* (1987:333, italics mine).

To enter the culture, learn to speak and listen in the language of the people, Kurdish. When the gospel comes to the Kurds, it will come in the heart language of the people.

PUT ON HOSPITALITY

Abraham entertained three visitors with a feast (Gen 18:1–15); it sounds like the hospitality of Kurds. The guest is the honor of the house, the family, the tribe. Even political parties have special guest houses in the major cities of northern Iraq, where the tribal chief, *in absentia*, can welcome you, and where his loyal minions wait to make you coffee.

In the past, it was the agha who maintained the guest house. "Since the agha represents his people to the outer world, his treatment of foreigners is the honour of the village" (van Bruinessen 1992:81). However, the village guest houses (*mehvan khane* or *diwan khane*) have lapsed into decay as the economic dependency of the village on the agha lessens. The mechanization of agriculture in the 1950s and 1960s "made the aghas less dependent on the villagers' labour" (1992:84). Yet, hospitality remains a virtue in the Kurdish home. A foreign visitor will have to pray for strength to maintain the social schedule that it will be his or her privilege to keep. Especially a married couple will be entertained a great deal (Kurds may regard single foreign women as honorary males). Woe to the foreigner whose energy runs out and the knock comes on the door after the dinner is cleared, and here is a guest. Nowhere is the clash of east and west more apparent than in the use of time: the westerner has something to *do*, and that is *business*; the Kurd has something to *be*, and that is a *guest* or a *host*. The westerner stands perplexed when his best Kurdish friend is jealous of any time spent with other Kurds. Hospitality gone sour can be possessive.

PUT ON CHRIST'S GOOD WORKS

"Jesus went about doing good" (Ac 10:38). He commanded the same of His followers, "that men might see your good works and give glory to the Father" (Mt 5:16). Missionaries in Kurdistan combined medicine with their message. It is a lesson to follow. Today's workers should bring medical healing to Kurds, as did the missionaries before us. To be sure, the day of missionary hospitals is over. Government hospitals have replaced them. However, beyond the reach of the government hospitals are multitudes of sick people. The afflicted are like Jesus Christ to those who find Him among the sick.

Visit the prisoners. Prisoners are rejected, neglected, and sick. Christ is in the prison with them. Be certain that the missionary must follow Him there.

"Honor all men." Kurds, like lost people everywhere, honor persons of higher status and, correspondingly, dishonor those lower than themselves. Someone will work until another person, below him or her, arrives; then the first worker sits and directs the second to work. Confound the system. Honor all people. However, sometimes the outsider must sit in the place of honor because he or she is the guest; this is also a duty. There will be many opportunities to honor the least, and thus follow the One who is servant of all.

Teach the children. Kurdish children are at the bottom of a grinding system. Kurdish girls are beneath Kurdish boys. Pay attention to the children. They are not change-agents in the society, so children cannot help you reach your goals. The kingdom of God, upside down from the world, values the overlooked, underfed, and disregarded youth.

PUT ON KURDISH CULTURE

It was Donald McGavran, I believe, who emphasized language learning as the chief aspect of culture. If one is learning the language, he or she is more than half way into the secret knowledge of a people. However, the worker will want to care for other parts of Kurdish culture as well.

Music and Dance

Kurds, in contrast to the Arabs, have no tradition of calligraphy. This, along with the "prohibition of figural image in Islamic art" (Haddad, et al. 1984:137) has evoked certain Kurdish art forms, namely, music and dance, story and proverb. Three days of dancing usually accompanies Kurdish weddings. A special caste of musician plays the drum and horn (*dohoul* and *zarna*). The mullah may scorn the wedding celebration, saying that dancing encourages women to mingle with men. However, the people pay no attention, unless they have a mullah in their family. Singles mingle with one another at weddings. The instinct is basic.

Middle Eastern people sing their love and their lament. The singer takes his hearers up to the stars and down to the depths of misery. By music he or she takes them back to the village of their youth. Kurdish music will be a means of telling the gospel story. Kurds are poets, and they themselves will write, sing, and listen to Bible stories set to music.

Foreign workers should resist translating their choruses and hymns into Kurdish. However, an ethnomusicologist should sift through the Kurdish music and find those forms of prose, poetry and dance that will convey the gospel.

Stories and Proverbs

A foreigner who learns local stories and proverbs will delight his or her Kurdish friends. A notebook and pencil will unlock the doors leading to Kurdish thoughts and feelings about friends, loyalty, enemies, generosity, suffering, hypocrisy, minorities, mercy, injustice, power, women, and, in short, their entire worldview.

Marxists proved the power of dramatic presentation in moving the Kurds to a new worldview:

> It was in 1945 that the Komala [Kurdish Communist Party] finally came into the open [in Iran]. The Soviet Consul from Rezayeh was an honored guest. The main feature of the programme was an "opera" in which a woman called Daik Nishteman (Mother Native Land) was represented as abused by three ruffians, "Iraq," "Iran," and "Turkey," finally to be rescued by her stalwart sons. The audience, unused to dramatic representations, was deeply moved, and blood-feuds generations old were composed as life-long enemies fell weeping on each other's shoulder and swore to avenge Kurdistan (Chaliand et al. 1993:125–126).

The *Jesus* Film in Kurdish has proven a powerful communicator of the life of Christ. When we translated a brief summary of Don Richardson's *Peace Child* (1974) story into Bahdini Kurdish, the effect on the listeners was immediate and profound.

Kurdish Clothing

Workers should adapt to Kurdish dress when appropriate. No one else from the outside—not Turks, Arabs, Persians, or United Nations workers—wears Kurdish clothing. This small effort will net a good response from friends.

Margaret Kahn, who lived in Kurdish Iran during the late 1970s, describes women's clothing as "something of a fortress—layer upon layer, with heavy pantaloons, a slip, several dresses, an overcoat, a vest, and several scarves, even on hot summer days" (1980:3–4). Chaliand describes the Kurdish man's clothing in Iran; it consists

> of a tasselled turban of blue silk, embroidered vest, baggy grey pants of homespun wool, and a huge crimson cumberbund, intricately knotted in front, from which protrudes a pipe, the top of a tobacco pouch, and a long curved dagger. The Kurds, like Iranians

forced to abandon their native dress by Reza Shah, kept their clothes hidden in their homes, a symbol of their national pride, until the Allied invasion, when they suddenly blossomed out in them. The Kurds are incorrigible dandies and a poor man among them would rather spend his last coins on fine clothes than on a good kebab. Reza Shah's restrictions on their dress had served to make him and his regime all the more hated (Chaliand 1980:151).

Kurdish clothing is the wrapping of their national identity. In Iraq, Kurdish friends will invite the missionary to wear Kurdish clothes.

Kurdish Carpets

The design in Kurdish carpets—and in the various lace and embroidery work of women—may have once held symbols of the search for God. The symbolic meaning, if it was ever deliberate, is now forgotten.

PUT ON THE SUFFERINGS OF CHRIST

What the Kurds suffer, missionaries may suffer. Are missionaries willing to pay that price? The price is not only disease, danger, rickety housing, lack of privacy, guns, cigarette smoke, sameness of food, primitive toilets, and homesickness. Nor is the suffering limited to the brute effort by which all work is done, although this will drive the western person to the brink of madness. There being no sense of the public good, the neighbor tosses her garbage in the empty lot. Miseries which can be prevented persist; "no revolution, no evolution in the Middle East," to borrow Father Henry Ayrout's phrase (Bailey 1976:31).

THE DIFFICULT FAMILY LIFE IN KURDISTAN

Missionaries who have families will suffer in Kurdistan. Frederick Coan recalled his lonely missionary childhood in Kurdistan. He felt deprived of "a sufficient number of playmates to enable him to fit in easily to the social life of American schools and colleges." However, there were compensations as well for the young boy or girl:

He enjoys many unusual opportunities. Living in a foreign land and traveling back and forth with his parents he learns to know different countries and peoples, gaining thereby a far wider vision of the world and more tolerant attitude than the ordinary child at home. There is, for one thing, the association with none but people of high ideals, earnest deep purpose, education, and refinement. His reading matter is of the best (F. Coan 1939:14).

MUST KURDS BECOME CHRISTIANS IN ADDITION TO FOLLOWING JESUS?

Must the missionary want Kurds to call themselves *Christians?* Must Kurds do more than Peter and Andrew, who followed Jesus but never became Christians? The word "Christian" carries a foreign meaning in Islamic culture. The trajectory for a people movement begins with this question. If we will see thousands and tens of thousands of Kurds follow Christ, they must feel able to *follow Him as Kurds*, without becoming Chaldeans, Assyrians, or American evangelicals. What does the New Testament call the people who follow Jesus?

NEW TESTAMENT BELIEVERS USUALLY DID NOT BECOME "CHRISTIANS"

The New Testament apostles did not require the followers of Jesus to become *Christians*; other designations satisfied the New Testament writers. For example, the Lord's servants (Lk 1:38), the believers (Ac 1:15), children of Abraham (Ac 13:26), followers of the Way (Ac 9:2), disciples, and followers of Jesus. These names suggest that the New Testament uses some terms interchangeably to describe Christians.[7] When a Kurd hears "Christian neighborhood" or a "Christian village," he or she hears "foreign, off limits, no trespassing." When he or she hears the word "Christian" he may even hear "infidel," "dirty person."[8] In

---

7 We are not raising a credal issue of what constitutes the "faith once delivered to the saints" (Jude 3). However, we suggest that the New Testament offers a choice of terms to describe the person who follows Jesus Christ.

8 In June 1995 burglars entered my home while I and the family were away. One wrote on the wall and on the door, "Death to the missionary who makes Kurds to become Christians." I felt like a failure since the burglars did not realize they could follow Jesus without applying the foreign word "Christian" to themselves.

the Kurdish worldview 1) missionaries should not make Kurds into Christians; and 2) Kurds who become Christians are betraying their people; such a Kurd would be an infidel.

Shall we require Kurds, in addition to following Jesus in obedience (the scandal of the cross that every believer must accept) *but also* to be banished by his or her family and community? Few Kurds pace the floor at night, pondering whether faith requires that they be banished; however, most Kurds admire Jesus. Many wish they could follow Him. The title "Christian" is like the title "circumcised" in the early church; it is not necessary for Gentiles who follow Jesus.

WERE GENTILES CALLED JEWS WHEN THEY FOLLOWED JESUS?

Paul knew that it was not necessary for Gentiles (*ethné*) to become Jews. He was emphatic that the ethné *not* become Jews. The crisis that hastened the Jerusalem Council was what to call these new Gentile followers. Were they Jews? Were they second-class believers? Paul argued that Gentile followers were the new men and the new women. They were Followers of the Way, sons and daughters of Abraham by faith, grafted on to the tree of Israel. But they were not circumcised, and they were not Jews. At last the council decided with Paul, "Let's not make it difficult for the *ethné* who are turning to God" (Ac 15:19).

Some readers may feel anxious to move on to more important points. The worry about what to call new believers is frivolous, he or she may feel. However, when the persecution comes, and Muslims hurl threats and insults and in every way shake apart the pillars on which the believer perches, he or she must know that he belongs to Christ. When enemies say to the Kurdish believer that he or she should go live with the Assyrians or Armenians or Americans, that Kurd must know that he belongs to Christ by faith alone, not faith plus leaving the Kurdish culture. The Kurd who feels the sting of rejection because he or she has followed Jesus must believe that he or she is still a Kurd. He did not become an American; he did not become a Chaldean; the Kurdish believer did not lose his or her identity. "I am a Kurd, I follow Jesus Christ, as you can too." If we expect thousands of Kurds to follow Jesus into new life, they must come by faith alone when they hear, "Follow Me, and I will make you fishers of men." In this way Kurds follow the Way of the New Testament.

In Antioch they were first called Christians, but this word (*falah* in Kurdish) is chained to a meaning in Kurdish that makes it undesirable. Give up the word. The book of Acts suggest that the more normal term for believers was Followers of the Way.

Followers of the Way

The Book of Acts repeatedly uses "the Way" to describe the church:

Acts 9:2—If Paul found any there [in Damascus] who belonged to the Way, whether men or women, he might take them as prisoners to Jerusalem.

19:9—But some of them became obstinate; they refused to believe and publicly maligned the Way.

19:23—About that time there arose a great disturbance about the Way.

22:4—[Paul speaking] I persecuted the followers of this Way to their death, arresting both men and women and throwing them into prison.

24:14—[Paul speaking] I admit that I worship the God of our fathers as a follower of the Way, which they call a sect.

24:22—Then Felix, who was well acquainted with the Way, adjourned the proceedings.

In the early church the Jews and Gentiles followed the Way together. The Way was a neutral term that believing men and women could apply to themselves while remaining Jews or non-Jews. I suggest such a term for workers among Kurds. (One Kurdish believer calls himself a Holy Spirit Muslim.) Calling oneself by a neutral term will not prevent persecution (four of six references above prove that members of the Way suffered for their faith). A neutral term permits Kurds to consider Jesus Christ as Lord while remaining in their culture. We must "not make it difficult for the *ethné* who are turning to God" (Ac 15:19), then we must permit Kurds to turn to God without also requiring them to become circumcised Jews (i.e., *falah* Christians).

May Kurds Follow the Jesus Way as Muslims?

Thousands of Kurds would follow Jesus if they did not fear that they would be outcast from the Muslim community. Might Kurds reject the Islam of Muhammad (as they must do as followers of Jesus) and remain *Muslims*? Islam already has two meanings to Kurds in Iraq. First, Islam is "what we all believe," meaning the Muhammadan religion. Second, Islam is the severe doctrine of the fundamentalists. The second is a serious commitment of its men and women to coerce the rest of the Kurds into strict observance of shariah law. However, Islam has an etymological meaning: submission to Allah.[9] In his submission, Abraham was a Muslim. So were Noah, Esther, Ruth and David. Kurds who submit as Abraham should remain Muslims. Kurds who follow the Way are Muslims in this meaning of the word. The word Islam cannot be surrendered to Muhammadans.

Naqshibandi brotherhoods "were independent of the formalized Muslims institutions of the state" (McDowall 1996:50). The community of Muslim-background believers may form a brotherhood (order) which is independent in this same way. For the sake of community relations some Islamic terms may be used with new meaning by the believers.

Many Kurds are finished with the religion of Muhammad; it no longer holds them in its sway. Fourteen centuries of bowing to Arab holy places and praying in Arabic has lost its appeal to many Kurds. Many Kurds left faith for secularism or atheism. For some, this atheism is a major step toward belief in Christ. They must first discard the old wineskin. Then, after a period, these Kurds can consider the new wine.

Many Kurds are not finished with the word *Islam*. They did not even leave Islam when the Islamic government of Iraq persecuted them. Saddam Hussein, who added the words *Allahu Akbar* (God is the greatest) to the Iraqi flag after invading Kuwait in 1990, is widely viewed by Kurds in northern Iraq as a bad Muslim. Saddam Hussein invoked the Qur'an when he

---

[9] See Qur'an 2:112/106; 3:64/57. "Muslim" is also used in the Qur'an to describe Jesus' disciples (5:111, 112)

ordered the *anfal* (permission to plunder) against the Kurds from 1986–1989, a permission that Islam reserves against unbelievers. Did the Kurds renounce the religion that killed them? Even persons whose homes were destroyed five times in the last decade, even families whose dead and missing are victims of Saddam Hussein's war with Iran, have not renounced the religion of Muhammad.[10]

Kurds in northern Iraq reject all things *Arab*. That may lead to a break with Muhammad. A new meaning of Islam (following Jesus) may interest some who want to remain Muslims. However, the new meaning of Islam will not attract the Kurds who have turned their back on Islam.[11]

THE GOSPEL, NOT NATIONALISM

The missionary should teach Christ, not Kurdish nationalism. Nationalism was the false gospel of some early missionaries in Syria and Lebanon. They, failing to evangelize the Arabs, began to teach a dignity based on the pride of Arab nationhood. Nationalism is a cult in the Arab world today. The wheat of nationhood and the chaff of pompous ethnic pride are baked together in the bread of Middle East nationalism. It is a false gospel.

WHAT THE GOSPEL REQUIRES OF KURDS

When the gospel comes to Kurds, it must come with power to bless "all the families of the world." The gospel must take hold of men and women as it took hold of Abraham, when "God announced the gospel to him in advance, saying, 'All nations [*panta ta ethné*] will be blessed through you'" (Gal 3:8).

---

10 In 1991, one Kurdish woman said to my wife, "All of my family [in Sulaimania] have taken your religion; they do not want the religion of Saddam. My sister has hung a picture of Jesus and Mary on the wall. And all of their neighbors have done the same." This occurred apart from any contact with Christians.

11 According to this view, the etymological root of the Islam—submission to God—is preserved, while the imperial meaning of Islam—submitting to Arabization—is pitched overboard.

THE GOSPEL CALLS KURDS
TO LOVE THEIR ENEMIES

The gospel among Kurds must evoke love for their enemies; otherwise, it is not the gospel. A more fractious society than the Kurds can hardly be found on the planet. Sadly, they are bound by ancient chains that their fathers wore before them: the cursed manacles of the blood feud. Christ's words and His love are the good news that will rescue the Kurds:

> Love your enemies and pray for those who persecute you, that you may be sons of your Father in heaven. . . . If you love those who love you, what reward will you get? Are not even the tax collectors doing that? And if you greet only your brothers, what are you doing more than others? Do not even pagans do that? (Mt 5:43–47).

This is no small hope. I remember at Kurdish picnics in California, which brought together Kurds from different Middle Eastern countries, that some Kurds of Iraq would not mingle or befriend some Kurds from Iran. This was partly because the political alignment, if it can be described at all, looks like this:

Iraqi Government + Iraqi Kurds + Iranian Kurds

vs.

Iranian Government + Iraqi Kurds

vs.

Turkish Government + Iraqi Kurds

vs.

Syrian Government + Turkish Kurds

vs.

shifting alliances among governments and tribes

Kurds reserve their most exquisite hatred for rival Kurds who fight against them. For example, the Iraqi government pays Kurdish tribes to fight against Kurdish insurrectionists. The anti-government *pesh merga* Kurds mockingly refer to the mercenary Kurdish tribes as *jash* (young donkeys); *jash* forces

> were mostly recruited from among the large tribes and operated under their own tribal chieftains. . . . The tribal jash had no political motivations, and several had in the past *repeatedly changed sides from the government to the insurgents and vice versa* (van Bruinessen 1992:40, italics mine).

When the gospel comes to the Kurds, it must cause men and women to love their enemies in tangible ways: putting away the sword, breaking bread with all, and calling on all to follow Christ.

THE GOSPEL CALLS KURDS
TO A WORLDWIDE CHURCH

The Islam of the Arabs has failed to include Kurds in its worldwide fellowship. Accordingly, many Kurds reject Muhammad's Islam today. Kurds are open to a new worldwide fellowship; they tried to organize as Communists in Iran, in Iraq, and in Turkey. But communism did not reconcile Kurds with one another, and it denied the very God whom they know in their hearts. More than ever, Jesus Christ offers to Kurds their place in holy fellowship under God. Writing in the third century, Bardesanes of Edessa (now Sanliurfa in Kurdistan of Turkey) did not feel himself to be the leader of a sect; rather, he belonged to the universal Church:

> What shall we say about ourselves, the "new race" of Christians whom Christ has caused to be raised in all countries as a consequence of his own coming? We are all Christians by the one name of Christ wherever we may be found (Joseph 1961:19).

Bardesanes proceeds to speak of the brethren in Gaul, Parthia, India, Persia, and Mesopotamia without making any distinction (1961:19). This "new race" of humanity is superior to nationalism, which is based on false pride and allows no criticism of the group. When the gospel comes to the Kurds, it must bring them to belong to the one international fellowship of Jesus Christ. That fellowship will allow confession to one another, which creates a fellowship of forgiven sinners.

THE GOSPEL CALLS KURDS TO MAKE PEACE

Paul's missionary role was to proclaim Christ, the Man who would speak to God on our behalf: "God our Savior wants all men to be saved and to come to a knowledge of the truth. For there is one God and one mediator between God and men, the man Christ Jesus, who gave himself as a ransom for all men" (1 Ti 3b-5).

Well-known in the Middle East is the importance of mediators in making peace between hostile factions. Only a worthy go-between can negotiate a settlement in a dispute. Sometimes the worthy can prevent death, sometimes war, or, having once begun, war can be halted by his influence. His sense of fairness, and his persistence make him or her a highly respected person. Van Bruinessen writes of the Kurds that

> A peaceful end to the conflict is not spontaneously reached; it is the result of mediation by an influential person. The threatened party takes recourse to someone whose authority it knows or expects to be acknowledged by those from whom it expects a revenge attack. . . . The higher the level of confrontation between feuding units, the more difficult it will be to find an acceptable (or sufficiently powerful) mediator. . . . "Chiefs are many, but rare is the chief to whom (other) chiefs listen," says a proverb from northern Kurdistan (1992:68).

When the gospel comes to the Kurds, it must prove that Christ Himself is the peacemaker for a fragmented humankind.

HOW THE MISSIONARY KNOWS
WHEN THE TASK IS FINISHED

A great and distant goal focuses all of our energy in one direction. The goal, as Nevius set for missionary work in China, is a church that is self-governed, self-financed, and self-propagated (Nevius 1895). From its beginning, only Kurds can lead and finance such a church. Roland Allen, also a missionary in China, helps us to understand how from its beginning the missionary work must set the local church on its road to independence:

> Many years ago my experience in China taught me that if our object was to establish in that country a church which might spread over the six provinces which then formed the diocese of North China, that object could only be attained if the first Christians who were converted by our labours understood clearly that they could, by themselves, without any further assistance from us, not only convert their neighbors, but establish churches. That means that the very first groups of converts must be so fully equipped with all spiritual authority that they could *multiply themselves without any necessary reference to us*: that, though, while we were there, they might regard us as helpful advisers, yet our removal should not at all mutilate the completeness of the

church, or deprive it of anything necessary for its unlimited expansion (1962:1, italics mine).

Roland Allen was a member of a missionary order, the Society for the Propagation of the Gospel (SPG) of the Anglican Church. From its beginning, mission orders enable committed Christians to attain the principles of self-reliance and expansion.

THE CHURCH IS SELF-GOVERNED

Paul's method was to appoint local leaders for the churches. The Holy Spirit chose local teachers, evangelists, pastors, administrators, and deacons. Many books teach the spiritual gifts, so we do not need to dwell on the subject here.

The church that governs itself must also discipline its own members. The missionary lives a holy life, and demands holy living from the new church. Very soon the new believers should examine one another, to see if they are in the faith.

Many "one another" texts direct the church to govern itself: Love one another; Forgive one another; Encourage one another; Care for one another; Bear one another's burdens; Be useful and kind to one another; Serve one another; Watch over one another; Admonish one another; Confess to one another; Pray for one another; Be hospitable to one another; Comfort one another.

Other texts begin with "do not": Do not complain against one another; Do not speak against one another; Do not hate one another; Do not lie to one another; Do not challenge and envy one another; Do not consume one another. When the gospel comes to the Kurds, they must govern themselves in the way of Christ as directed in these passages.

THE CHURCH IS SELF-FINANCED

What more intractable problem hinders the growth of the developing church than its dependence on foreign money? From its beginning, the worker and church leaders must plan to fund the church with money that is in the country. This might be what Mrs. Shepard of Aintab had in mind, when she withdrew from medical work in 1893 in order to devote herself to her family "and the extensive lace and handwork industry which had developed" (A. Edmonds 1979:6). She had begun an enterprise that the church women could continue. The strings that tied the local church to the missionary money would thus be loosened.

The need for money in the Third World church seems as great as food itself. How shall the church arrange itself—a place of worship, a custodian, simple furnishings, and then the salaries? Shall the missionary open his pockets to supply the church's needs? The missionary may hope that in the future the local church will stand on its own feet. Yet the results are depressing. Writes Roland Allen,

> Nothing is so weakening as the habit of depending upon others for those things which we ought to supply for ourselves. Nothing more undermines the spirit which should express itself in spontaneous activity. How can a man propagate a religion which he cannot support, and which he cannot expect those whom he addresses to be able to support? (1962:35).

The missionary may despair of any good solution. At his door are poor converts or inquirers; they tell him or her that their faith in Christ has guaranteed their poverty, as they cannot find work. They may further say that the New Testament obliges the one with means to help the poor. So the missionary is inclined to supply foreign capital, and pray that the church grows more independent in the following generation. Can a source from the outside generate a source of continuing supply? There may be a way, and we turn to consider it below.

A Plan for Self-Financing of the Local Church

The mission order should start a business. The object of business is to make money. The object of making this money is to provide for the members of the mission order and for charity. A mission order that runs a business builds its capacity to grow.

The Order Should Start a Business

Kurds in northern Iraq have a proverb, "A man who does not work shall not eat." Real work needs to be done in exchange for food. When a man or woman joins the mission order, he or she goes to work. He joins not only a teaching community but a working community. That is the historic method of the monastery. That is the legacy that the Church of the East leaves for us today. The mission order supports itself; it never depends on the outside for money; nor does it depend on the congregation of the local church. Its members go to work. I think the missionary can help by helping the mission order to develop a business plan. The missionary can supply the start-up costs. This means that initial money comes from the outside. However, no continuing source of outside funding should be provided.

A Business Ends Dependence on the Outsider

From its start, the business belongs to the members of the missionary order. Business generates money for the members of the mission order. The practice of tithing also comes with business. From the business, local believers move towards equal footing with the missionaries. Accordingly the business-owning national can argue with the missionary as a fellow adult.

THE CHURCH IS SELF-PROPAGATING

The missionary desires a Kurdish church that reproduces new members. Kurds will evangelize Kurds. First, the missionary should show that he or she talks daily of faith to unbelievers. Second, he or she must disciple believers who will disciple others. Pray with the believers that they might have fruit, for this was Christ's prayer. The church will increase by adding new numbers; it should also have in mind the forming of new churches.

"RESENTMENT OF SUPERINTENDING MISSIONARIES"

The reader should not fault us here, in emphasizing self-finance, self-governing, and self-propagation, as if we meant that the local church should not rely upon Divine Providence. The local church should grow up, the same as its missionary parent. Once an adult, the local church should expect to enter a new and permanent relationship with the church everywhere in the world, based on partnership. This partnership, or interdependence, means cooperation between the missionary church and daughter church in the work of mission to the world.

Trust the young church to make its own government, financing, and growth. Roland Allen points the way:

If the first groups of native Christians are not fully organized churches which can multiply themselves, but must wait upon a foreign bishop to move, they are in bondage. . . . Sooner or later they must awake and then I do not see how they can fail to feel resentment. If I were an Indian, or a Chinese, or an African, *I should resent most bitterly the attempt to establish the Faith in my country by men who took it for granted that they must control and direct our spiritual life and progress.* I should resent most bitterly the domination of foreign bishops and superintending missionaries (1962:2, italics mine).

Appendix A

Nestorian, Chaldean, Assyrian, and Syriac

These four—Nestorian, Chaldean, Syriac, and Assyrian—all refer to the Church of the East. However, in using these four terms for the Church of the East, they do not all mean the same thing. The great scholar on this subject is John Joseph. We will rely on his book, *The Nestorians and their Muslim Neighbors* (1961). In this Appendix we will present only his conclusions; students who wish to hear his proofs should read the book.

THE NESTORIANS

The Church of the East was called Nestorian by outsiders. However, it was founded earlier than Nestorius, the 5th century patriarch of Constantinople. For Nestorius, Mary was the Mother of Christ, not the mother of God [*thcotokos*]. For this he was excommunicated. The Church of the East refused to recognize the excommunication of Nestorius, and the Persian rulers protected his adherents as they fled the Greek Orthodox cities. For these reasons the Church of the East became known in the West as the Nestorian Church. Many centuries later (12th or 13th century) the Church of the East called itself Nestorian.

THE CHALDEANS

The Church of the East was called Chaldean because its headquarters was situated in ancient Chaldea. The Chaldean

Christians are not the same people as the ancient Chaldeans (who spoke Akkadian). All suggestions that the Chaldeans today are descended from the ancient Chaldeans should be doubted. It was "because of the geographic location of their patriarchate that the East Syrians or Nestorians were called Chaldeans and not because of their ethnic origin" (Joseph 1961:8).

When the Roman Catholics won back a large portion of the Church of the East (in the 15th century but most successfully in the 17th century), the Pope forbade the title "Nestorian" for his Catholic subjects from that church. The title "Chaldean" came to mean those members of the Church of the East who entered the Catholic fold. The remaining (non-Catholic) members of the Church of the East dropped the name Chaldean.

THE ASSYRIANS

The Anglican missionaries in 1842 gave the name Assyrian to the remaining Church of the East that did not become Roman Catholic. Most Protestant missionaries worked among the Assyrians. All suggestions that the modern Assyrians are related to the ancient Assyrians (evidence supposedly based on physical resemblance and language) have been disproved.

THE SYRIAN ORTHODOX

Various rival heirs to the original Church of Antioch claim the title of Syrian Orthodox. Besides the Nestorians, "several different bodies of Christians—Jacobites, Maronites, Syrian and Chaldean Uniates, and the Church of St. Thomas in Malabar—call themselves Syrian, the term being nearly equivalent to 'Orthodox Christians'" (Joseph 1961:11). No church wants to surrender orthodoxy (the connection to the Church of Antioch) to a rival. Westerners who do not feel part of this rivalry "can take 'Syrian' to mean simply Christians who use or have used Syriac [Aramaic] in their liturgical services or as a vernacular" (1961:12). All the Churches of the East use Aramaic in their liturgical services, as do the other bodies mentioned here.

The Syrian Church people are not related to the Assyrian people of old. In Aramaic, "the two words [Syrian—Suryaya and Assyrian—Aturaya] are of completely different origin" (1961:12).

THE JACOBITE CHURCH

Jacob Baradeus organized a reform movement in the Syrian Church. It became known as the Jacobite Church. Cell groups existed throughout Anatolia, Mesopotamia, Syria, and Egypt. Jacob and his followers were condemned by the Byzantines and the Nestorians alike. Jacobite churches and monasteries can still be found in Kurdistan.

Appendix B

An Assyrian Liturgy
from the 19th Century

E. L. Cutts of the Anglican Church translated the Assyrian liturgy. The following portion is one of the morning praises. Where the text says "1st" and "2nd," the choir chants antiphonally:

Semi-choir:

1st: At the dawn of the day we praise Thee, O Lord: Thou art the Redeemer of all creatures, give us by Thy mercy a peaceful day, and give us remission of our sins.

2nd: Do not cut off our hope, shut not Thy door against our faces, and cease not thy care over us. O God, according to our worthiness reward us not. Thou alone knowest our weakness.

1st: Scatter, O Lord, in the world love, peace, and unity. Raise up righteous kings, priests, and judges. Give peace to the nations, heal the sick, keep the whole, and forgive the sins of all men.

2nd: In the way that we are going may Thy Grace keep us, O Lord, as it kept the child David from Saul. Give us thy mercy as we are pressing on, that we may attain to peace according to Thy will. The Grace which kept the prophet Moses in the sea, and Daniel in the pit, and by which the companions of Ananias were kept in the fire, by that Grace deliver us from evil.

Whole choir:

In the morning we all arise, we all worship the Father, we praise the Son, we acknowledge the Holy spirit. The grace of the

Father, the mercy of the Son, and the hovering of the Holy Spirit, the Third Person, be our help every day. Our help is in Thee. In Thee, our true Physician, is our hope. Put the medicine of thy mercy on our wounds, and bind up our bruises that we be not lost. Without thy help we are powerless to keep thy commandments. O Christ, who helpest those who fulfill thy will, keep Thy worshipers. We ask with sighing, we beseech Thy mercy, we ask forgiveness from that merciful One who opens His door to all who turn unto Him. Every day I promise Thee that tomorrow I will repent; all my days are past and gone, my faults still remain. O Christ, have mercy upon me, have mercy upon me (Bird 1891:269–270).

Appendix C

Translations of Scripture into Kurdish

Missionaries and Kurds have put their pen to Kurdish Bible translations for more than 160 years. Here is a chronicle of their efforts. Wycliffe Bible Translators made the basic compilation. Comments by Gardiner come from his personal recollections. Additional comments come from a source who asked to remain anonymous.

Kurmanji Translations from the 19th Century
1827: Hakkari-Kurdish Bible portions
An Armenian Uniate (Catholic) Bishop, named Schevris, employed Mullah Mohammed, a Kurd from Urumia, to translate into Kurmanji from an Arabic Bible. However, when it became known that a translation was being done, the Kurd had to flee and even the bishop was threatened. Several revisions of this translation followed. Hoernle mentioned however that Kurds living in Hakkari could not understand it (anonymous source).

1856: *St. Matthew's Gospel* (Constantinople)—16.5 + 11 cm 112 pages[1]
Translated by an Armenian of Haineh, named Stephen, whom American missionaries employed in Diyarbakir. This gospel was written in the Kurmanji dialect as spoken at Kharput; being primarily designed for the Kurdish-speaking Armenians, it was in Armenian characters. Published by the British Foreign Bible

---

[1] In this and succeeding references, the book size is mentioned.

Society (BFBS) in Constantinople on the recommendation of W. Goodell of the ABCFM.

1857: *The Gospels* (BFBS)— 18 + 10 cm 398 pages
By the same translator mentioned above.

1872: *The New Testament* (ABS, Constantinople)—19.5 + 13 cm 624 pages, followed by a list of errata.

In this edition of the New Testament the Gospels were reprinted from the 1857 edition, while the other books were translated apparently by an Armenian under the direction of J. G. Bliss, the American Bible Society (ABS) agent in the Levant.

According to Marcellus Bowen, a later ABS agent for the Levant, this version was intended for Armenians in that part of Kurdistan which extends from Marash to Kharput and Diyarbakir and beyond towards Urumia. "It was, I suppose, mainly in the Koormanj dialect, but it became so mixed with Zaza and other dialects as to be almost useless" (letter from Bowen, 7 June 1913).

Comments Gardiner, probably about this translation, "Armenians I have showed the work to could spell out the words but no Kurds now exist who can read Armenian script" (1982:5).

The written history of the LOMS refers to a poor translation that may be this one:

> Another attempt of the same sort gave a portion of the New Testament in Assyrian character in one of the dialects in the neighborhood of Urumia and a third in the dialect used in the vicinity of Diyarbakir either in Armenian or Syrian character. Its usefulness was limited. . . . An attempt was made some years ago which resulted in the four Gospels in a mixture of dialects used in Kermanshah. The translating was done by a Persian who, though making an awkward attempt to have it in Kurdish idiom, succeeded in making it more Persian than Kurdish (Jensen and Oberg 1985:6).

1891: *The New Testament*

This was a fresh Kurdish translation made by Armenian pastors in the neighborhood of Kharput, under the direction of

American missionaries. Two editions were intended, one in Armenian character and the other in Arabic, but only that in Armenian character was published.

Kurmanji Dialect Translation in the 20th Century

American and English missionaries have translated portions of the New Testament into several Kurdish dialects, but "these translations in so far as they have been printed at all, have been printed for the most part in Armenian letters, unintelligible to the majority of the uncultured clans" (Richter 1910:325–6).

When the Lutherans accepted the challenge of working directly with the Kurds, they noted the need for a new Scripture translation:

> A very few inadequate attempts have been made to put the Gospel into the language of the Kurds. The best of these is the New Testament in Armenian character in one of the dialects of northern Kurdistan about Mush [1881?], done in the earlier days of mission to the Armenians when there was still hope that the old church would rise to its privilege (Jensen and Oberg 1985:6, quoting Blanche Wilson Stead's *Kurdistan for Christ*, 1920).

1911: *St. Matthew's Gospel* (ABS, Constantinople)—13.5 + 9 cm, 148 pages

1911: *St. Mark's Gospel* (ABS, Constantinople)—13.5 + 9.5 cm 87 pages. Uniform with the above

1911: *St. Luke's Gospel*—Uniform with the above

1911: *St. John's Gospel*—Uniform with the above

1911: *The Acts*—Uniform with the above

Lost Manuscript of *Luke*

Fossum supervised a translation of Luke before the First World War, but the manuscript "was lost in crossing a river when the translator was fleeing to the mountains with the whole of his village at the approach of the Russians. Thus Kurdistan remains practically without the Word of God in her own tongue" (Jensen and Oberg 1985:7).

1919: *The Gospels* (BFBS, and ABS, New York)—18.5 + 13 cm, 306 pages

Translated by L. O. Fossum, of the LOMS, with the assistance of two Kurds and a converted Jew. The above-mentioned translation of St. Mark's Gospel was revised and incorporated in this translation of the Gospels.

Each Gospel was also issued as a separate portion: Matthew, 87 pages; Mark, 53 pages; Luke: 94 pages; John: 72 pages.

The impact of the Gospel translations on Gardiner was pivotal,

> His [Fossum's] translation of the four Gospels into separate well-bound volumes in the Arabic script (the only one at that time) I used and studied from and I cleared out all stocks of these for my use from the London and Beirut Bible Societies. I did not find the Grammar till later. I really learnt my Kurdish from these and spent many hours with my tutor and a Mullah pouring over them and gave many away. It was while studying the Sermon on the Mount in Matthew that I was challenged and accepted what became a clear call to devote my life to the Kurds (1982:5).

In addition, Fossum wrote a *Kurdish Grammar* and *Hymnbook*.

1922: *St. Matthew's Gospel* (ABS, Constantinople)

A transliteration by H. H. Riggs' 1891 *St. Matthew's Gospel* in Arabic script. The ABS called this form "Arabo-Kurdish" and the same Gospels in Armenian character "Armeno-Kurdish."

Until 1947, nothing of the Bible was published in the Roman alphabet. Gardiner writes,

> My teacher at London University, Major Edmunds, with Kurdish helpers in Mosul really put the Roman Kurdish script on the map which was taught in schools in Iraqi Kurdistan. The older people and those who could only cope with the national Arabic script continued in this. A Kurdish newspaper which used to be printed and sent to me contained articles in Roman and Arabic script. Major Edmunds, five years ago, published a very excellent Kurdish vocabulary and lexicon in the Roman script (published as with his other books by Kegan Paul, Trench and Trubner, British Museum Street) (1982:5).

However, no Kurds in Iraq learn Kurdish in the Roman script. Sorani has been taught in the Arabic script for many years in

Sorani-speaking Iraq Kurdistan. The Kurdish department of education has tried to teach Bahdinani-speaking pupils in Zakhu and Dohouk to read Sorani in the Arabic script. This will fail, since not even the teachers understand what they are reading.

1947: *Proverbs/Methelokên Hezretê Silêman* (ABS & BFBS, Beirut)—15.5+12 cm/ 84 pages

Translated by Emir Dr. Kamuran and Bedr-Khan, revised by Father Thomas Bois, O.P. The script was in New Roman characters. Gardiner doubts whether anyone could make use of this translation:

> Christian workers in Damascus in cooperation with the B & F Bible Society who gave the money arranged for a Dr. Bedr Khan who was a Moslem but professed his conversion to Christ. As a result of his work translated the New Testament and the Psalms into Kurdish. I corresponded with him and was consulted by the Bible Society at the time. Parts of this was published by the society in combined Arabic and Roman scripts on opposing pages. However the small Kurdish group in Damascus and in Beirut (which I visited and knew American missionaries working among them) were not truly representative of any large Kurdish language group. Most were illiterate and doing menial portering tasks and the learned doctor himself spoke a Kurdish very much overlaid with Arabic. I could not make use of them and I do not think that the L.O.M. workers in N. Iraq found them much use. Sad to say the Roman script was different from the Edmunds script though of course the reader would be able to convert if he already knew the latter. However the whole concept was a brave one (1982:5).

1953: *St. Luke* (Civata Kitaba Micedes, Beirut)—17 + 12 cm 208 pages

A translation made by the above mentioned Bedr-Khan and Thomas Bois, in Arabic and Roman characters in parallel columns. This translation was re-printed in 1981 by Orientdienst.

Kermanshahi (Iranian Kurdish) Dialect

Translations of this dialect date from the end of the 19th century. Five references are cited below.

1894: *St. John's Gospel* (BFBS)—17 + 12 cm 161 pages

Translated by a Persian convert named Mirzaq Yahya Khan, who worked from R. Bruce's revised version of the New Testament in Persian, under the supervision of T. R. Hodgson, BFBS's agent in Persia. Persian characters. This edition was printed by lithography at the Henry Martyn Memorial Press of the Church Missionary Society (CMS) at Julfa.

1900: *The Gospels* (BFBS)—16 + 10.5 cm, pages not numbered

Translated from the Greek by W. St. Clair Tisdall, of the CMS with the help of a Kermanshahi convert named Mirza Ismail. The above-mentioned St. John's Gospel, 1894, was revised for this edition. Printed in Persian character by photo-zincography. English at the end.

1918: *The Gospels*

Gardiner of Iran adds,

> There are some very old New Testaments printed off hand-engraved plates possibly originating from missionaries with the Nestorians in the 19th century. Only Kurdish scholars I have asked have been able to make them out. (Arabic Script) (1982:5).

1926: *Gospel of Matthew in the Sanandaji dialect*—Arabic script

1926: *The Four Gospels*

Arabic script (This is perhaps the same translation as the one above done in 1918.) Despite these early 20th century efforts in Iranian Kurdish, Gardiner, who owned as large a collection of translations as anyone in the world, had nothing useful in his hands:

> There were no Kurdish translations for the Kurds I worked among in Northern Iran, though Gospel messages, prayers, and readings were given in Kurdish by translation from Farsi or by Kurds. Kurdish in Iran was not a written language and steps were taken to prevent it being one. . . . We instead distributed hundreds of whole Gospels or New Testaments in Farsi to Kurds who, if they had been to government Farsi schools, would have had no difficulty in reading them and could have and I am sure still do translate them verbally to their illiterate friends and families (1982:6).

Mukri-Sorani Dialect

This is the Kurdish dialect of northern Iraq east of the Zab River. Bahdinan is spoken west of the Zab River.

1909: St. Mark's Gospel (BFBS)—Philippopel, 18.5 + 12.5 cm 8 pages

Translated by Detwig von Oertzen of the Deutsche Orient Mission, with the help of Mirza Jawtat. Printed at J. Awetararian's press at Philippopolis.

1973: *St. John* (LBI, Beirut, Lebanon)—11.5 + 8.5 cm

A paraphrased translation based on the English "Living" version. A new edition of this translation was printed by Sådd and Skörd Publishing House, in Gothenburg, Sweden, 1986, under the title *The Life and Message of Jesus the Messiah.*

1979: *New Testament, Pentateuch, Psalms, and Proverbs* (LBI)

A new translation was made by a group of Kurdish scholars inside Iraq. The manuscript was confiscated and kept in Baghdad during part of the Iran-Iraq war. In 1984 someone smuggled it out of Iraq to Europe. However, the translation was called "hopelessly Islamicized"[2] and was never printed.

1987: The Gospel of John—This translation is now considered a linguistic failure.

1990: *St. Luke* (LBI, Holland)— 14.5 + 10.5 cm 103 pages

1991: *St. Luke* (LBI)— England 16 + 11 cm 93 pages

This was a revised edition of the 1990 St. Luke, now with notes. It first printing ran to 60,000 copies, and later another 100,000 copies were printed to be taken into Iraq Kurdistan.

Since 1991, translation efforts have accelerated in many dialects. Much of the work requires confidentiality.

---

[2] Islamization might not be a drawback, but a help, as with the *Injil Sharif* in Bangladesh.

ADDRESSES

Many Psalms and scripture readings in Kurmanji of Turkey and Armenia are now available from Orientdienst in Germany:

Postfach 45 46
65035 Wiesbaden
Germany

Gospel Recordings worked briefly in Kurdistan of Iran in the late 1970s (Muhr 1982:64–65). Evangelistic cassettes in the Sorani, Laki, Luri and Khorasani Kurdish dialects are available from:

Gospel Recordings
1222 Glendale Blvd.
Los Angeles, CA 90026

Audio Scriptures International has produced Scripture portions on tape as well.

Audio Scriptures International
P.O. Box 460634
Escondido, CA 92046
760 745-8105

Glossary

Agha	Kurdish tribal ruler, also as beg or shaikh
Alevi	religious sect in Turkey, Iran and Syria which exalts Ali as a manifestation of the Supreme Being. Kurds are numerous in this sect, which is also known as the Ahli-al-Haqq or Alowi
Ba'ath Party	meaning "renaissance party" the Arab socialist totalitarian regime of Syria and of Iraq, though the two are enemies of one another.
Darwish	Member of a Muslim mystic order, sometimes called *dervish*
Dyophysite	the teaching of the Orthodox, Catholic and Protestant churches that within the one person of Christ there are two inseparable natures, one divine and the other human. Rejected by the Church of the East (Nestorian).
Ethné	word in the Greek New Testament for ethnic group, usually translated Gentiles
Falah	a Christian of the ancient churches of Mesopotamia
Falahi	the language of the Church of the East, modern Aramaic
Firman	an official order, a decree
Gewor	Kurdish for Christian "infidels," from the Arabic *Kaphir*
Hamidiye	special Kurdish militia which operated against Armenians in the Ottoman Empire at the end of the 19th century
Hajj	a Muslim who has made the pilgrimage to Mecca; hajj is also the pilgrimage itself

245

Jash	a mercenary Kurd who has fought alongside the government of Iraq (literally, "little donkey")
Kairos	Greek word for "time," referring to the mystery of God's intervention in human affairs
Khan	a chief over several tribes
Kizilbash	a pejorative term given by the Turks to the Ali (Alevi) sect (literally, "red heads")
Millet system	the minorities groups in the Ottoman Empire
Monophysite	teaching of the Armenian Church that Christ was only divine
Mukhtar	village head man
Naqshibandi	a missionary mystical order from India which found acceptance among Turks and Kurds.
Pesh Merga	Kurdish freedom fighters in Iraq (literally, "those who face death")
Porte	The seat of power in Constantinople during the time of the later Ottoman Empire
Regula	rules of a brotherhood or mission order
Sayyid	a Muslim holy man, considered a descendant of the Prophet Muhammad
Sanliurfa	city in southeastern Turkey, previously known as Urfa, Edessa, and Callirhoe
Shariah law	Islamic legal code favored by Islamic fundamentalists
Soujbulakh	Older name for the city of Mahabad, Iran
Tarika	"Way," referring to the Naqshibandi and Qadiri religious orders
Wilayet	an ethnic group allowed self-rule during the time of the Ottoman Empire

References Cited

ABCFM (American Board of Commissioners for Foreign Mission)
1859 *Annual Report.* Boston, MA: T. R. Marvin and Son.
1860a *Annual Report.* Boston, MA: T. R. Marvin and Son.
1860b *Missionary Herald.* Boston, MA: T. R. Marvin and Son.
1877 *Missionary Herald.* Boston, MA: T. R. Marvin and Son.
1899a *Missionary Herald.* Boston, MA: T. R. Marvin and Son.
1899b *Annual Report.* Boston, MA: T. R. Marvin and Son.

Abdulla, Jamal Jalal and Ernest N. McCarus
1967 *Kurdish Basic Course.* Ann Arbor, MI: University of
Michigan.

Allen, Roland
1962 *The Spontaneous Expansion of the Church.* Grand Rapids,
MI: Wm. B. Eerdmans Publishing Co.

Amnesty International
1995 *Iraq: Human Rights Abuses in Iraqi Kurdistan since 1991.*
London: Amnesty International.

Anderson, Rufus
1872a *History of Missions*, vol. 1. Boston, MA: Congregational Publishing Society.
1872b *History of Missions*, vol. 2. Boston, MA: Congregational Publishing Society.
1873 *History of Missions of the American Board of Commissioners
for Foreign Missions.* Boston, MA: Congregational Publishing Society.

Arfa, Hassan
1966 *The Kurds.* London: Oxford University Press.

Assyrian Democratic Movement
1992 *Light magazine.* (April 11). Northern Iraq.

Bailey, Kenneth E.

1976   *Poet and Peasant and Through Peasant Eyes.* Grand Rapids, MI: Wm. B. Eerdmans Publishing Co.

1989   *A Tale of Three Cities.* Pasadena, CA: Presbyterian Center for Mission Studies.

Barrett, David

1997   "Annual Statistical Table on Global Mission." *International Bulletin of Missionary Research* 21:1 (January):24.

Bible, The Holy

1985   *The Holy Bible.* New International Version (NIV). Grand Rapids, MI: Zondervan Publishing. All Bible references in this thesis are from the NIV.

Bird, Isabella

1891   *Journeys in Persia and Kurdistan II.* London: Virago Press. Reprinted 1989.

Brewster, Thomas and Betty Sue

1976   *Language Aptitude Made Practical* (LAMP). Pasadena, CA: Lingua House.

Buchanan, John

1997   Address, PCUSA Synod Mission Rally, Bel-Air, CA, February 1.

Buteyn, John

1989   Address, New Brunswick Theological Seminary, New Jersey.

Chaliand, Gerald, et al.

1980   *People without a Country: The Kurds and Kurdistan.* London: Zed Press.

1993   *People without a Country* (Reprint). New York: Olive Branch Press.

Coakley, James

1989   Address, New Brunswick Theological Seminary, New Jersey, May 13.

Coan, Frederick G.

1939   *Yesterdays in Persia and Kurdistan.* Claremont, CA: Saunders Studio Press.

Cochran, Joseph P.

1983   *Memoirs of Joseph P. Cochran.* Privately published.

Cochran, Richard
1996 Personal interview with author. Poulsbo, WA, November.

Cumberland, Roger
1926 "The Kurds." *The Moslem World* 16:2 (April).
1938 Board Minutes, Part II. Presbyterian Church in the USA. Philadelphia, PA: Office of the General Assembly.

Daniel, Robert L.
1970 *American Philanthropy in the Near East, 1820–1960*. Athens, OH: Ohio University Press.

Darke, Diane
1987 *Guide to Eastern Turkey and the Black Sea Coast*. London: Hippocrene Books.

Dwight, Henry Otis
1913 *What is the Near East Mission?* New York: Revell.

Eddy, David Brewer
1913 *What Next in Turkey?* Boston, MA: The American Board of Commissioners for Foreign Mission in the Near East.

Edmonds, Anna G.
1979 *The Near East Mission Medical Work in Gaziantep*. Istanbul: Near East Mission United Church Board for World Ministries.

Edmonds, C. J.
1957 *Kurds, Turks, and Arabs*. London: Oxford University Press.

Farnham, Bruce
1985 *My Big Father*. Waynesboro, GA: OM Lit.

Fidelis Society
1993 *A Hundred Years and Still Cooking*. Fresno, CA: H. Markus Printing.

Fleming, Glenn
1981 "An Ethnographic Study of the Kurdish People." Master's thesis, Loma Linda University.

Franciscan Mission
1982 "Franciscan Mission Among the Muslims." Assisi, Italy: Franciscan Mission.

Fromkin, David
1989 *A Peace to End all Peace*. New York: Avon Books.

Gardiner, Richard
1982   Correspondence to Patrick Johnstone. July 19.

Garnett, Lucy
1891   *The Women of Turkey and Their Folklore.* London: David Nutt.

George, Evelyn
1997   Personal interview with author. San Mateo, CA, January.

Glover, Robert Hall
1928   *The Progress of World-Wide Missions.* Garden City, NY: Doubleday, Doran and Company.

Guest, John
1987   *The Yezidis.* New York: Methuen Inc.
1993   *Survival Among the Kurds: A History of the Yezidis.* New York: Kegan Paul International.

Habib, Gabriel
1988   Open letter to the Lausanne Committee on World Evangelization, Manila meeting.

Haddad, Yvonne, et al.
1984   *The Islamic Impact.* New York: Syracuse University Press.

Hansen, Henny Harald
1960   *Daughters of Allah.* London: George Allen and Unwin Ltd. Museum St.

Heazell, M. A. and Mrs. Margoliouth
1913   *Kurds and Christians.* London: Wells, Gardner, Darton & Co.

Horner, Norman A.
1989   *A Guide to Christian Churches in the Middle East.* Elkhart, IN: Mission Focus Press.

Hymns
1976   "I Sought the Lord." *Hymns II.* Music by George Chadwick. Author of lyrics unknown. Downer's Grove, IL: InterVarsity Press.

Izady, Mehrdad
1992   *The Kurds: A Concise Handbook.* Washington D.C.: Taylor and Francis.

1993   "The Archaeology of Kurdish Tribal Names." Part 1. *The International Journal of Kurdish Studies*. Brooklyn, NY: The Kurdish Heritage Foundation.

Jensen, J. A. and Oberg, Einer
1985   *The Messengers of God: The History of the Lutheran Orient Mission Society*. Part I: 1910–1950. Part II: 1950–1985. Minneapolis, MN: LOMS.

Joseph, John
1961   *The Nestorians and their Muslim Neighbors*. Princeton, NJ: Princeton University Press.

Kahn, Margaret,
1980   *Children of the Jinn*. New York: Seaview Books of Harper and Row.

Kaplan, Robert D.
1993   *The Arabists*. New York: The Free Press of Macmillan.

Kerr, Stanley E.
1973   *The Lions of Marash: Personal Experiences with the American Near East Mission, 1919–1922*. Albany, NY: State University of New York Press.

Kinross, Lord
1977   *The Ottoman Centuries*. New York: Morrow Quill Paperbacks.

Kreyenbroek, Philip and Stefan Sperl, eds.
1992   *The Kurds*. New York: Routledge Publishing.

Latourette, K. S.
1945   *Advance through Storm: A History of the Expansion of Christianity*. Vol. 7. New York: Harper.
1975   *History of the Expansion of Christianity*. New York: Harper & Row.

Livingstone, Greg
1990   "A Team Approach to Urban Church Planting in the Muslim World." D.Min. dissertation, Biola College.

Lohre, N. J.
1918   "The Highlanders of Kurdistan." *The Moslem World* (c 1918).

Marr, Phebe
1985   *The Modern History of Iraq*. Boulder, CO: Westview Press.

Marsh, Dwight W.

1869 *The Tennesseean in Persia and Koordistan.* Philadelphia, PA: Presbyterian Publication Committee.

Masters, William M.

1953 "Rowanduz: A Kurdish Administrative and Mercantile Center." Ph.D. dissertation, University of Michigan, Ann Arbor.

McCurry, Don M., ed.

1978 *The Gospel and Islam: A 1978 Compendium.* Monrovia, CA: MARC.

McDowall, David

1996 *A Modern History of the Kurds.* London: I. B. Taurus.

McGilvary, Margaret

1920 *The Dawn of a New Era in Syria.* New York: Revell.

Meyer, Craig

1986 *A Clash of Swords.* Grand Junction, CO: Friends of Turkey.

Miller, William M.

1971 "The Future Role of Western Missions to the Muslim World." *Evangelical Missions Quarterly.*

Minorsky, V.

1927 *Encyclopedia of Islam: Kurds.* New York: E. J. Brill. Reprinted 1993.

Muhr, Marlene

1982 *Along Unfamiliar Paths: The Story of Gospel Recordings in Europe.* Los Angeles, CA: Gospel Recordings Inc.

Nevius, John L.

1895 *Planting and Development of Missionary Churches.* Philadelphia, PA: The Presbyterian and Reformed Publishing Company.

Newshirwan Mustefa

1992 *Kurds and Turks* (in Sorani Kurdish). Iraq: Erbil Cultural Printing House.

Olson, Robert

1989 *The Emergence of Kurdish Nationalism and the Sheikh Said Rebellion, 1880, 1925.* Austin, TX: University of Texas Press.

Parshall, Phil
1980   *New Paths in Muslim Evangelism.* Grand Rapids, MI: Baker
       Book House.

Pryce-Jones, David
1989   *The Closed Circle.* London: Paladin.

Rasooli, Jay, and Allen, Cady
1957   *Dr. Sa'eed of Iran.* Pasadena, CA: William Carey Library
       (Republished).

Reuters Wire Service
1993   "Pope Calls on Iraqi Christians Not to Emigrate." *Jordan
       Times* (May 4).

Richardson, Don
1974   *Peace Child.* Glendale, CA: Regal Books.

Richter, Julius
1910   *A History of Protestant Missions in the Near East.* New York:
       Revell.

Riggs, Alice Shepard
1920   *Shepard of Aintab.* New York: Interchurch Press.

Rizgar, Baran
1996   *Dersen Kurdi.* London: published by author.

S., Rick
1984   Private correspondence.

Sanneh, Lamin
1987   "Christian Mission and the Western Guilt Complex." *Christian Century*
       (April 8).

Shaad, David
1997   Personal interview with author, February.

Sheehan, Neil
1988   *A Bright Shining Lie: John Paul Vann and America in Vietnam.* New York: Random House.

Shepard, Mary Alice
1970   *Doctor's Care: Medical Mission in Turkey.* Istanbul: American
       Board.

Shireen
1996   *Ni Roj Language Learning Series.* Longview, TX: published by author.

Speer, Robert E.
1911   *The Hakim Sahib, The Foreign Doctor: Biography of Joseph Plumb Cochran, M.D. of Persia.* New York: Revell.

Stead, Blanche Wilson
1920   "Kurdistan for Christ." *The Moslem World* 10:3 (July): 241–248.

Stewart, John
1928   *Nestorian Missionary Enterprise.* Edinburgh, Scotland: T & T Clark.

Taylor, J. G.
1866   *A Tour in Armenia, Kurdistan, and Upper Mesopotamia.* published by author.

Teague, David P.
1992   *Turning Over a New Leaf: Protestant Missions and Orthodox Churches of the Middle East.* Lynnwood, WA: Middle East Media.

UN (United Nations High Commissioner for Refugees)
1992   *Time* (June 8).

UPCUSA (United Presbyterian Church, U.S.A.)
1936   *A Century of Mission Work in Iran, 1834–1934.* Beirut, Lebanon: Presbyterian Church U.S.A. Iran Mission.
1953   *Presbyterian Church General Assembly Minutes.* New York: United Presbyterian Church, U.S.A.

van Bruinessen, Martin
1991   "Religion in Kurdistan." *Kurdish Times* vol. 4.
1992   *Agha, Shaikh and State.* London: Zed Books.

Vander Werff, Lyle L.
1977   *Christian Mission to Muslims: The Record: Anglican and Reformed Approaches in India and the Near East, 1800–1938.* South Pasadena, CA: William Carey Library.

Waldburger, A.
1983   *Missionare und Moslems—Die Basle mission in Persien 1833–1837.* Basel, Switzerland: Basilea Verlag.

Werda, Joel E.
1924   *The Flickering Light of Asia.* published by author.

Wheeler, Mrs. Crosby H.
1899   *Missions in Eden: Glimpses of Life in the Valley of the Euphrates, Harput.* New York: Revell.

Winter, Ralph D.
1977   *The Warp and the Woof.* South Pasadena, CA: William Carey Library.
1992   *Mission Frontiers.* Pasadena, CA: U.S. Center for World Mission.

Wittler, Mel
1992   Personal interview with author. Istanbul, Turkey, November.

Yacoub, Jacob
1986   *The Assyrian Question.* Chicago, IL: Alpha Graphic.

Yonan, Isaac Malek
1934   *The Beloved Physician of Teheran.* Nashville, TN: Cokesbury.

Yonan, Jesse Malek
1895   *Martyrdom in the Orient: The Kurds and their Massacres.* published by author.

Young, Herrick B.
1939   *Roger Craig Cumberland.* New York: The Board of Foreign Missions of the Presbyterian Church in the United States of America.

Zwemer, Samuel
1941   *The Cross above the Crescent.* Grand Rapids, MI: Zondervan Publishing.

Index

258   *Ethnic Realities: Lessons from Kurdistan*

262　*Ethnic Realities: Lessons from Kurdistan*

About the Author

Robert Blincoe graduated with a B.A. in history from the University of Oregon in 1973. His Master of Divinity and Master of Theology degrees are from Fuller Theological Seminary. He is a Presbyterian minister and general director of the Presbyterian Order for World Evangelization. He and his wife, Janice, have three children.